There is a richness and diversity in this edited collection which makes it an important addition to a challenging and necessary debate within the field of public policy and between practitioners and decision makers. What this set of essays brings are insights into those 'stories less told' and the ways in which conventional thinking and actions can be challenged. From 'action tanks' to valuing dialogue and listening as a way of shaping action. This is a welcome contribution.

John Diamond, *Professor and Director of the Institute for Public Policy and Professional Practice, Edge Hill University, UK*

If ever there was a time for new thinking about how to shape and deliver public policy; it is now. Old problems are piling up and new ones are emerging. Both call for more productive approaches that harness the diversity of expertise, resources and commitment held by various groups within and across sectors. Despite the rhetoric, actually making the shift to such a multi-party approach to policy and its implementation is largely unchartered territory. The set of chapters compiled within this book take a strong step forward, by opening up the debate as well as providing practical strategies for action.

Robyn Keast, *Professor, Southern Cross University, Australia*

Success in tackling the large challenges in social policy and service delivery increasingly depends on how well the public sector can work with civil society and other organisations. This requires collaboration and dialogue instead of traditional models of bureaucratic authority and expertise. This book showcases the experience of diverse leaders across three sectors – government, civil society and research – and across several policy arenas. It is clear that leading practitioners and reflective analysts are now proceeding in parallel.

Brian Head, *Professor, University of Queensland, Australia*

This collection offers a potentially valuable set of insights to bridge gaps and provoke debate between policy makers inside government and those outside – whether in academia or civil society. Particularly useful is its recognition that, in a democracy, politics is a legitimate and intrinsic part of policy making.

Jill Rutter, *Programme Director, Better Policy Making, Institute for Government, UK*

This book brings together the creative ideas of some of the best thinkers in the field. It offers new ideas about the policy process, as well as how to change policy. It is a rich smorgasbord of theories and practical insights informed by cutting edge research... a must read.

Rosemary O'Leary, *Professor, University of Kansas, USA*

T0330493

Creating and Implementing Public Policy

In order to address major social policy problems, governments need to break down sectoral barriers and create better working relationships between practitioners, policymakers and researchers. Currently, major blockages exist, and stereotypes abound. Academics are seen as out of touch and unresponsive, policymakers are perceived to be justifying policy decisions, and the community sector seeks more funding without demonstrating efficacy. These stereotypes are borne out of a lack of understanding of the work and practices that exist across these three sectors.

Drawing on ground-breaking research and partnerships, with contributions from senior public servants, this book explores the competing demands of different actors involved in policy change. It challenges current debates and assumptions and reflects a unique diversity of experiences. Combined with differing theoretical perspectives, it provides a uniquely practical insight for those seeking to influence public policy.

This innovative text provides essential reading for community sector practitioners, academics and advanced level students in public policy, social policy and public administration, as well as for public service professionals.

Gemma Carey is a Research Fellow with the Regulatory Network at the Australian National University, Australia.

Kathy Landvogt is a social worker with experience in service delivery, management, policy research and further education. Kathy is currently a social policy researcher in Good Shepherd Australia New Zealand, Australia.

Jo Barraket is Director of the Centre for Social Impact Swinburne at Swinburne University of Technology, Australia.

Routledge critical studies in public management
Edited by Stephen Osborne

The study and practice of public management has undergone profound changes across the world. Over the last quarter century, we have seen

- increasing criticism of public administration as the over-arching framework for the provision of public services;
- the rise (and critical appraisal) of the 'New Public Management' as an emergent paradigm for the provision of public services;
- the transformation of the 'public sector' into the cross-sectoral provision of public services; and
- the growth of the governance of inter-organisational relationships as an essential element in the provision of public services.

In reality these trends have not so much replaced each other as elided or co-existed together – the public policy process has not gone away as a legitimate topic of study, intra-organisational management continues to be essential to the efficient provision of public services, while the governance of inter-organisational and inter-sectoral relationships is now essential to the effective provision of these services.

Further, while the study of public management has been enriched by contribution of a range of insights from the 'mainstream' management literature, it has also contributed to this literature in such areas as networks and inter-organisational collaboration, innovation and stakeholder theory.

This series is dedicated to presenting and critiquing this important body of theory and empirical study. It will publish books that both explore and evaluate the emergent and developing nature of public administration, management and governance (in theory and practice) and examine the relationship with and contribution to the over-arching disciplines of management and organisational sociology.

Books in the series will be of interest to academics and researchers in this field, students undertaking advanced studies of it as part of their undergraduate or postgraduate degree and reflective policymakers and practitioners.

Creating and Implementing Public Policy

Cross-sectoral debates

Edited by Gemma Carey,
Kathy Landvogt and Jo Barraket

Routledge
Taylor & Francis Group

LONDON AND NEW YORK

First published 2016 by Routledge

2 Park Square, Milton Park, Abingdon, Oxon, OX14 4RN

605 Third Avenue, New York, NY 10017

Routledge is an imprint of the Taylor & Francis Group, an informa business

First issued in paperback 2020

British Library Cataloguing in Publication Data
A catalogue record for this book is available from the British Library

Library of Congress Cataloging-in-Publication Data
Creating and implementing public policy : cross-sectoral debates / edited by Gemma Carey, Kathy Landvogt and Jo Barraket.
    pages cm. – (Routledge critical studies in public management)
    Includes bibliographical references and index.
    ISBN 978-1-138-80650-4 (hardback) – ISBN 978-1-315-75165-8 (ebook) 1. Social policy. 2. Public welfare. 3. Social service.
    I. Carey, Gemma editor. II. Landvogt, Kathy, editor. III. Barraket, Jo, editor.
    HN18.3.C74 2016
    306–dc23   2015023166

ISBN: 978-1-138-80650-4 (hbk)
ISBN: 978-0-367-73755-9 (pbk)

Typeset in Bembo
by Wearset Ltd, Boldon, Tyne and Wear

This book is dedicated to all those trying to make a difference in policy and civil society.

Contents

Figures

Tables

Boxes

Contributors

Verity Archer is a lecturer in sociology at Federation University, Melbourne, Australia. She has a PhD in history from the Australian National University and writes about welfare, class, political ideologies and social enterprise.

Jo Barraket is Director of the Centre for Social Impact Swinburne at Swinburne University of Technology, Melbourne, Australia. She is a leading researcher in social enterprise, and the relationships between government and the third sector in public policy design and implementation.

Toba Bryant is an Assistant Professor in the Faculty of Health Sciences at the University of Ontario Institute of Technology, Oshawa, Canada. She earned her PhD specializing in health and social policy at the University of Toronto. She is the author of *An introduction to health policy*, co-editor of *Staying alive: critical perspectives on health, illness, and health care* and has published book chapters and articles on policy change, housing and health, and women's health. Dr Bryant's research focus is on the social determinants of health, welfare state analysis and health and social policy change.

Gemma Carey is a Research Fellow with the Regulatory Institutions Network at the Australian National University. She holds a PhD in social policy and population health from the University of Melbourne. Her research sits at the critical interface between public health, public administration and social policy. Dr Carey has published widely on different aspects of public administration and public health. In addition to her academic research, she runs a policy forum – the Power to Persuade (PTP) (an annual symposium and blog). PTP is aimed at improving the relationships between policymakers, academics and the community sector. Running since 2011, PTP is sponsored by the Victorian Government and a range of NGOs and peak bodies (www.powertopersuade.org.au).

John Chesterman is Manager of Policy and Education at the Office of the Public Advocate (OPA), State Government of Victoria, Australia. The OPA is Victoria's guardian of last resort for adults with decision-making incapacity. He is a trained lawyer and he leads OPA's systemic reform activities. Before joining OPA he lectured in politics at the University of Melbourne and has previously worked at James Cook University's School of Indigenous Australian Studies in Townsville. He has written a number of books, including *Civil rights: how Indigenous Australians won formal equality* (University of Queensland Press) and (with Louise Chappell and Lisa Hill) *The politics of human rights in Australia* (Cambridge University Press).

Rachel Clark is currently leading the integration of evidence into England's new National Diabetes Prevention Programme at Public Health England, London. Prior to this, and at the time of writing this chapter, she held a research and knowledge exchange position at the Centre of Excellence in Intervention and Prevention Science (CEIPS) in Victoria, Australia. Rachel worked in a range of academic and practice positions in Wales before commencing work in knowledge exchange at the University of Melbourne, where she was involved in design and implementation of a trial to increase evidence-informed decision making in local government. Her work at CEIPS involved knowledge exchange practice, and research into the systemic drivers of evidence use in local government. She has led and supported a number of systematic evidence reviews in previous roles and as a consultant. Her current work continues to focus on supporting evidence-informed decisions but from within a policy environment.

Deborah Connolly Youngblood, PhD is a cultural anthropologist with expertise in social services, applied research and developing pathways out of poverty for low-income families. She is the author of the book *Homeless mothers: face to face with women and poverty* (2000) and numerous articles and reports. She was the Vice President of Research and Innovation at Crittenton Women's Union in Boston, MA (USA) from 2007 to 2015. She is now the Commissioner of Health and Human Services for the City of Newton, Massachusetts.

Brad Crammond is a public health lawyer in the Michael Kirby Centre for Public Health and Human Rights at Monash University. Brad's work combines elements of law, political philosophy and social theory to understand the causes of, and solutions for, persistent health inequalities.

Helen Dickinson is Associate Professor of Public Governance at the School of Social and Political Sciences, University of Melbourne, Australia. Her expertise is in public services, particularly in relation to topics such as governance, commissioning and priority setting and decision making. Helen has authored, co-authored or edited twelve books on these topics in the last six years and has also published in journals such as *Public Administration, Public Management Review, Social Science and Medicine* and *Evidence and Policy*. Helen is co-editor of the *Journal of Health, Organization and Management* and the *Australian Journal of Public Administration*. Helen has worked with a range of different levels of government, community organisations and private organisations in Australia, UK, New Zealand and Europe on research and consultancy programmes.

Jennifer Doggett is a Fellow of the Centre for Policy Development and editor at Crikey Health Blog, Australia. She works as a consultant in the health sector for a number of professional, industry and consumer groups. She has previously worked within the Federal Department of Health, as a political advisor and in a community health organisation. Jennifer has written a number of papers on public policy issues including 'A new approach to primary care for Australia' and 'Out-of-pocket: rethinking co-payments in the health system'. She is a contributing author of the books *More than luck: ideas Australia needs now* and *Pushing our luck: ideas for Australian progress*.

Mary Gatta is Senior Scholar at DC-based advocacy Wider Opportunities for Women, and Associate Professor of Sociology at Guttman College in the City University of New York (CUNY) system. Mary's expertise includes the integration of a gender lens into social and economic policy analysis. Before working at Wider Opportunities for Women, Mary was the Director of Gender and Workforce Policy at the Center for Women and Work at Rutgers University. While at Rutgers University, Mary explored the experiences of women as they navigate unemployment which led to Mary's latest book, *All I want is a job! Unemployed women navigating the public workforce system*, released from Stanford University Press in April 2014. Mary is also the author of *Not just getting by: the new era of flexible workforce development* and *Juggling food and feelings: emotional balance in the workplace* and is the editor of *A US skills system for the 21st century: innovations in workforce education and development*. Mary received a Bachelor of Arts degree in social science from Providence College and her Master's degree and PhD in Sociology from Rutgers University.

Sue Grigg has been working in the field of welfare for over 20 years with experience in the community sector, consulting, research and government. Sue managed the J2SI program and is currently managing the Learning and Practice Development Unit at Jesuit Social Services.

Michelle Haby is a researcher at the University of Sonora, Mexico and an Honorary Senior Fellow at the Centre for Health Policy, the University of Melbourne, Australia. She is an epidemiologist with extensive experience in both research and policy roles. Her most recent position was with the Victorian Government Department of Health where she led a program of work to encourage and facilitate the use of research evidence in policy decision making and evaluation of programs. Since moving to Mexico in 2012 Michelle has undertaken a number of consultancy projects with the World Health Organization, conducting systematic reviews of interventions to inform policy development. Her most recent project is on methods for rapid reviews to support evidence-informed decision making in both policy and practice.

David Hayward is currently Dean of the School of Global, Urban and Social Studies, one of the largest Schools at the Royal Melbourne Institute of Technology, Melbourne, Australia. He has just completed his second term as non-executive Director of Melbourne Health, which is one of Victoria's largest health services, incorporating the Royal Melbourne Hospital. In that role he was also Chair of the Finance Committee for four years. By invitation from the Government of Tasmania, in 2011 he was a member of the Expert Advisory Group advising the Tasmanian Social Inclusion Commissioner Professor David Adams on a Cost of Living Strategy. An economist and sociologist, David has edited or co-written four books and more than 20 refereed articles and book chapters. He sits on the editorial board of Urban Policy and Research, of which he was Chair from 2002 to 2007. In 2011 he was awarded life membership of the Victorian Council of Social Service in recognition of his years of service. He is a regular media commentator on economic and social affairs.

Guy Johnson is the Deputy Director at the Centre of Applied Social Research at RMIT University Melbourne, Australia. He has been involved in the area of homelessness for almost three decades, initially as a practitioner and more recently as a researcher. Since completing his PhD in 2006, Guy has published extensively on homelessness and is a co-author of *On the outside: pathways in and out of homelessness* and *Young people leaving state out-of-home care: Australian policy and practice*, and recently co-edited *Homelessness in Australia: an introduction*.

Kathy Landvogt is a social worker with experience in service delivery, management, policy research, and further education. Kathy is currently a social policy researcher in Good Shepherd Australia New Zealand, engaging in action research, policy research, program development, evaluation and system advocacy focused on women's safety, financial security and education pathways out of disadvantage.

Ruth Liberman is the Vice President of Public Policy at Crittenton Women's Union, Boston, USA. She directs CWU's advocacy efforts to shape public policy and achieve social change that will help lift low-income families out of poverty. Her previous public policy experience includes serving as the Director of Public Policy for Planned Parenthood in Los Angeles and a Senate Fellowship in the California Legislature. She earned her Master's in Public Administration at Harvard's Kennedy School of Government.

Chris Mason is Senior Research Fellow at the Centre for Social Impact Swinburne, Swinburne University of Technology in Melbourne. His research explores political, social, organisational and critical questions of social enterprises.

Mark Matthews is a UK-based public policy specialist with experience that bridges management consulting, academic research, running a government-funded policy unit and also heading up a science diplomacy unit. His work focuses on science and innovation policy and also on the ways in which governments can improve their ability to cope with uncertainty and risk. In addition to practising as a management consultant he has research affiliations with the Overseas Development Institute, the Australian Centre for Biosecurity and Environmental Economics, and with the Crawford School of Public Policy, at the Australian National University.

Shawn McMahon is Vice President for Policy and Programs at Wider Opportunities for Women (WOW), where he oversees diverse research and federal and state-level advocacy. His former positions at WOW include President and CEO and Manager of Research and Innovation. He works across WOW programs and with partners across the United States to advocate for workforce, education and public supports policies and practices that improve the economic security of women, families and seniors. He is the lead author of WOW's Basic Economic Security Tables (BEST) Index, and the author of *Fight for equality: international medical graduates in the United States.*

Dennis Raphael is a Professor in the School of Health Policy and Management at York University, Toronto, Canada. He earned his PhD in educational psychology at the University of Toronto. He is the author of *Poverty in Canada: implications for health and quality of life*, editor of *Social determinants of health: Canadian perspectives* and *Tackling health inequalities: lessons from international experiences* and co-editor of *Staying alive: critical perspectives on health, illness, and health care*. He researches the health effects of income inequality and poverty, the quality of life of communities and individuals, and the impact of government decisions on Canadians' health and wellbeing.

Helen Sullivan is Foundation Director of the Melbourne School of Government, the University of Melbourne and a public policy scholar. Her research and teaching explores the changing nature of state–society relationships including the theory and practice of governance and collaboration, new forms of democratic participation, and public policy and service reform. Helen's work reflects a long-term commitment to finding new ways to bridge the gap between research and policy. She has published widely in academic and practitioner media. Her latest book is *Hybrid governance in European cities: neighbourhood, migration and democracy* (2013). She is a Fellow (Victoria) of the Institute of Public Administration Australia.

Yi-Ping Tseng is a Senior Research Fellow in the Labour Economic and Social Policy program, Melbourne Institute of Applied Economic and Social Research, the University of Melbourne, Australia. She joined Melbourne Institute in 1999 as a research fellow after completing her PhD at the Australian National University. Yi-Ping's research is primarily in the area of labour economics and social policy with a focus on program evaluation, economics of homelessness, and early childhood development.

John Wiseman is Deputy Director of the Melbourne Sustainable Society Institute, the University of Melbourne, Australia. John has worked in a wide range of public sector, academic and community sector settings including as Foundation Director of the McCaughey Centre, School of Population Health, the University of Melbourne; Professor of Public Policy, Victoria University; and Assistant Director, Policy Development and Research, Victorian Department of Premier and Cabinet. The main focus of his current work is on the social and political transformations needed to prevent runaway climate change and achieve a rapid transition to a just and resilient post-carbon future.

Andrew Wyatt is a Principal Consultant at Oxford Policy Management. Prior to this, he served for over 23 years in the UK public service as a policy adviser, manager, and trainer and facilitator. Andrew's experience includes working with permanent secretaries, chief executives and the boards of public bodies to strengthen parliamentary accountability, and with civil servants at all levels to improve policy processes and policy management. As a consultant he has experience of supporting all stages of the policy cycle, from analysis and appraisal to implementation to evaluation. He has substantial experience as a manager in the civil service, and as team leader, project manager or project director of complex consultancy projects, and has designed and taught public policy modules on Public Sector MBA programmes at two UK universities. He is currently managing a major project to strengthen parliamentary financial oversight in Bangladesh.

Foreword

The ability of governments to address major social policy problems is contingent upon better working relationships between community sector practitioners, policymakers and researchers. Yet, there are few opportunities for these groups to come together and share knowledge and there is a paucity of material that examines these issues from different perspectives or that creates opportunities for dialogue and learning across these actors. Currently, major blockages exist between these different policy actors. Specifically, academics are seen as out of touch and unresponsive to the needs of government, policymakers are perceived to only seek evidence to justify policy decisions that have already been made, and the community sector is seen as continuing to seek more funding without demonstrating efficacy.

In 2012, the 'Power to Persuade: Building Capacity for Social and Political Change' (PTP) Symposium (held in Melbourne, Australia) was designed to challenge these stereotypes and break down the barriers between sectors. Now entering its third year, the one-day Symposium series has attracted over 120 invited participants annually, including public servants, CEOs and practitioners from community organisations and academics. This book brings together speakers from PTP, with other leading international thinkers and researchers, to share these insights with a broader audience and extend the conversations begun in the symposium.

While there are a range of texts that deal explicitly with public administration, theoretical perspectives on the policy process and issues relating to the community sector, there is a paucity of work that brings these different perspectives together. Each of these sectors – government, academic and community – has different demands and expectations when engaging with policy design and implementation. By providing a window into these sectors, and insight into how to enhance cross-sectoral collaboration and working, the book aims to meet an important need for those working in all aspects of policy.

Drawing on ground-breaking international research and partnerships, the book will shed light on the policy process, presenting and examining the perspectives of different sectors on what is needed to create policy change. In doing so, the book will explore the complexity of the policy process, the competing demands of sectors, and the role of evidence in policy development.

The book aims to provide new insights into the policy process by drawing on real life experiences informed by diverse theoretical frameworks (from policy studies, public health and sociology). The diversity of experiences it captures, coupled with differing theoretical perspectives, provides practical information and guidance for those seeking to influence policy.

Preface

That power and persuasion are central themes in this book should be no surprise. First, notions of power and persuasion figure in most debates about public policy whether they are contemporary, historical, practical or academic. Second, many of these contributions have their genesis in the annual 'Power to Persuade Symposium', a forum which is fast developing an enviable reputation for bringing together people from across the community, private and public sectors with academics, to tackle a range of public policy issues.

In this engaging and insightful collection, I see a commitment to breaking through in several ways: through the perceived gap between practitioner and scholars, through established ways of doing, and through the silos and barriers that lock us into well-rehearsed scripts for why things can't work even if we want them to. I am drawn to the big themes that the editors stake out in the introduction: understand, influence, disrupt. These notions capture the collection of contributions from across a broad range of actors – a diversity of voices rarely drawn together in a single collection – and they speak to the guiding principles of many of them. Many stress how important *understanding* the world and how it works, both practically and abstractly, is; most consider how we can go about *influencing* others to get change; and many look at *disrupting* existing routines to innovate and embed new ways of operating. The authors map out a range of factors and take stock of what works, who blocks, and how to break through. And, while they might not agree on much, one thing that shines through in this collection of analysis, reflection and wisdom is that the power to persuade is critical.

As a pragmatist I'm more inclined to accept that practitioners and scholars will always have different interests and incentives, and for the most part believe they should. As an optimist, however, I don't see why we can't have common goals. Trying to 'fix' this gap, rather than work with it, seems like an exhausting endeavour. Perhaps, in a preface to such a collection, I can advocate for a pragmatic acceptance that it exists, that a little distance is not such a bad thing, and for more attention to how we can work with it. My own experience in collaborative ventures with practitioners mirrors the well-rehearsed frustrations, and they would say the same, but also showed me the power of collaboration based on trust-based relationships, how empathy with the position of the other matters, and how our differences and the creative conflict that can spark can drive great innovations. It might just be here that we make breakthroughs and build powerful platforms for persuasion. But we need to accept the different worlds we operate in, focus on the bigger picture, and grunt up and do the hard grind that we all know can, and will, make a difference in the day-to-day lives of those we say we are trying to change the world for.

I also think it is time we looked beyond the usual suspect countries and policy areas for new horizons. I am increasingly drawn to the radically different approaches held outside the relatively rich and Western nations that dominate the public policy and management agenda. Mostly I learn about these from practitioners, often those who come into my classroom at the University of Melbourne. Year after year I see how these practitioners are making a difference through their day-to-day lives, whether that be about opening up education access for girls in rural Pakistan, developing corruption education programs for children in Bolivia, or addressing procurement weaknesses in Sierra Leone. They shake up my assumptions, challenge my thinking, and keep me coming back to my constant refrain, "it all depends". The other thing that they constantly remind me is that passion is important in catalysing change.

Power and persuasion are critical, but passion matters. All three are critical ingredients in understanding and enacting public policy to change the world and make a difference. And in the end, this has to be the end goal that we can overcome our differences to focus on, doesn't it?

Janine O'Flynn
Professor of Public Management
Melbourne School of Government
The University of Melbourne

Acknowledgements

The editors would like to acknowledge all those who have made the 'Power to Persuade' initiative possible, with special thanks to its foundational designers and long-time supporters, Gavin Dufty, Tanya Corrie and Michael Horn. A special thanks also to Celia Green for her assistance with editing the collection.

Introduction

Crossing boundaries for better public policy

Gemma Carey, Kathy Landvogt and Jo Barraket

Whether working in the community sector, research, advocacy or perhaps even government, individuals want to know how to get heard and how to have an impact on policy. But for the most part, as Clavier and De Leeuw suggest, the "complex and shifting rationalities of public policy making still largely elude" many of us (Clavier and de Leeuw 2013, p. 3). Both in the academic literature and in practice, two different views of policy exist which often sit in tension with one another. One depicts the policy process as a rational act, typically following a cycle (albeit not necessarily in a linear fashion). The other (and increasingly popular) presents policy as messy, inherently political and frequently inscrutable.

We begin with outlining this tension because, not only does it run throughout the collection of writings contained in this book, it is central to the book as a whole. Through bringing together different views of policy, from widely different perspectives (i.e. from the world of government, advocacy and academia), this collection presents readers with a 'toolbox' approach to understanding and engaging with public policy. By this we mean that no one view of policy (design or implementation) is privileged over another, recognising that, under varying circumstances, different ideas about how policy processes function and how best to engage with them may be more or less valid. Rather than providing an academic critique or overview of the state of policy research and theory, this volume presents a resource for those wanting to engage with policy debates, design and implementation. It draws on the perspectives of individuals well versed in the 'art' of government and policy as well as those active in theorising policy processes and effects.

Individual chapters, and the collection as a whole, create a picture of policy design and implementation that involves interplay between politics, values, ideas and evidence. Which of these elements is perceived to dominate depends upon the author, their world view, their role in policy and their experiences. From this diversity, we encourage readers to take away inspiration – just as no single chapter provides a roadmap for how you or your organisation can best navigate the world of policy, nor does the book as a whole. Instead, we anticipate this collection will function as a 'jumping off point', providing encouragement and inventiveness for finding new ways to move towards social change through engagement with the policy process and other policy actors.

Structure of the book

The construction of public policy and its effects differs according to one's position in the process. Part I, 'Understanding the policy process', examines the mechanics and machinations of government largely from the perspectives of insiders. Its purpose is to help elucidate and explain what occurs within policy-making circles.

Yet, this leaves the question of how to influence policy unanswered. Part II, 'Influencing policy' demonstrates a range of ways that different actors (both individuals and organisations) have worked to shape policy. While the first two sections of the book help to navigate policy 'as is', a secondary goal of this collection is to move thinking forward on how policy can be 'done' better. The final Part, 'Disrupting business as usual' poses a challenge to current thinking from research to practice with regard to how policy is designed and implemented. The chapters in this final section begin from a common premise that things can be done better in the world of policy, particularly with regard to governance. They range from the micro (i.e. practices involved in policy making), through to the organizational (i.e. tools for pursuing cross-sectoral collaboration) and structural barriers.

In his chapter 'Lost in translation: knowledge, policy, politics and power', John Wiseman draws on his diverse career experience as a senior public servant and then academic to examine differences in motivations, values, time frames and assumptions between sectors. In doing so, he sets out the ideological divide – or 'parallel universes' that exists between those engaged in policy making, and those charged with the creation of knowledge and evidence. Despite the growth in debate regarding evidence-based policy and the challenges of working across the government–academia divide, Wiseman contends that the gap is in fact growing in terms of the difference between public perception and the lived experience of working in different sectors. Indeed, stereotypes abound – academics are combative and unwilling to compromise, policymakers only seek out evidence to justify decisions that have already been made, and the community sector just says the same old thing. In describing these 'parallel universes', Wiseman sets the scene for the chapters to come – each of which seeks to outline ways to bridge the tensions and deal with the different languages that each sector speaks.

Wiseman's real life experience is complemented in Chapter 2, where Toba Bryant and Dennis Raphael provide a range of policy models and theories – each of which shines a different light on policy and politics. From drawing these differing models together, they argue that politics is often the most neglected yet important determinant in whether governments and government agencies act on social issues (termed, in this context, 'the social determinants of health'). They suggest that advocates and academics harness communities more effectively in the fight to change politics. Andrew Wyatt's chapter (Chapter 3) provides another (more traditional) model of policy – the policy cycle model. While his analysis places the matter of politics to one side, he argues that there is still a role for policy cycle heuristics to provide guidance (for those inside and outside of government) on the core elements of the policy process.

Our roles in relation to public policy are not fixed. In the final chapter of Part I (Chapter 4), John Chesterman returns to the personal to reflect on his experiences of moving from academia into government, specifically an unusual government agency from an advocacy perspective – The Office of the Public Advocate. By recounting his personal struggle with his 'insider–outsider' status, Chesterman delves deeper into issues raised in Chapter 1 regarding how to negotiate differing values and deal with disjunctures between action and evidence, while retaining credibility within the policy sphere.

Part II of the book turns attention from policy theories and challenges to the more practical ways in which one might engage with policy. In Chapter 5, Jennifer Doggett provides 'tips and tricks' for engaging with policy actors, particularly public servants and politicians. In doing so, she provides techniques for navigating the divides (in values, ideology and so on) noted in Part I. From the individual, we then move to the organisational – as Shawn McMahon and Mary Gatta explain how their organisation, Wider Opportunities for Women (WOW), uses metrics and measures of wellbeing to advocate for policy change. They argue that measures of wellbeing can be inserted into nearly any stage of policy change processes, providing they have sufficient methodological rigor, accessibility and timeliness, and are tailored towards the needs of decision makers (as suggested by Doggett). WOW's strategic use of metrics is particularly powerful, when viewed in light of Doggett's practical strategies for how to engage policymakers and politicians on an individual level.

The theme of developing and using an evidence-base to impact policy continues in Rachel Clark and Michelle Haby's contribution (Chapter 7). The last 20 years has seen the rise of the evidence-based policy paradigm. This trend has its roots in the evidence-based medical movement, which began in the 1970s under Archie Cochrane. Cochrane argued that Randomised Controlled Trials offer the most effective means by which to judge the value of health interventions (Cochrane 1972). Recently, there has been a push back against evidence-based policy discourses – that evidence-based policy should be seen as an aspiration, and the closest we may come is evidence-informed policy (Head 2010). Despite these recent trends, Clark and Haby put forth the case for why an evidence-based approach to policy is still valuable and should not be abandoned.

The final two chapters in Part II support Clark and Haby's arguments – that evidence generation has a place in advancing policy. Chapters 8 and 9 outline two innovative approaches to developing policy-relevant evidence, and using it as a basis for policy engagement. Guy Johnson, Sue Griss and Yi-Ping Tseng describe the 'J2SI' pilot – a first of its kind randomised control trial (RCT) to evaluate a support intensive homelessness intervention. They show that, although RCTs are rarely used in social policy settings, they can provide powerful evidence for policy change. This cross-disciplinary theme is continued in the discussion of creating an integrated model of social services based on insights from brain science, by Ruth Liberman and Deborah Connolly Youngblood. Here, evidence from the natural sciences forms the basis for an innovative program design at the local level which, in time, can be scaled up.

In the final Part of the book, we attempt to unsettle the status quo and suggest (or inspire) new ways of 'doing' research and practice. In Chapter 10, Jo Barraket, Verity Archer and Chris Mason describe the ways in which social enterprise can unsettle (and thereby improve) the practice of policy and government at the local level by harnessing organisational hybridity. The authors explore how hybrid organisations, which span the social and the economic, can act as alternate policy actors with the potential to reshape and disrupt local governance.

In Chapter 11 Mark Matthews draws upon his work as a policy think tank practitioner to explore how government can develop better methods for coping with uncertainty, ambiguity and risk. In doing so, he explores the technical issues faced in articulating evidence-based policy in an uncertain and changing policy environment. His proposed approach ('intelligence-based policymaking'), based on a more explicit use of structured hypothesis testing to define and learn by doing in implementing government interventions, opens up new avenues for civil society engagement in the policy process, engagement which is critical in the context of risk management, because of the different types of knowledge generated and held at the 'local level' by civil society organisations.

In Chapter 12, David Hayward similarly attempts to draw us away from old, potentially out-dated, practices – with a focus on how governments engage with and manage civil society organisations. Hayward contends that governments need to empower individuals not just to work with government, but to get the most from community organisations themselves by engaging them actively in the process of setting public management targets. These arguments tie in with Gemma Carey and Brad Crammond's chapter on joined-up government (Chapter 13); they similarly state that we must challenge conventional and intuitive ways of working across sectors and boundaries. They argue that as much as evidence of the 'problem' and 'solution' is important, so too is evidence of the process (i.e. *how* we work to implement policies).

Carey and Crammond largely argue for a change in approaches at the meso-level, re-thinking how organisations and sectors engage. However, change at this level naturally requires new ways of working at the micro level. This issue is picked up by Helen Dickinson and Helen Sullivan in their chapter on collaborative performance. Here, Dickinson and Sullivan argue that, if we want to work more effectively across boundaries and sectors, we need to place a much finer analytical lens over the question of collaboration itself. In Chapter 14, they set out a new research agenda for examining collaboration and social and cultural performance – an agenda which is, by its very nature, bound with practice.

While the chapters clearly display a diversity of perspectives, approaches and ideas, they are underpinned by the normative objective of this collection – that for better policy (design, implementation and outcomes) we need to engage in public learning, new and more effective forms of cross-boundary collaboration and develop the necessary 'soft' skills that success in this domain requires.

References

Clavier, C and de Leeuw, E (eds) 2013, *Health promotion and the policy process*, Oxford University Press, London.

Cochrane, A 1972, *Effectiveness and efficiency: random reflections on health services*, Nuffield Provincial Hospital, London.

Head, B 2010. 'Evidence-based policy: principles and requirements', in *Strengthening evidence-based policy in the Australian federation 1*, Roundtable Proceedings, Productivity Commission, Canberra, pp. 13–26.

Part I

Understanding the policy process

1 Lost in translation

Knowledge, policy, politics and power

John Wiseman

Introduction

Policy paralysis. Political gridlock. Governance failure. These are the familiar phrases which academic, community and public sector researchers and policymakers use with increasing frequency to describe their frustration in addressing a growing array of complex and interconnected social, ecological and economic policy challenges. This chapter aims to strengthen understanding of these frustrations and challenges at two interrelated levels. The first section focuses on the widening gap between the parallel universes within which researchers and policymakers produce, analyse and communicate evidence, knowledge, ideas and policies. The second section draws on recent research on the roadblocks standing in the way of decisive action on climate change to briefly open up broader debates about the increasingly disconnected realms of democratic decision making, political agency and corporate power.

Parallel universes? Bridging the knowledge–policy gap

Working in a variety of research and policy-making settings, I have, like many others, been both intrigued and concerned by the number of times I have heard public sector decision makers dismiss university-based researchers as ivory tower academics, hopelessly out of touch with the 'real world' expectations and requirements of policymakers. I have also heard an equal number of disparaging comments from academics berating public servants as unreflective, bureaucratic pragmatists with little understanding of the time and care needed to fully address complex, wicked policy problems. While the relationship between research and policy making continues to evolve, anecdotal accounts of the dysfunctional divide between policymakers and researchers are supported by an extensive body of empirical research (Shonkoff 2000; Lewig *et al.* 2006; Farfard 2008; Bammer *et al.* 2010; Wu 2011). Edwards (2005) for example notes that the research–policy nexus continues to be affected and infected by a range of factors including:

Demand side issues (i.e. from policymakers)

- lack of awareness of existence or relevance of research
- anti-intellectualism
- limited capacity to absorb and use research;

Supply side issues (i.e. from academic researchers)

- capacity (funding, time, skills)
- access to relevant data and evidence
- researcher understanding of needs of policymakers
- communication by researchers ineffective; and

Socio-cultural factors

- disconnect between researchers and policymakers
- competing research paradigms and domains.

In an extensive review of relevant research literature, Landry *et al.* (2003) argue that key factors determining utilisation of university research by policymakers include:

- policy makers valuing of research knowledge
- credibility of researchers
- research products adapted for ease of use by policymakers
- clear implications for policy action (the capacity to answer the 'so what' question)
- strength of formal links between researchers and policymakers
- strength of informal, respectful, trusting relationships between researchers and policymakers.

While all of these factors are clearly important there is also consistent empirical and anecdotal evidence that the last of these factors – the level of respect, trust and shared understanding between researchers and policymakers – is particularly crucial (Stone *et al.* 2001; Landry *et al.* 2003; Giles-Corti *et al.* 2014). This makes good sense intuitively and conceptually, given that respectful, shared understanding of differing values, assumptions and priorities is an essential precondition for genuine and effective collaboration between different cultures (see Said 1997). A useful initial step in cultural bridge building is therefore for all parties to have a clear picture of the range and extent of differing values and assumptions. Table 1.1 provides an overview of the range of differing drivers, assumptions and expectations between public sector policymakers and university-based researchers.

Table 1.1 Differing drivers, assumptions and expectations between public sector policymakers and university-based researchers

Key drivers, assumptions and expectations	Public sector policymakers	University-based researchers
1. Core aim and motivation	Informing policy advice, development and implementation; Solving policy problems	Identifying, exploring and answering research questions; Building knowledge
2. Primary responsibility for framing problems and questions	Ministers and their advisers; Central agencies and senior public servants	Individual researchers, research teams and colleagues; Funding agencies
3. Time frame for results	Short–medium term: usually months	Medium–long term: often years
4. Assumptions about impact of research evidence on decision making	Research evidence is one of many inputs into policy decisions; Pragmatism is more important than rigour	Research evidence should be primary driver of policy decisions; Rigour is more important than pragmatism
5. Key risks to be managed	Criticism of government for wrong action – or inaction	Low research productivity; Loss of reputation for academic rigour
6. Organisational context and culture	Risk averse bureaucracies; Increasing focus on contract management	Universities with multiple responsibilities for teaching, research and engagement – and income generation
7. Most valued communications media and approach	1–2 page policy briefs; Powerpoint slides; Concise policy reports; Keep messages as clear and simple as possible	Peer reviewed articles; Conference papers; Chapters and books; Full complexity of issues needs to be addressed
8. Importance of personal authorship and attitude to intellectual property	Low; IP belongs to funder (i.e. government)	High; IP belongs to knowledge producer (i.e. researcher and/or university)
9. Individual performance criteria	Policies and programs developed and implemented on time and on budget	Peer reviewed publications; Competitive grant income
10. Employment context	Relatively secure	Increasingly insecure

The parallel universes of public sector policymakers and university-based researchers

Core aim and motivation

The core driver and motivation for most government policymakers is the search for credible, affordable, politically feasible solutions to complex problems. The range of potential answers and solutions should ideally be kept reasonably small and not overly complicated by reflections on competing discourses, perspectives and paradigms.

While academic researchers are also commonly driven by an interest in addressing important complex issues, there is often a stronger focus on critical analysis and on ensuring that the full range of relevant theoretical perspectives and methodological possibilities are taken into account. Opening up and exploring new questions and conceptual frameworks is at least as important as arriving at clear, definitive answers.

Primary responsibility for framing problems and questions

The problems for which policymakers are seeking solutions are usually selected and framed by others. In the end the dominant driver for public service policy advice is the achievement of the government's political priorities as specified in election platforms or as decided by Ministers. Public service priorities are also powerfully driven by input and advice from external stakeholders and Ministerial staff with an even sharper focus on short-term political risk management and media impacts.

Many academics still (perhaps naïvely) prefer to see themselves as working in a culture of independent intellectual inquiry, in which the choice of research projects, questions and methods should primarily be determined by the expertise of individual researchers and research teams in identifying and addressing knowledge gaps.

Time frame for results

The time frame for most government decision making is severely constrained by the electoral cycle which, in Australia, is rarely more than three or four years. In fact most policy development processes have an even shorter time scale, with outcomes expected in months rather than years. The relentless pressure of the annual budget cycle, political crises generated by unforeseen events and criticism from political opponents and the media also frequently lead to extreme pressures for quick answers.

Academic research traditionally operates at a very different rhythm and pace. Applications for significant research grants frequently take several years to develop and prepare, particularly if they require bringing together large, multi-disciplinary research teams or collaborative partnerships. Assessment and approval by government funding bodies of research grant applications is likely to take a further six to nine months. Once approved, additional time is needed to finalise research contracts, hire staff and obtain the necessary accommodation and equipment. Large-scale data collection and analysis is likely to involve several years of work, with publication timetables affected by the lengthy processes involved in securing publication in peer-reviewed journals. Ironically government expectations in relation to research performance metrics are tending to further overload and extend journal editorial and peer review processes.

Assumptions about impact of research evidence on decision making

Many academic researchers cling tenaciously to the belief that empirical evidence and the scientific method are – or should be – the primary driver of policy decisions (Sanderson 2002; Jensen 2013). Some continue to be shocked and disappointed by the extent to which calculations about political risks and benefits can and do trump evidence obtained from carefully constructed, methodologically robust research. Compelling ideas and robust evidence are a necessary but not sufficient basis for achieving policy change. Evidence does need to be communicated with the punch and precision required to cut through the noise of information surrounding politicians and public servants. And the capacity to demonstrate the link between evidence, action and outcomes – to clearly answer the 'so what' question – is crucial.

However there is also now a clear body of research showing the ways in which all of us – including politicians and public servants – filter evidence through the lens of individual values and experience (Lorenzoni *et al.* 2007). That is why the best predictors of views on policy issues such as climate change are more often views about individualism, egalitarianism and the role of government rather than exposure to the latest scientific evidence. It is also why stories fuelled by experience and passion generally trump even the most robust statistics.

Most policymakers start from the assumption that scientific and research-generated knowledge are only one ingredient in the complex stew of 'facts', narratives and power that infuses and influences policy decisions. (Stone *et al.* 2001; Farfard 2008) The diverse sources of knowledge feeding into policy decisions include Ministers and Ministerial staff; public policymakers, program managers and service deliverers; books, journals, newspapers, TV, radio and internet; think tanks; consulting firms; public hearings and consultations; lobbyists; community organisations, clients and consumers – as well as university-based researchers.

Most policymakers also have a favourite anecdote about the Minister whose decision was triggered by encounters or conversations with a particular constituent, friend or family member. The primary role of public sector policymakers is therefore to identify and sort relevant policy knowledge from diverse sources leading to an integrated 'policy narrative' which takes account of a wide range of issues including effectiveness, cost, implementation issues, stakeholder reactions and risks. While overly crude and simplistic narratives are clearly undesirable, this suggests that there may be value in researchers becoming more skilled in constructing and telling 'stories' which can assist policymakers, journalists and the general public understand the key messages and implications arising from their research.

Key risks to be managed

Risk management is a crucial component in the job description of any public sector policymaker. The problem however is working out how to balance the risks of taking no action with that of taking the wrong action. Public sector culture is full of apocryphal stories about the dangers of rushing complex policy choices – particularly those with significant unintended consequences or implementation challenges. In the Australian context, debates about the consequences of poor risk management in the high speed implementation of household insulation as a response to the Global Financial Crisis have added a further chapter to this manual (Commonwealth of Australia 2014). At the same time politicians are under constant media scrutiny to show that they have implemented election policies and other commitments on time and on budget. Careful attention to detail and respect for consultative processes can be rapidly portrayed as indecisive dithering. This reinforces the pressure to ensure that the evidence informing policy decisions provides clear and sharp guidelines for action – not a case for further questions and evidence gathering.

The greatest risk facing university researchers remains failure to demonstrate personal research productivity. While many university performance and promotion criteria now include some reference to 'knowledge translation' and 'community engagement', the dominant performance metrics remain success in winning competitive research grants and publications in high status, high impact peer-reviewed journals.

Organisational context and culture

There is a growing gap between public perception and reality in relation to the experience of working in both public sector and academic organizations. The media and general public still tend to visualise the public service as a legion of slow-moving, time-serving bureaucrats. In reality rolling waves of managerialism, privatisation, outsourcing and 'efficiency dividends' have created a far leaner and more corporate organisational culture. Work expectations and demands have become increasingly intense. Effective management of projects, programs, relationships, contracts and risks has increasingly overtaken policy analysis and advice as the primary focus of most job descriptions.

At the same time, ongoing reductions in government funding for tertiary education have intensified pressures on universities to cut costs, develop new sources of income and generally operate more like competitive businesses than ivory towers. With the exception of a small number of eminent research leaders, the working life of most academics has become highly pressured, juggling a complicated mix of research grants, teaching, post graduate supervision, publication and administrative commitments. Communicating and engaging with policymakers can often look like one task too many, particularly in the absence of explicit recognition, incentives and rewards.

Most valued communications media and styles

Internal public sector communications are dominated by one to two page policy briefs, PowerPoint slides, email exchanges and face-to-face briefings. Internal public sector communications products with real impact are usually those which can cut through the vast amount of informational noise to which Ministers and policymakers are exposed, providing clear answers to the vital 'so what' questions – what action should I take as a result of this advice? Numbers, graphs, maps and pictures are all powerful assets. Importantly these are also the primary media and communications products employed by consulting firms – which is one of the reasons for the increasing influence of consultants in most policy making arenas.

The communications products traditionally valued by academics are very different – and importantly reflect considerable variation across disciplines. The disciplines of science and medicine tend to privilege relatively short, multi-authored articles in highly regarded academic journals. Social science and humanities academics have a stronger tradition of single authored publications. Articles tend to be longer and more discursive with the old fashioned medium of 'the book' still highly valued. Researchers from the disciplines of design, architecture and engineering also place considerable value on visual communication outputs including diagrams, pictures and models. While many academics do recognise the importance of producing concise 'summaries for policymakers', the reality is that these outputs are generally of limited value in maximising promotion and research funding prospects.

Importance of personal authorship

One of the toughest challenges faced by academics moving into public sector positions is to learn to embrace – or at least tolerate – the process of collaborative, collective authorship through which most policy briefings and reports are constructed. This process is often perplexing and challenging for researchers drilled in the importance of intellectual work being produced and owned by the individual author – and by the need to rigorously avoid any suggestion of unacknowledged influence or plagiarism. Policymakers tend to find this emphasis on the individual ownership of ideas and the need to provide dense thickets of footnotes and references precious, unnecessary and annoying.

These differing traditions and perspectives about authorship also help to drive prolonged and sometimes bitter negotiations about intellectual property. Academics and their university-based lawyers are very focused on protecting the right and ability of individual researchers to publish the outcomes of their research. Public servants and their equally pugnacious legal departments are far more concerned about making sure that the outcomes of the research are captured and controlled by the client and purchaser of the product – the public sector.

Individual performance criteria

The performance and promotion criteria of public servants tends to emphasise the provision of timely and concise policy advice, the successful management of projects and programs and the avoidance of policy and political risks. Research academics are working to a very different set of drivers, with high quality peer-reviewed publications and income from competitive research grant applications at the top of the list. For many academics, research is only one task, sitting alongside teaching, supervision, administration and community engagement.

Job security

While the work pressures on most public servants continue to intensify, job security remains relatively strong, certainly compared to most of the Australian workforce. For most academics the idea of 'tenure' is a fondly remembered myth. For many, a contract of two to three years is the maximum expectation. Many junior staff are on even shorter contracts of six to 12 months. This further intensifies the pressure to focus energy on the core teaching and research activities most likely to result in contract renewal.

Towards shared understanding of the key challenges facing policymakers and researchers

Policy practitioners and researchers have offered a variety of practical suggestions for building shared understanding of the key challenges facing policy makers and university based researchers (Crewe and Young 2002; Edwards 2005; Landry *et al.* 2003; Lewig *et al.* 2006; Wu 2011; Giles-Corti *et al.* 2014). These include, for example:

- clear understanding of the respective contexts and priorities of researchers and policymakers;
- regular formal and informal opportunities for information sharing and discussion (e.g. joint roundtables, seminars and conferences);
- joint working groups, task forces and project teams;
- joint agenda setting, project design and implementation;

- increased emphasis on interdisciplinary and collaborative research projects;
- joint appointments, secondments, exchanges and scholarships;
- legal, contractual, IP and financial arrangements designed to facilitate collaboration and mutual benefit rather than solely risk management and IP capture and control;
- professional development courses and joint workshops which encourage and strengthen high level communications, diplomatic and negotiating skills;
- continuing to broaden university selection and promotion criteria to include knowledge translation, exchange and engagement as core elements;
- the development of models and templates for a variety of policy communication media, such as concise policy briefs and Power Point presentations;
- appointment by both public sector agencies and universities of skilled and experienced relationship managers and knowledge translation brokers.

The problem of political agency: the widening gap between politics and power

While improved bridge building between the parallel universes of academic researchers and public sector policymakers is important, it is also essential to locate this task in the context of the broader and more complex challenge of the rapidly widening gap between the realms of politics and power.

As Bauman and Bordoni (2014) note the initial driver of the split between *politics* ('the ability to decide which things ought to be done' and *power* ('the ability to get things seen through and done') was the failure of state-based institutions to effectively manage the rolling crises of energy, economic, social and environmental insecurity emerging in the mid-1970s. The ensuing hollowing out of the state by neo-liberal strategies of deregulation, outsourcing and privatisation has been further exacerbated by the accelerating impact of corporate globalisation, with many crucial economic and financial decisions now largely beyond the control of national governments. Bauman and Bordoni summarise the outcome and implications of this process in the following way:

> The present crisis differs from its historical precedents in as far as it is lived through in the situation of a *divorce between power and politics*. That divorce results in the *absence of agency* capable of doing what every crisis by definition requires: choosing the way to proceed and applying the therapy called for by that choice.... On the one hand we see power safely roaming the no-mans land of global expanses free from political control and at liberty to select its own targets; on the other there is politics squeezed/robbed of all or nearly all of its power, muscles and teeth.
>
> (2014, pp. 12 and 22)

The accelerating disconnect between localised politics and globalising power has significant implications for policymakers and researchers working on challenges as diverse and as complex as refugee and migration flows; the prevention and management of pandemics; the regional employment impacts of changes in corporate investment, trade and labour hire policies; and the achievement of reductions in global greenhouse gas emission at the speed and scale required to reduce the probability and risks of extreme climate change.

As the recent 'Post-carbon pathways' review of large-scale de-carbonisation strategies concludes, the overall suite of actions required to reduce the risk of dangerous climate change is now widely understood: rapid replacement of fossil fuels by renewable energy; rapid reductions in energy consumption and improvements in energy efficiency; and the drawdown and sequestration of carbon into sustainable carbon sinks (Wiseman *et al.* 2013). There is now also widespread understanding that the biggest roadblocks preventing rapid de-carbonisation are social and political rather than technological. The key roadblocks preventing rapid implementation of post-carbon economy transition strategies (each of which reflect the accelerating decline of political agency) include the following:

- denial of the necessity and urgency of action
- the power and influence of vested interests
- political paralysis and 'short termism'
- technological, social and economic path dependencies and lock ins
- financial, governance and implementation constraints.

Denial of the necessity and urgency of action

Clear and effective communication of the most robust scientific evidence of climate change trends, causes and risks remains the essential foundation for overcoming climate change denial and strengthening understanding of the necessity and urgency of action. Evidence of the ways in which climate change is increasing the frequency and severity of extreme weather events will be particularly important in enabling individuals to 'join the dots' between personal experience and broader climate change trends and patterns.

As noted above, the evaluation and interpretation of climate science messages is, however, profoundly influenced by pre-existing value frameworks and political perspectives. The core messages of climate science therefore need to be augmented by action to expose and overcome climate denial disinformation campaigns and by framing and communication strategies which reach and appeal to a variety of audiences. For some audiences, an ethical concern about the consequences of catastrophic climate change for the most vulnerable people and species now and in the future will be a sufficient motive for action. For others, recognition of more immediate and personal risks to their own families and communities will be crucial. Others again may be most influenced by imagining and understanding the potential social and economic opportunities and co-benefits of a healthy and sustainable post carbon future.

The power and influence of vested interests

As Professor Ross Garnaut has recently noted, drawing on his extensive experience in leading work on Australian climate change policy options, the role of vested interests is increasingly central to an adequate understanding of the relationship between policy, politics and power:

> It is inherent in the human condition that where most people stand depends on where they sit. Many Australian business people have a vested interest in the failure of global efforts to mitigate the dangers of climate change. One consequence is that our business leadership contains an unusually high number of people who express the opinion that the best of climate science is wrong on global warming.
>
> (Garnaut 2013, p. 250)

The most effective strategies for overcoming the influence of the fossil fuel lobby – and ending the mining of fossil fuels – include ceasing public subsidisation of fossil fuel industries; a concerted campaign to encourage private sector disinvestment in fossil fuel corporations; a sufficiently robust carbon price; and legislation and regulation driving a rapid shift in investment from fossil fuels to renewables. Equitable structural adjustment programs for communities and households affected by the phase out of fossil fuel industries and employment will also be vital, both for ethical reasons and to maintain community and electoral support for the implementation of tough political decisions.

Political paralysis and short termism

Courageous moral leadership, at multiple levels and in many sectors, is an essential precondition for the effective implementation of rapid emissions-reduction strategies. In addition to the corrosive influence of denial campaigns and the lobbying of vested interests, other obstacles standing in the way of decisive climate change leadership include competing and more immediate economic and political demands, the pressure not to be seen to be politically naïve or unrealistic; and the sense that the transformational change required is simply not possible (Rickards *et al.* 2014). The imagination and communication of 'parallel narratives' visualising a just and resilient post-carbon future combined with 'living laboratories' demonstrating what life in such an alternative future might be like can also provide a valuable foundation for sustaining the belief that transformational change is indeed socially and politically feasible.

Technological and social path dependencies

The crucial role of individual and organisational change agents, social entre-preneurs and demonstration projects in opening up 'niche spaces', challenging path dependent thinking and imagining and communicating disruptive ideas and technologies is now widely understood. Many researchers and policy-makers also note the importance of a proactive role for government in setting long policy directions and in mobilising the investment required to drive the rapid, scaled-up commercialisation and deployment of game-changing social and technological innovations. Professor John Schellnhuber, Director of the Potsdam Institute for Climate Impact Research, draws these conclusions, for example, from his reflections on the speed with which renewable energy is replacing fossil fuels in Germany:

> Public will, individual psychology, and technological innovation come together to create tremendous innovation dynamics, tremendous substi-tution dynamics. In a few years renewable energy has already overtaken, at least in installed capacity, the nuclear power industry in Germany. So this is 'proof of concept' – that yes we can create big transitions.
> (cited in Wiseman *et al.* 2013, p. 35)

As Westley (2002) also notes, innovative networks of activists and academics can catalyse public participation to levels which push policy debates towards experimentation with alternatives and bridge the gap between intention and action. Such approaches highlight the role of 'shadow networks' operating both within and outside the dominant system in developing alternatives which can potentially replace the dominant regime if and when the oppor-tunity arises.

Financial, governance and implementation constraints

An equitable strategy for implementing rapid emissions-reduction policies will need to include internationally verifiable de-carbonisation road maps; a shared approach to carbon pricing; a strengthened role for international gov-ernance institutions; structural adjustment assistance to support workers and communities shift away from fossil fuel-based employment; and the embed-ding of renewable energy and climate change resilience investment resources in international aid and development programs. The urgency of the timetable for emissions reductions and the limited likelihood of immediate progress towards binding global treaties mean that there will also need to be a major focus on alliances and collaborations between nation states, provinces and cities. There will also be an important and increasing role for local govern-ment and community organisations in exploring and implementing innov-ative post-carbon-economy transition solutions.

Towards a theory and practice of transformational change

In the end, the most challenging question in relation to the design and implementation of effective climate change policy responses remains the relationship between political agency and power. How might the transition to a just and resilient post-carbon future actually occur? What theories and practices of social and political change could plausibly deliver this transformation at sufficient speed and scale? To explore the question of pathways to transformational change in more depth, researchers, policymakers and activists interviewed for the Post Carbon Pathways project were asked to provide a brief response to the following 'back casting' question:

> Imagine it is 2030.... Imagine we now live in a world in which the transition to a just and resilient post-carbon society has occurred so there is now real hope that catastrophic climate change will be avoided. How did this happen?

Responses to this question highlight four interconnected and interlinked drivers of transformational change.

Evidence and education which broadens and deepens understanding of the necessity and possibility of an emergency speed reduction in greenhouse gas emissions

Reflecting on the campaigns which overcame the threat of ozone depletion or the power of the tobacco corporations might lead us to imagine emissions reduction scenarios driven first of all by scientific evidence, persuasion and regulation. The key question which remains here is whether the speed with which climate tipping points are approaching will allow us the time for primarily incremental strategies.

Creative and disruptive technological, social and economic innovation

The speed and spread of game-changing technologies such as the printing press, the steam engine or the silicon chip provide a second, plausible narrative of swift and transformational change. The speed with which renewable energy technologies and systems are improving in efficiency and falling in cost is certainly impressive, although it is also increasingly clear that social as well as technological innovation will need to be a central part of any real solution to climate change.

Visionary leadership, courageous advocacy and skilful implementation by communities, business and government

A third pathway might be created though the kind of visionary leadership and community mobilisation that led to the achievement of women's rights and the overthrow of apartheid. James Goldstene, former CEO of the California Clean Air Board, noted, for example, the following leadership lessons arising from the successful implementation of robust climate change policies in California:

> In 2006 the timing was right for passing the Californian Clear Air Act, AB32. People understood the science, we had the right mix of politicians, we had a governor who was very energetic on the issue and all these things coalesced, to make that possible. You never know when that's going to happen – and that's where leadership really comes in. As soon as you see the opening you've got to strike; that's the challenge. We are the incubator – we're developing these programs so others can adopt them, and copy them.
>
> (cited in Wiseman *et al.* 2013, p. 44)

Decisive action at critical moments of ecological, economic and social crisis

Bearing in mind the speed with which climatic tipping points are bearing down on us, many experienced climate researchers and activists have come to the conclusion that a devastating series of crises on the scale of Hurricane Katrina and Hurricane Sandy will be needed to create the 'Pearl Harbor' political tipping points in which visionary political leadership, community mobilisation, technological innovation and social creativity can come together to drive transformational change at the necessary scale and speed.

While his role in formulating and driving the neo-liberal economic agenda makes his advice somewhat ironic, Milton Friedman provides us with a useful reminder of the ways in which alternative visions of the future can play a significant role in driving transformational change, particularly at moments of economic, social and ecological crisis.

> Only a crisis – actual or perceived – produces real change. When the crisis occurs, the actions that are taken depend on the ideas that are lying around. That, I believe, is our basic function: to develop alternatives to existing policies, to keep them alive and available until the politically impossible becomes politically inevitable.
>
> (cited in Klein 2007, p. 6)

Conclusion: bridging the divides between knowledge and policy, politics and power

The formidable obstacles standing in the way of an adequate and timely response to global warming are a useful reminder of the scale of the challenges facing policymakers in responding to an increasingly complex web of economic, social and environmental policy problems. As noted in the first section of this chapter, an adequate response to these interconnected challenges certainly calls for increased skill in creating, communicating and deploying knowledge and evidence in ways which maximise impact and usefulness to decision makers. Strengthening understanding of the parallel universes of academic researchers and public sector policymakers is an important first step in this process. The ongoing difficulties encountered in creating just and sustainable climate change solutions are also, however, a stark reminder of the broader political context within which policymakers and academics operate and of the urgent need to find new ways of navigating the growing gap between local political agency and globalising corporate power.

References

Bammer, G, Micheaux, A and Sanson, A 2010, *Bridging the know–do gap*, ANU Press, Canberra.

Bauman, Z and Bordoni, C 2014, *State of crisis*, Polity Press, Cambridge.

Commonwealth of Australia, 2014, *Royal commission into the home insulation program: final report*, Commonwealth of Australia, Canberra.

Crewe, E and Young, J 2002, *Bridging research and policy: context, evidence and links*, Overseas Development Institute, Working Paper 173.

Edwards, M 2005, 'Social science research and public policy: narrowing the divide', *Australian Journal of Public Administration*, vol. 64, no. 1, pp. 68–74.

Farfard, P 2008, *Evidence and healthy public policy: insights from health and political sciences*, Canadian Policy Research Networks, May.

Garnaut, R 2013, *Dog days: Australia after the boom*, Black Inc. Publishing, Melbourne.

Giles-Corti, B, Sallis, J, Sugiyama, T, Frank L, Lowe, M and Owen, N 2014, 'Translating active living research into policy and practice: one important pathway to chronic disease prevention', *Journal of Public Health Policy*, vol. 36, no. 2, pp. 231–243.

Jensen, P 2013, *What is evidence-based policy?*, Melbourne Institute Policy Brief No. 4/13, August.

Klein, N 2007, *The shock doctrine*, Metropolitan Books, New York.

Landry, R, Lamari, M and Amara, N 2003, 'The extent and determinants of the utilization of university research in government agencies', *Public Administration Review*, vol. 63, no. 2, pp. 192–205.

Lewig, K, Arney, F and Scott, D 2006, 'Closing the research–policy and research–practice gaps: ideas for child and family services', *Family Matters*, no. 27, pp. 12–19.

Lorenzoni, I, Nicholson-Cole, S and Whitmarsh, L 2007, 'Barriers perceived to engaging with climate change among the UK public and their policy implications', *Global Environmental Change*, vol. 17, no. 3, pp. 445–459.

Rickards, L, Kashima, Y and Wiseman, J 2014, 'Barriers to effective climate change mitigation: the case of senior government and business decision makers', *Wiley Interdisciplinary Reviews: Climate Change*, vol. 5, no. 6, pp. 753–773.

Said, E 1997, *Covering Islam: how the media and the experts determine how we see the rest of the world*, Random House, New York.

Sanderson, I 2002, 'Making sense of "what works": evidence-based policymaking as instrumental rationality?', *Public Policy and Administration*, vol. 17, no. 3, pp. 61–75.

Shonkoff, J 2000, 'Science, policy and practice: three cultures in search of a shared mission', *Child Development*, vol. 71, no. 1, pp. 181–187.

Stone, D, Maxwell, S and Keating, M 2001, *Bridging research and policy: An International Workshop funded by the UK Department for International Development* Radcliffe House, 16–17 July, Warwick University.

Westley, F 2002, 'The devil in the dynamics: adaptive management on the front lines' in L H Gunderson and C S Holling (eds), *Panarchy: understanding transformations in human and natural systems*, Island Press, Washington, DC, pp. 333–360.

Wiseman, J, Edwards, T and Luckins, K 2013, *Post carbon pathways: towards a just and resilient post carbon future*, Centre for Policy Development and Melbourne Sustainable Society Institute, Melbourne.

Wu, I 2011, 'Bridging the policy–research divide from the practitioner's point of view', *The Forum*, vol. 9, no. 2.

2 Opening policy windows with evidence and citizen engagement

Addressing the social determinants of health inequalities

Toba Bryant and Dennis Raphael

Introduction

It has been known since the mid-1850s that the primary factors that determine whether one lives a long, healthy life or a short, sick one are the living conditions experienced over the lifespan (Engels 1845/1987; Virchow 1848/1985). It has also been known that these factors result from actions taken by governing authorities (Raphael 2014). Despite an apparent endorsement of these understandings by Canadian authorities, Canadian public health discourses and public understandings concerning the determinants of health have come to be dominated by genetic and behavioural risk explanations (Low and Therault 2008). Increasing Canadian interest in the social determinants of health concept as detailed in international, national and local reports is an attempt to counter these dominant explanations (Butler-Jones 2008; Sudbury and District Health Unit 2011; World Health Organization 2008).

Drawing upon theoretical insights from the social inequality and political economy literatures as well as empirical research studies, the public policy and public health communities are increasingly concerned with the same problems and challenges: creating public policy that will reduce the social inequalities that create health inequalities (Banting and Myles 2013; Clavier and de Leeuw 2013). In essence, they are creating opportunities for public policy that enhances the quality of the social determinants of health and makes their distribution more equitable (Graham 2007). We call this addressing the 'social determinants of health inequalities' (SDHI).

Drawing on Canadian experiences, this chapter examines how the public health community can learn from public policy models to create opportunities by using evidence and promoting citizen engagement. These models suggest how combinations of activity with local elected officials, community partners, and mainstream and social media can move a health promotion agenda forward. Such activity will also involve public education to create a demand for governmental action on the SDHI. Such efforts are necessary as public policy action on the SDHI in Canada lags well behind other wealthy developed nations (Bryant *et al.* 2011; Hancock 2011; Low and Therault 2008). To help understand these developments, we engage with various models of the public policy process to illuminate both the barriers to action and the means by which the public health community can surmount them.

Canadian scene: conceptual contributions vs policy development and implementation

Canada's contributions to conceptualising health promotion in general and the SDHI in particular are significant (Hancock 2011; Restrepo 2000). In 1986, Canada hosted the inaugural International Conference on Health Promotion in Canada's national capital. It produced the Ottawa Charter on Health Promotion, the first of many health promotion documents outlining the importance of public policy that provides the prerequisites – now called the social determinants – of health (World Health Organization 1986).

Even before this, the Canadian government identified broader determinants of health inequalities. In 1974, *A new perspective on the health of Canadians* recognised the role physical and social environments play in shaping health (Lalonde 1974). This was followed by *Achieving health for all: a framework for health promotion* in 1986 which argued for reducing health inequalities by enhancing public policy in the areas of income security, employment, education and housing, among other non-health care areas (Epp 1986). The Population Health Working Group of the Canadian Institute for Advanced Research identified a number of determinants of health (Evans *et al.* 1994). These health determinants were adopted by the Public Health Agency of Canada (PHAC) and form the basis of ongoing governmental statements and reports exploring these issues. The Healthy Cities movement also began in Canada (Awofeso 2003).

There have certainly been efforts to address these issues. During the 1990s, the Toronto Healthy Cities Office drew upon the principles of health equity, democratic participation and healthy public policy to recommend governmental actions (Wigle 1998). Canadian government-funded research institutions such as the Canadian Population Health Initiative and the Health Council of Canada have since reported on the extent and determinants of health inequalities in Canada (Canadian Population Health Initiative 2008; Health Council of Canada 2010).

The Canadian Institute for Health Research funds research into these issues and Canadians are certainly not under-represented in academic publishing on these issues (Raphael 2012). A series of reports from the Chief Health Officer of Canada and complementary reports from provincial health authorities and national and provincial public health associations speak of the importance of addressing the SDHI (Butler-Jones, 2008, 2010, 2011). Finally, PHAC provided funding for two WHO Commission on Social Determinants of Health's knowledge hubs – Early Child Development, and Globalization and Health – which were based in Canada (World Health Organization 2008).

Despite these efforts, the consensus is Canada lags well behind other nations in implementing these concepts through public policy action (Bryant *et al.* 2011; Hancock 2011; Health Council of Canada 2010; Low and Therault 2008). As one example, the Healthy City Concept, which is robustly implemented in Europe, is now moribund in Canada (Raphael 2001). And addressing SDHI is not on the public policy agenda of the federal or any provincial government. Associated with this governmental neglect is a dearth of media coverage of these issues (Hayes *et al.* 2007) and evidence that the Canadian public has virtually no understanding of the importance of addressing the SDHI (Canadian Population Health Initiative 2004; Lofters *et al.* 2014).

Despite this rather dismal state of affairs, there are new and innovative efforts to place the SDHI on the public policy agenda through gathering and disseminating evidence to the public with the goal of fostering citizen engagement. In the following sections, we situate these efforts within various theories of the public policy process with the goals of first identifying and then surmounting these barriers to Canadian public policy action. These analyses should be relevant in other nations where the SDHI are not receiving significant public policy attention.

Models of public policy change and their role in understanding public policy inaction

Addressing the SDHI through public policy action is contested, with implementation anything but assured (Graham 2007; Milio 1986; Robert Wood Johnson Foundation 2010) Analysis of public policy processes can both identify barriers to action and enable the surmounting of these barriers (Clavier and de Leeuw 2013). Kickbusch calls for a *health political science* focused on these issues (Kickbusch 2013).

The aspects of a health political science include analysis of policy content, policy processes, policy actors, and the politics behind decision making by authorities (Clavier and de Leeuw 2013). Models of policy development and change can help: (1) explain how public policy is made; (2) identify barriers to achieving action on given public policy issues; and (3) suggest means of surmounting these barriers. Existing models differ in how they see society and the public policy process but all have implications for moving an SDHI agenda forward. Three models illustrate the range of existing approaches and are relevant to this inquiry: Kingdon's model of agenda setting, Hall's policy paradigms model, and Esping-Andersen's welfare state regime approach. The first two are consensus models in assuming public policy is generally made on the basis of rational cost and benefit analyses by governmental authorities. The last one is a conflict model in seeing public policy made on the basis of the distribution of power and influence of various sectors of society such that public policy may systematically benefit some at the expense of others.

Kingdon's agenda-setting model

Kingdon's model is representative of a family of pluralist models that examine how various sectors act to influence policy development (Kingdon 2010). The public policy-making apparatus consists of three process streams – problems, policy and political – which initially function independently by their own set of rules. Policy outcomes depend on how these streams come together to create windows of opportunity. In the problems stream, government decides which problems are worthy of action. In the present analysis the question is: *Are the SDHI seen as worthy of public policy action by governmental authorities?*

The policies stream is where a community of experts develop policy proposals to respond to recognised problems. The question here is: *What are some public policies that can address the SDHI?* These experts or specialists are usually civil servants, planning and evaluation analysts, political staff and others. The political stream is where the ideologies and belief systems of ruling authorities shape receptivity to these issues. This stream also determines the ability of advocacy and opposition groups to have their views acknowledged by these authorities. The question here is: *Is addressing the SDHI through public policy consistent with the political ideology of ruling authorities?* Table 2.1 answers these questions in relation to the SDHI in Canada.

In addition to the political ideology of current ruling authorities, the politics stream can be affected by specific events and changes in political dynamics. These events can be changes in administration or public opinion, global economic collapses such as the events of 2008, which triggered significant social and economic changes, and the actions of advocacy organisations. Applied to the SDHI, Kingdon's model emphasises that moving any issue onto the public policy agenda is shaped by the orientation of government and its receptivity to an issue and its proposed remedies. In short, it is essential to

Table 2.1 The Canadian scene: Kingdon's policy streams and addressing the SDHI

Are the SDHI seen as worthy of public policy action by governmental authorities?	By public health authorities, yes. By governmental authorities, no. Addressing SDHI is not on the agenda of any governmental authority in Canada at any level.
What are some public policies that can address the SDHI?	Public health authorities, advocates and researchers have identified a wide range of public policies that would address the SDHI.
Is addressing the SDHI through public policy consistent with the political ideology of ruling authorities?	Apparently not. Analysis of political activity in Canada indicates that virtually all political parties have eschewed public policy actions to address the SDHI.

understand how an issue takes root and receives government attention. In Canada, addressing the SDHI requires attention to both the *problems* and *political* streams. Later sections consider how public health community actions may remedy the situation.

Hall's policy paradigms model

Hall's model is representative of the family of learning models of policy change in that it focuses on the structures and processes of government and how these structures and processes are shaped by previous experience (Hall 1993). The policy paradigms model outlines different kinds of policy change with a particular focus on how radical departures in policy decisions come about. As an institutional model, it sees previous policy decisions as important guides to future public policy action. These institutional dispositions are called policy legacies. Policy legacies refer to past government decisions shaping future public policy decisions (Pierson 2000). A policy paradigm refers to the system of ideas and principles in which policymakers work. Policy paradigms prescribe policy goals and the type of policy instruments to be deployed to achieve policy goals. Importantly, policy paradigms determine which types of problems will even be addressed.

Central to Hall's model is a policy change typology: *first-order, second-order,* and *third-order changes* (Hall 1993). *First order policy change* involves no changes to the overall goals and objectives of a public policy area but rather minor or incremental modifications to policy. These may involve increasing funding to programs that address specific health issues that may or may not include the SDHI. *Second-order policy change* refers to a change in policy instruments. For example, a government may decide that issuing guidelines for jurisdictions to address SDHI has not been successful and therefore now make these guidelines mandatory with accountability mechanisms employed. Similar to *first-order* change, *second-order* change is incremental. The policy goals and objectives remain the same. Finally, *third-order* policy change refers to paradigmatic or radical policy change (Hall 1993). For example, a government may decide to shift from a biomedical and lifestyle approach to promoting health and preventing illness to an SDHI approach enacted through public policy. This entails redefining the policy goals and objectives to reflect the change in orientation required by an SDHI approach.

Hall considers a shift in paradigm as being driven by societal shifts rather than changes in scientific knowledge. Governmental authorities are driven to adopt a new paradigm when anomalies related to the current paradigm accumulate. Such an anomaly may be declines in the rank of a nation in life expectancy or infant mortality, or evidence of growing health inequalities, which adherents of the new paradigm will use to critique the dominant or received policy paradigm. Indeed, in a later work, Hall argues that a new economic paradigm drove public policy transitions especially during the period from the end of World War II through to the 1980s (Hall 2013). This critique may lead to a shift to a new paradigm. In Canada, this would involve taking seriously the problems that could be remedied by adopting public policy that addresses the SDHI.

Esping-Andersen's welfare regime typology

Esping-Andersen's model is representative of the family of political economy models concerned with how political ideology and power operates through economic and political systems to distribute material and social resources. Central to this perspective is that politics and economics are intrinsically related and this dynamic shapes public policy development (Coburn 2004; Esping-Andersen 1990, 1999). Esping-Andersen's model conceives ideas and institutions – and the public policy that flows from these – as evolving from societal arrangements influenced by historical traditions. The central features of welfare regimes are their extent of social stratification, decommodification and the relative role of the State, market, and family in providing economic and social security to the population. Importantly, the State's role is influenced by class mobilisation in that the loyalties of the working and middle class determine the forms by which the economic and political systems operate. These differing patterns of loyalties have contributed to the formation and maintenance of these welfare state regimes.

The Social Democratic welfare state has been strongly influenced by social democratic politics. Its concern with equality outlines a key role for the State in addressing inequality and providing the population with various forms of economic and social security (Saint-Arnaud and Bernard 2003). Its provision of programs and supports on a universal basis is consistent with its goal of reducing social stratification and decommodifying the necessities of life. In essence, the Social Democratic welfare state strives to provide the means by which one can live a decent life independent of employment market involvement. The Conservative welfare state is distinguished by its concern with maintaining stability (Saint-Arnaud and Bernard 2003). Historically, governance is by Christian Democratic parties that maintain many aspects of social stratification, a moderate degree of decommodification of societal resources, and an important role for the family in providing economic and social support. The Church played a significant role in its development. Finally, the Liberal welfare state's emphasis is on liberty and is dominated by the market and ruled by generally pro-business political parties (Saint-Arnaud and Bernard 2003). Little attempt is made to reduce social stratification and its degree of decommodification is the lowest. There is little State intervention in the operation of the economic system.

Esping-Andersen's distinction between Social Democratic, Conservative and Liberal welfare states has much to do with the making of public policy that addresses the SDHI. Figure 2.1 shows the basic elements and characteristics of these differing forms of welfare state. Their alignment with SDHI-related public policy is apparent. These differing forms of the welfare state

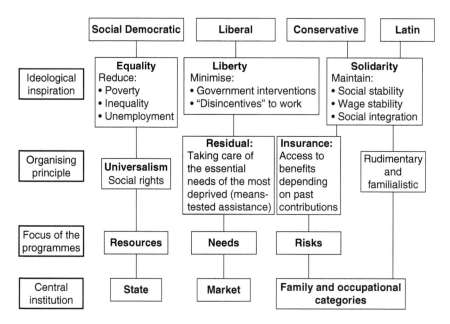

Figure 2.1 Ideological variations in forms of the welfare state (Saint-Arnaud and Bernard 2003, p. 503).

have not come about by accident but are shaped and maintained by ideologies of governing authorities informed by the politics of political parties.

The political economy approach provides a critical analysis that identifies how some sectors of society benefit at the expense of others. It draws a direct line between neoliberalism – a political ideology of the market (Coburn 2010; Teeple 2000) that emphasises free enterprise and freer trade between nations which emerged during the 1970s – and the retrenchment of the welfare state during the 1980s. The approach specifies that Liberal welfare states such as Canada are especially susceptible to its effects. Indeed, political economists attribute growing inequality in the distribution of the social determinants of health in many nations to these effects (Coburn 2010). In Canada and elsewhere, governments reduced social spending ostensibly to enhance the competitiveness of their economies in the new global economy. In actuality, these changes usually led to the enhancement of one sector – the business and corporate sector – at the expense of organised labour and civil society (Langille 2009).

The political economy approach is important as it considers how the ideological views of governments shape receptivity to timing and content of public policies. This model suggests that addressing the SDHI through public policy action in Liberal welfare states such as Canada will require no less than shifting the role of the State. This shift will occur as a result of addressing

Table 2.2 Summary of key aspects of models for public policy development and implementation

Kingdon's policy stream model of public policy development and implementation	Hall's policy paradigms model of public policy development and implementation	Esping-Andersen's welfare regime model of public policy development and implementation
Problems stream: Government identifies problems/issues for which action will be considered. *Policy stream*: Policy experts develop public policy proposals to address identified problems. *Political stream*: Ideology and beliefs of the government of the day influence government receptivity to public policy responses. *The model is an example of an agenda-setting approach.*	Applies *policy paradigms* concept to explain different forms of policy change. *Policy legacies* influence future developments. *Identifies three orders of policy change: First-order* involves minor changes to policy such as increasing social assistance rates. *Second-order* consists of change in policy instruments, e.g. shifting from voluntary to involuntary measures such as mandating provision of job benefits. *Third-order* change refers to a radical shift in policy goals and objectives, e.g. shift from a biomedical and behavioural risk conception of health promotion to one concerned with developing public policy to address the SDHI. The shift from one policy paradigm to another is largely socially determined with politicians arbitrating these shifts. *The model is an example of an historical institutional approach.*	Identification of welfare state clusters – Social Democratic, Liberal and Conservative – based on the degree of State intervention that shapes social stratification, decommodifies societal resources, and balances roles of the State, market, and family in providing market and social security. *Social Democratic* regimes are the most decommodified (i.e. extensive State intervention in the economy) and most concerned with public policy activation. The State provides comprehensive economic and social support to citizens. *Liberal* regimes are the least decommodified. The market is the most important institution in providing economic and social security. *Conservative* welfare states have some decommodification of societal resources. The family is the most important institution in providing economic and social security. *The model is an example of a class mobilisation approach, informed by a political economy analysis.*

imbalances in power and influence that at present favour the business and corporate sector. Interestingly, many public health activities designed to address the SDHI may help facilitate such a shift.

All three models are concerned – at some level – with knowledge creation and dissemination. Kingdon and Hall's models focus on knowledge creation and dissemination to elites such as government authorities and policymakers. Esping-Andersen's model suggests a need to expand these activities to the public in order to shift existing power imbalances. Each model is also concerned with political ideology and how political dynamics shape public policy. The political economy model, however, explicitly considers how political power of various sectors shapes State activities. It calls for more than knowledge creation and transmission to elites, but rather the development of social and political movements that will challenge existing economic and political structures and processes. Employing these models, it can be seen that the SDHI-related public policy arises from a particular set of societal arrangements. As such, the SDHI are socially created and therefore amenable to change through public policy. Table 2.2 summarises key aspects of these models.

The current state of the public health community's efforts to address SDHI

There appears to be vigorous and sustained Canadian public health community activity that is creating evidence concerning the SDHI. There are many government reports, public health and health care association declarations and statements, as well as conferences and meetings concerned with the SDHI (Raphael 2010).

Federal and provincial funding is available for research on SDHI. The federal government established a number of National Coordinating Centres to address these issues and of particular note are those concerned with Healthy Public Policy and Determinants of Health (National Collaborating Centre for Healthy Public Policy 2014). Canadian researchers publish extensively on these issues. Local public health units investigate and respond to these issues (Joint OPHA/ALPHA Working Group on the Social Determinants of Health 2010).

But despite these efforts, there is little if any impact of these activities on public policy development and implementation (Bryant *et al.* 2011; Hancock 2011). Why, despite abundant evidence, is there little public policy implementation of findings? Some argue it is due to a lack of advocacy efforts and knowledge translation, while others argue that it is a result of governmental approaches that aim to remove state intervention in the operation of the market economy (Bryant, 2012). Governments continue to act within existing policy paradigms and see no reason to shift from these policy legacies. It also does not help that Canadian public policy making is consistent with the interests of the corporate and business sector, consistent with Canada being a

Liberal welfare state and being increasingly susceptible to neo-liberal ideology (Bryant *et al.* 2011; Langille 2009; Raphael 2014).

One of the reasons for this situation is that public health community evidence production and dissemination is limited to public health professionals and policymakers rather than the Canadian public (Brassolotto *et al.* 2014). This lack of understanding of SDHI issues by the public allows governments to avoid acting upon this evidence since there are no political repercussions for doing so from an uninformed public.

The approach taken to date by the public health community is not difficult to understand. Researchers, civil servants and advocates work on the assumption that gathering and dissemination of evidence to the professional community and policymakers is in itself sufficient to effect public policy that addresses the SDHI (Institute of Population and Public Health 2011; National Collaborating Centre on the Determinants of Health 2008). In essence, they assume that focusing on Kingdon's problem and policy streams will lead to the desired outcomes. In addition to ignoring Kingdon's political stream, they overlook Hall's insights into the difficulty of enacting paradigmatic policy change, especially in the light of long-standing policy paradigm legacies. They certainly do not consider Esping-Andersen's analysis of the role of political power and influence and how these shape the making of SDHI-related public policy. What is required to address these deficiencies?

Key developments in the public health community's efforts to address SDHI

Each model suggests means of overcoming these barriers and opening policy windows that address the SDHI. Table 2.3 identifies the implications of these for Liberal welfare states such as Canada. All three models suggest a need for public education about the importance of the SDHI. It is important for: (a) agenda setting; (b) shifting policy paradigm legacies; and (c) correcting existing power imbalances among societal sectors. All three models suggest barriers exist to having Liberal welfare states take the SDHI seriously. For Kingdon, these barriers include the political ideologies of ruling authorities; for Hall, existing policy paradigm legacies; and for Esping-Andersen, power imbalances among societal sectors. The last model is unique in indicating the need to engage in activating an engaged public, strengthening the labour movement and electing political parties of the left. Such activities would certainly represent a paradigm change for the public health community in Canada!

All these models suggest educating the public and using strength in numbers to promote an SDHI public policy agenda. Educating the public with regard to the SDHI has not been a priority of governing authorities in Canada and, in response, grassroots public health activity has done so (Raphael *et al.* 2014). The welfare regime model and to some extent policy paradigms highlight the role of politics and political ideology in shaping public policy change outcomes.

Table 2.3 Implications of public policy models that address the SDHI

Implications of Kingdon's policy stream model for creating public policy that addresses the SDHI	Implications of Hall's policy paradigms model for public policy that addresses the SDHI	Implications of Esping-Andersen's welfare regime model for public policy that addresses the SDHI
Problems stream: Public education as to the importance of the SDHI will force governing authorities to respond to challenges. *Policy stream:* Continue to provide public policy solutions to SDHI issues but provide these to the public as well. *Political stream:* These efforts will force governing political parties to address SDHI issues under threat of electoral defeat or will build support in political parties receptive to addressing the SDHI through public policy action.	*Policy legacies:* Recognise the historical dominance of biomedical and behavioural approaches to health promotion and their making addressing the SDHI through public policy action difficult. *Recognise need for paradigmatic change:* Recognise the profound barriers to paradigmatic shifts among well-established liberal welfare states. *Promote paradigmatic change:* Collate evidence concerning policy failures and implications of not addressing the SDHI. *Build public support for paradigmatic change:* Confront governmental authorities by lobbying for changes to public policy that does not address the SDHI.	*Build citizen support for enhanced role of the State:* Strengthen citizen support for public policy that addresses the SDHI through public education and community organising. *Balance imbalances in societal power and influence:* Work to offset dominance of the public policy agenda by corporate and business interests by strengthening the labour movement and political parties of the left. Activation of the working and middle classes in their own interests will spur development of SDHI-related public policy.

Local public health units across Canada are engaging in public education activities concerning the SDHI (Brassolotto *et al.* 2014; Raphael *et al.* 2014). Importantly, one local public health unit in Ontario created a video animation *Let's start a conversation about health and not talk about health care at all* (Sudbury and District Health Unit 2011), which has been adapted for use by no fewer than 17 other public health units in Ontario (out of the total of 36), numerous others across Canada and jurisdictions in the USA and Australia (Raphael 2012).

Mikkonen and Raphael created the public primer on the SDHI entitled *Social determinants of health: the Canadian facts*, which has been downloaded over 250,000 times since April 2010. Canadians made 85 per cent of these downloads (Mikkonen and Raphael 2010). And a new Canadian organisation *Upstream Action* aims to create a movement to create a healthy society through dissemination to the public – as well as policymakers – of evidence-based, people-centred ideas (Upstream Action 2013). It is hoped that these activities will create a groundswell of public interest and concern that will *force* policymakers to take the SDHI seriously. Each model sees a role for an engaged citizenry that can come to influence the public policy-making process.

With regard to other implications of our analysis, there has been virtually no public health community effort to engage with the labour movement to strengthen union influence and power. Such engagement would be consistent with findings that SDHI-related public policy is more likely where the organised labour movement is strong (Navarro and Shi 2002; Raphael 2013). There has also been little engagement with political parties that draws upon findings that social democratic parties are more receptive to – and successful at – implementing public policies that address the SDHI (Brady 2009; Navarro and Shi 2002; Raphael 2012; Swank 2005).

There is an opportunity to do so, as the 2011 federal election elevated the social democratic New Democratic Party (NDP) in Canada to Official Opposition in Ottawa. In fact, the NDP raised the SDHI in its campaign for the 2015 election (New Democratic Party of Canada 2013) following a cross-Canada consultation. There clearly is an opportunity to influence political developments: a pathway implicitly or explicitly suggested by all three policy models discussed in this chapter.

Conclusion

As Clavier and de Leeuw note, there is frequently resistance to policy change with respect to the SDHI and other health promotion concepts (Clavier and de Leeuw 2013). This is especially the case in Liberal nations such as Canada. We have identified different elements of the public policy development process that influence government receptivity to acting on the SDHI through public policy action. We agree with Clavier and de Leeuw that public policies are "socially and historically embedded" (Clavier and de Leeuw 2013, p. 9) such that previous public policy decisions and institutional arrangements shape future courses of government action and their willingness to implement public policies to address identified issues. These policy legacies lead to path dependence, a concept that explains much of Canadian governments' policy continuity.

In Canada, the disjuncture between conceptual development and implementation of public policy that addresses the SDHI has much to do with the political and economic organisation of Canada's Liberal welfare state and the congruence of neo-liberal political ideology and individualised biomedical and behavioural approaches to health promotion (Raphael *et al.* 2008). Not surprisingly, health-related public policy is focused on health care and lifestyle approaches to promoting health. The task for the public health community is to shift these policies to an SDHI stance.

Kingdon's model provides insights into how opportunities for influencing the public policy development process can emerge. The notion of three independent process streams and their role in implementing solutions suggests specific public health actions as detailed in Table 2.3. Hall's model categorises policy change outcomes and identifies the barriers to paradigmatic change. Hall shows that politicians can use the ideas of experts to support a new paradigm but will do so only when existing policy legacies prove inadequate for emerging problems. But governments must be motivated to actually respond to these problems and this will require an engaged public to raise these issues.

Implicit but not developed in Kingdon and Hall's models is how power and influence shape the public policy process. It is here that the insights of Esping-Andersen as to the nature of the Liberal – as well as Social Democratic and Conservative – welfare states provide important added value. As a class mobilisation model it requires addressing the underlying politics of power and influence that shape public policy. In Canada, unless the undue influence of the corporate and business sector is remedied, there will be little public policy action that addresses the SDHI. It may be that these emerging public health community activities described may help right these imbalances. If these activities do not open up the necessary policy windows for SDHI-related public policy, then alternatives responses by the Canadian public health community must be formulated and implemented.

References

Awofeso, N 2003, 'The healthy cities approach – reflections on a framework for improving global health', *Bulletin of the World Health Organization*, vol. 81, no. 3, pp. 222–223.

Banting, K and Myles, J (eds) 2013, *Inequality and the fading of redistributive politics*, UBC Press, Vancouver.

Brady, D 2009, *Rich democracies, poor people: how politics explain poverty*, Oxford University Press, New York.

Brassolotto, J, Raphael, D and Baldeo, N 2014, 'Epistemological barriers to addressing the social determinants of health among public health professionals in Ontario, Canada: a qualitative inquiry', *Critical Public Health*, vol. 24, no. 3, pp. 321–336.

Bryant, T 2012, 'Applying the lessons from international experiences', in D Raphael (ed.), *Tackling health inequalities: lessons from international experiences*, Canadian Scholars Press Incorporated, Toronto, pp. 265–285.

Bryant, T, Raphael, D, Schrecker, T and Labonte, R 2011, 'Canada: a land of missed opportunity for addressing the social determinants of health', *Health Policy*, vol. 101, no. 1, pp. 44–58.

Butler-Jones, D 2008, *Report on the state of public health in Canada 2008: addressing health inequalities*, Public Health Agency of Canada, Ottawa.

Butler-Jones, D 2010, *Report on the state of public health in Canada 2009: growing up well – priorities for a healthy future*, Public Health Agency of Canada, Ottawa.

Butler-Jones, D 2011, *Report on the state of public health in Canada 2010: growing older – adding life to years*, Public Health Agency of Canada, Ottawa.

Canadian Population Health Initiative 2004, *Improving the health of Canadians*, Canadian Population Health Initiative, Ottawa.

Canadian Population Health Initiative 2008, *Reducing gaps in health: a focus on socioeconomic status in urban Canada*, Canadian Population Health Initiative, Ottawa.

Clavier, C and de Leeuw, E 2013, 'Framing public policy in health promotion: ubiquitous, yet elusive', in C Clavier and E de Leeuw (eds), *Health promotion and the policy process*, Oxford University Press, Oxford, pp. 1–22.

Coburn, D 2004, 'Beyond the income inequality hypothesis: globalization, neo liberalism, and health inequalities', *Social Science & Medicine*, vol. 58, no. 1, pp. 41–56.

Coburn, D 2010, 'Health and health care: a political economy perspective', in T Bryant, D Raphael and M Rioux (eds), *Staying alive: critical perspectives on health, illness, and health care*, 2nd edn, Canadian Scholars Press, Toronto, pp. 65–92.

Engels, F 1845/1987, *The condition of the working class in England*, Penguin Classics, New York.

Epp, J 1986, *Achieving health for all: a framework for health promotion*, Health and Welfare Canada, Ottawa, Canada.

Esping-Andersen, G 1990, *The three worlds of welfare capitalism*, Princeton University Press, Princeton, NJ.

Esping-Andersen, G 1999, *Social foundations of post-industrial economies*, Oxford University Press, New York.

Evans, R G, Barer, M L and Marmor, T R 1994, *Why are some people healthy and others not? the determinants of health of populations*, Aldine de Gruyter, New York.

Graham, H 2007, *Unequal lives: health and socioeconomic inequalities*, Open University Press, New York.

Hall, P 1993, 'Policy paradigms, social learning, and the state: The case of economic policymaking in Britain', *Comparative Politics*, vol. 25, pp. 275–296.

Hall, P A 2013, 'Brother, can you paradigm?', *Governance*, vol. 26, no. 2, pp. 189–192.

Hancock, T 2011, 'Health promotion in Canada: 25 years of unfulfilled promise', *Health Promotion International*, vol. 26, (suppl. 2), pp. ii263–ii267.

Hayes, M, Ross, I, Gasher, M, Gutstein, D, Dunn, J and Hackett, R 2007, 'Telling stories: news media, health literacy and public policy in Canada', *Social Science and Medicine*, vol. 54, pp. 445–457.

Health Council of Canada 2010, *Stepping it up: moving the focus from health care in Canada to a healthier Canada*, Health Council of Canada, Toronto.

Institute of Population and Public Health 2011, *IPPH knowledge translation*, viewed 14 May, 2015, www.cihr-irsc.gc.ca/e/27155.html.

Joint OPHA/ALPHA Working Group on the Social Determinants of Health 2010, *Activities to address the social determinants of health in Ontario local public health units*, Joint OPHA/ALPHA Working Group on the Social Determinants of Health, Toronto.

Kickbusch, I 2013, 'Foreword: we need to build a health political science', in C Clavier and E De Leeuw (eds), *Health promotion and the policy process*, Oxford University Press, Oxford UK, pp. iii–iv.

Kingdon, J W 2010, *Agendas, alternatives and public policies*, Pearson, New York.

Lofters A, Slater M, Kirst M, Shankardass K and Quinonez, C 2014, 'How do people attribute income-related inequalities in health? A cross-sectional study in Ontario, Canada', *PloS one*, vol. 9, no. 1, p. e85286.

Lalonde, M 1974, *A new perspective on the health of Canadians: a working document*, Government of Canada, Ottawa.

Langille, D 2009, 'Follow the money: how business and politics shape our health', in D Raphael (ed.), *Social determinants of health: Canadian perspectives*, 2nd edn, Canadian Scholars Press, Toronto, pp. 305–317.

Low, J and Therault, L 2008, 'Health promotion policy in Canada: lessons forgotten, lessons still to learn', *Health Promotion International*, vol. 23, no. 2, pp. 200–206.

Mikkonen, J and Raphael, D 2010, *Social determinants of health: The Canadian facts*, viewed 1 November, 2010, http:/thecanadianfact.org.

Milio, N 1986, *Promoting health through public policy*, Canadian Public Health Association, Ottawa.

National Collaborating Centre on the Determinants of Health 2008, *KSTE in action: 3rd annual summer institute in knowledge synthesis, translation and exchange*, viewed 14 May 2015, http://nccdh.ca/resources/entry/making-sense-of-it-all.

National Collaborating Centre for Healthy Public Policy 2014, *What we do*, viewed 14 May 2015, www.ncchpp.ca/62/What_We_Do.ccnpps.

Navarro, V and Shi, L 2002, 'The political context of social inequalities and health', in V Navarro (ed.), *The political economy of social inequalities: consequences for health and quality of life*, Baywood, Amityville, NY, pp. 403–418.

New Democratic Party of Canada 2013, *Prevention is better than cure*, viewed 21 June, 2013, www.ndp.ca/prevention-better-cure.

Pierson, P 2000, 'Increasing returns, path dependence, and the study of politics', *American Political Science Review*, vol. 94, no. 2, pp. 251–267.

Raphael, D 2001, 'Letter from Canada: an end of the millennium update from the birthplace of the healthy cities movement', *Health Promotion International*, vol. 16, pp. 99–101.

Raphael, D 2010, *About Canada: health and illness*, Fernwood Publishing, Winnipeg.

Raphael, D 2012, 'Canadian experiences', in D Raphael (ed.), *Tackling health inequalities: lessons from international experiences*, Canadian Scholars Press, Toronto.

Raphael, D 2013, 'The political economy of health promotion: Part 2, national provision of the prerequisites of health'. *Health Promotion International*, vol. 28, pp. 112–132.

Raphael, D 2014, 'Beyond policy analysis: The raw politics behind opposition to healthy public policy', *Health Promotion International*, vol. 30, no. 2. pp. 380–396.

Raphael, D, Brassolotto, J and Baldeo, N 2014, 'Ideological and organizational components of differing public health strategies for addressing the social determinants of health', *Health Promotion International* (2014), dau022.

Raphael, D, Curry-Stevens, A and Bryant, T 2008, 'Barriers to addressing the social determinants of health: insights from the Canadian experience', *Health Policy*, vol. 88, pp. 222–235.

Restrepo, H (ed.) 2000, *Health promotion: an anthology*, Pan American Health Organization, Washington DC.

Robert Wood Johnson Foundation 2010, *A new way to talk about the social determinants of health*, viewed 14 May 2015, www.rwjf.org/vulnerablepopulations/product.jsp?id=66428.

Saint-Arnaud, S and Bernard, P 2003, 'Convergence or resilience? a hierarchical cluster analysis of the welfare regimes in advanced countries', *Current Sociology*, vol. 51, no. 5, pp. 499–527.

Sudbury and District Health Unit 2011, *Let's start a conversation about health ... and not talk about health care at all*, viewed 25 June 2011, http://tinyurl.com/7t8476f.

Swank, D 2005, 'Globalisation, domestic politics, and welfare state retrenchment in capitalist democracies', *Social Policy and Society*, vol. 4, no. 2, pp. 183–195.

Teeple, G 2000, *Globalization and the decline of social reform: into the twenty first century*, Garamond Press, Aurora Ontario.

Upstream Action 2013, *Upstream action is a movement to create a healthy society through evidence-based, people-centred ideas*, viewed 13 May 2015, www.thinkupstream.net/.

Virchow, R 1848/1985, 'Report on the typhus epidemic in Upper Silesia', in L J Rather (ed.), *Collected essays by Rudolph Virchow on public health and epidemiology, volume 1*, Science History Publications, Canton MA, pp. 205–319.

Wigle, J 1998, *Healthy cities/healthy communities*, viewed 22 May 2014, www.muniscope.ca/_files/file.php?fileid=fileynZstnCalg&filename=file_ICURR_LITERATURE_SUMMARY_NO2_a.pdf.

World Health Organization 1986, *Ottawa charter for health promotion*, viewed 14 June 2011, www.who.int/hpr/NPH/docs/ottawa_charter_hp.pdf.

World Health Organization 2008, *Commission on the social determinants of health*, viewed 15 March 2008, www.who.int/social_determinants/en/.

3 Policy cycle models

Are we throwing the baby out with the bath water?

Andrew Wyatt

Introduction

The purpose of this chapter is to examine some of the ways in which policy processes are commonly described and understood. Specifically, the intention is to confront what has in recent years become the somewhat orthodox dismissal of cyclical models of policy making, and to mount a defence of the 'policy cycle heuristic' as still providing a valuable – if limited – conceptual tool in specific contexts and for specific purposes. Referring here to policy processes in the plural acknowledges the fact that the sequences of activities and events through which public policy is formulated, implemented and changed may vary substantially from country to country and sector to sector, and between national, sub-national and supra-national levels of government. Nevertheless, in what follows it will generally be less cumbersome to use the singular term.

The critique of the policy cycle model

In *Theories of the policy process*, Paul Sabatier emphasises the complexity of the process of public policy making, and the consequent need for the analyst to find some way of simplifying the situation in order to understand it (Sabatier 2007). Amongst the theoretical frameworks available for this purpose, he identifies the 'stages heuristic', which divide the policy process into a series of discrete stages, and which he characterises as based on the assumption that there is a single policy cycle; he concludes that despite its value to scholars up until the mid-1980s, the stages heuristic has subsequently been subjected to devastating criticisms and has outlived its usefulness. These criticisms include the absence of causal drivers to propel the process across and within stages, oversimplification and inaccuracies in describing iterations and interactions between supposedly discrete stages, and a supposed legalistic, top-down focus typically focused on a single major piece of legislation.

In place of the stages heuristic a number of other theoretical frameworks are proposed by Sabatier and his contributors as offering more promising bases for study of policy processes. All are presented from the perspective of theorists or scholars of the policy process, and all endeavour from their different directions to capture more fully the complexity of the social and political interactions between the large numbers of institutions, interest groups and individual actors that constitute the policy environment.

Within the centre of UK central government, there have also been repeated attempts in recent years to replace cyclical models with other frameworks. The authors of a Cabinet Office report, *Professional policy making for the twenty-first century*, stated that:

> We started to try to represent the 'modernised' policy process in the traditional way, using a model ... showing sequential activities organised in a cycle. But we found that experienced policy makers reacted against such a presentation because they felt it did not accurately reflect the realities of policy making.
>
> (Cabinet Office 1999, Section 2.9)

This was the case even when the basic activities of a core policy process were explicitly presented as embedded in wider public, political and organisational contexts, to yield a much richer picture of the multiple factors bearing on the process and on the policymakers. The fundamental problem was perceived to be that "policy making rarely proceeds as neatly as this model suggests and that no two policies will need exactly the same development process" (Cabinet Office 1999, Section 2.9). The solution adopted was to replace the cycle with a 'descriptive model' – comprising a set of features, themes and competencies required for effective policy making, including such qualities as being forward- and outward-looking, innovative, evidence-based and inclusive – after which the authors report was accepted by policymakers "as a challenging and yet realistic representation of the policy process they experience in their day to day working lives."

More recently, and again in the UK, the Institute for Government's report *Policy making in the real world* (Institute for Government 2011) emphasises the critical importance of good policy for good governance, and also recognises the need not just to describe the desirable qualities of good policy making but also to have good processes in place. However, over-simplistic models that fail to engage with real-world challenges provide inadequate intellectual support for policymakers; in particular, policy cycle models "resemble a comforting narrative that imposes specious order on a complex reality" (Institute for Government 2011, p. 7).

Other commentators have adopted similar arguments. For example, Louise Shaxson contends that rationalist, cyclical models cannot accommodate the political, pluralist bargaining and negotiating approaches demanded by complex or chaotic policy issues, though she does concede that they may still be a useful guide in dealing with well or moderately structured problems (Shaxson 2008).

In defence of the policy cycle heuristic

In the light of the sustained criticisms, of which those cited above are only a small sample, what remains of the stages or cycle model of policy making? Can it still have value as a heuristic device, and if so for whom, and in what way?

It is the contention of this chapter that quite basic models of the policy cycle may provide an effective aid to improved management of policy processes by those whose task it is to try to impose some order on a chaotic flux of events and diverse competing interests, first intellectually and then through securing decisions on and implementing a course of action. It may well be that this conception of policy management is itself anathema to those whose focus is on the wider social, political and institutional background, the network of actors inside and outside government whose interests and preferences shape the choices that can be conceived of and carried out, or even the processes through which the idea of a particular policy domain is constructed in the first place. However, from a 'bureaucratic' position, it appears that the first imperative for governments is that they have to act and to be seen to act, either to carry out their own mandate or to respond to emerging problems, or preferably to do both of those things in combination. The second imperative is to act efficiently and effectively if at all possible, to deploy the finite resources of society so as to achieve the greatest positive impacts – and to ameliorate the most harm – in the time available.

From this perspective, the first requirement of policy management is for a set of tools that will help practitioners – those supporting and advising decision makers – to identify problems and their root causes correctly; define what can or should be achieved; analyse possible courses of action and their foreseeable and calculable consequences; secure decisions on the way ahead and oversee their execution; collect data on what is happening; evaluate and account for the results achieved; and learn lessons to shape future action. Hence the enduring appeal among practitioners of the policy cycle heuristic, as a clear and robust structure within which a wide range of analytic, administrative and managerial tools can be deployed as and when required. This is not to say that policy officials (and politicians) should not endeavour to acquire a deeper theoretical understanding of the determinants and characteristics of public policy, in order to become better informed and more reflective and reflexive practitioners of their profession and to shape better decisions. It is merely to argue that this deeper understanding will not obviate the need for more basic practical tools which may help them to impose order on apparent disorder in their day-to-day work.

Condemnations of the cycle model have emanated from two principal sources. First, there are the academic critics like Sabatier and his co-authors, whose strongly research-oriented, social science affiliation has already been noted. However, the differences in perspective between academics and practitioners (taken here to mean primarily officials employed in policy-related roles in government) with regard to the generation and use of policy-relevant knowledge has been often discussed, as for example by Peter M. Jackson, who rehearses a comprehensive list of reasons which may inhibit the engagement of academics with the world of practical policy making (Jackson 2008). The time-scales of serious research and those of emerging policy and political crises often differ drastically, and expert views on the weight which a given body of evidence can be asked to bear may well be at odds with the needs of decision makers for simplification and certainty. In the same way, conceptual frameworks which do not stand up well to the rigorous epistemological challenges which can be mounted by theoreticians in the course of a sustained critique may nevertheless still offer useful (and easily accessible) practical tools for practitioners who are struggling to understand and devise an immediate response to complex unfolding events and competing interests.

Like any model, the policy cycle must necessarily reduce complex processes to a relatively small number of elements. Social scientific analytical methods have been said to form a continuum between, at one extreme, approaches that favour descriptive accuracy and completeness and at the other those that build models of reality, making simplifying assumptions in order to arrive at parsimonious explanations which can illuminate aspects of the real world (Booth 2014). The same can be said of depictions of the policy process, where policy cycle models certainly lie at the parsimonious but potentially illuminating end of the spectrum, even though as such they necessarily abstract away from much descriptive detail.

The second principal source of criticism is found among reformers within or on the margins of government, who have tended to direct attention to the qualities of good policy making and the competencies required of policy-makers. The problem with this approach is that this kind of static description does not represent a process at all. That term unavoidably carries with it the connotation of a series of actions, steps, operations or natural changes leading to an intended or consequential result – which leads us back in the direction of a stages or cyclical model. Contrary to Sabatier's view that a stages model lacks causal drivers, such a model is inherently dynamic rather than static. The advantage for practitioners of a dynamic model is that it always indicates what needs to be done next in order to achieve results. It can thus help officials to keep attention focused on, for example, the need to move forward from analysis to decision, or to remind political leaders of the dangers inherent in attempting to implement solutions to poorly defined problems. As the authors of the *Australian policy handbook* have said:

> A policy cycle is just a heuristic, an ideal type from which every reality will curve away. It is designed to answer the daunting question "what do I do now?" Followed, a policy cycle might assist a public servant move from vague problem to authoritative government deliberation.
>
> (Bridgman and Davis 2003, p. 100)

However, because it addresses the question of *what* to do rather than *how* to do it, a model of this kind does need to be complemented and enriched by more static descriptions of the required features of good policy work; the argument here is for multiple perspectives rather than a single approach to understanding the complexities of the policy environment.

The four principal reasons adduced in *Policy making in the real world* for dismissing cycle models as divorced from the real world can be taken as typical of many such critiques. They are: (1) the stages of policy making do not just often overlap, they are often inseparable; (2) the process needs to support a greater emphasis on policy design and much more extensive and rigorous testing of policies; (3) policy making does not take place in a vacuum, where the government is in total control of its agenda; (4) the effects of policy interventions may be complex, wide-ranging and unintended (Institute for Government 2011, p. 6). These are all very valid observations about the nature of policy making and policy processes, but have little force as a critique of the cycle heuristic. There is nothing in this conceptualisation of the policy process, properly understood and applied, which necessarily contradicts any of these assertions.

Even the assumption that the model predicts that the stages of policy making are rigidly discrete, non-interpenetrating and irreversible has no rational basis. The whole notion of a process supposes a sequence that unfolds incrementally over time rather than a set of rigidly separated steps or platforms – becoming rather than being might be a useful rubric for the interpretation of such models. As the Institute's authors themselves say:

> In the real world, policy problems and policy solutions frequently emerge together, rather than one after another. In other words, plans may be present at the same time, or before, a need to act has been identified. This can lead to poorly conceived policies if ministers present a *fait accompli* solution that is flawed, or whose relationship to a policy problem is unclear – but will not hear it challenged.
>
> (Institute for Government 2011, p. 6)

This is an apt description of a situation with which very many policy practitioners, across many different jurisdictions, will undoubtedly be familiar. It identifies the sort of sequencing problem which the cycle model can pinpoint very easily, and in favourable circumstances help officials to find means of solving or at least mitigating. It is hard to see its force as an argument *contra* such models.

Putting the policy cycle to use

The policy cycle approach still potentially retains considerable value as a framework to support the understanding and management of policy processes. Much, however, depends on the way it is used: depicting a simple sequence of core activities will have little traction on reality, unless it is used as an armature on which to build a much more nuanced and context-specific analysis of the circumstances of a specific intervention, and is seen as embedded in and interacting with a complex web of social, political, economic, institutional and organisational factors. What is called for is a both-and rather than an either-or approach, which embraces the insights and concepts of many of the critics of the cyclical model, but retains the cycle at its heart to provide the essential dynamic force and cues for action without which the policy machinery risks becoming static and merely reactive to outside interests, and the rational structure without which it may become simply random and capricious in its actions.

The remainder of this section draws heavily on the present author's own experience of developing and delivering programmes of policy-related training for government officials both in the UK and in jurisdictions as diverse as South Africa and Bulgaria, and adapting some of the same tools to help improve policy processes for a number of governments of developing countries and territories. In general, in these training or consultancy assignments, the emphasis at the outset has been on building up a locally relevant version of the policy cycle based as far as possible on the experience of participants or counterparts. A typical diagrammatic representation is shown at Figure 3.1.

Around this framework, a great deal of material can then be woven to explain the necessary or possible activities and sub-routines within each stage, the most useful tools, techniques and methods for policymakers to master or be acquainted with at each stage, principal points of influence or leverage for interested parties outside and inside government, the nature of the likely iterations, overlaps and interdependence between activities, the nature of the relationship between political and official or technocratic actors at different stages, and the points at which political commitment and decision are essential.

Once an acceptable representation of reality has been agreed it can be developed into guidance, which can provide a practical resource for officials, political leaders and legislators, a basis for training, and a standard of best practice to be followed whenever practicable. The adoption of a shared conception of the process being undertaken and a common language for discussing the issues it generates may itself constitute a significant step in the direction of more effective policy making.

Typically this procedure has resulted in a nine-stage version of the policy cycle. Such a representation of the policy process is explored in more detail below, following an introductory note on the characteristics of good policy making The description of each stage of the process illustrates the features that are typically highlighted in the development of guidance materials, although the constitutional and institutional framework will of course differ from one administration to another, and the matters that are emphasised will reflect particular local concerns and problems. The aim is to demonstrate that even a simple depiction of the policy cycle can provide the basis for an

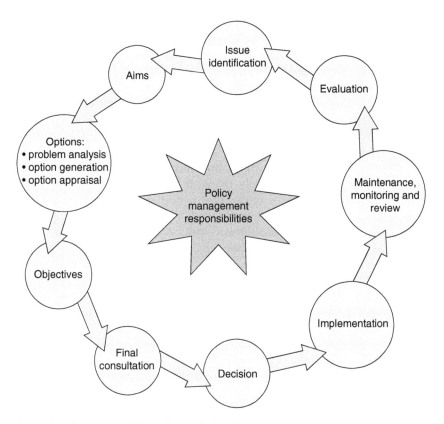

Figure 3.1 A version of the policy cycle heuristic.

effective, practical and nuanced examination of the policy environment that contradicts many of the criticisms levelled at this approach by its opponents. The text boxes provide examples of real world cases where the cycle model has played a positive role in the improvement of policy processes.

Characteristics of good policy making

The power to make policy, in the sense of making decisions on the course of action to be followed by the government, is the prerogative of the political leadership. It is, however, an integral part of the duties of senior public servants to support that decision making by playing a full and active part in the development of policy proposals, keeping policies within their area of responsibility under active review, and taking the initiative in identifying and drawing attention to the need for new or altered policies when circumstances demand.

The purpose of policy making is to establish clearly the course of action that the government intends to take, in response to a problem or difficulty that has arisen, or in order to realise the vision of the country's leadership for improvement in some aspect of life. Policy making is, in other words, a form of practical problem solving in the context of public affairs, linked to the exercise of legal and political authority. The key to good policy making is therefore that firm and unambiguous decisions should be made (with appropriate authority) about what is to be done, based on the best available evidence concerning the nature of the issue being addressed and what responses are most likely to be effective, coupled with an accurate assessment of the resources required to carry out the decisions and the means of ensuring that the required action is taken. Good policy making should result in a clear understanding of what is to be done, by what means and within what constraints.

Good policy making is unlikely to occur by chance. It depends on a complex sequence of activities requiring the professional support of a competent public service. The existence of a well-managed policy process enhances the chances that a good policy will result, and intended outcomes be achieved. Poor policy decisions, on the other hand, can harm the health, wealth and wellbeing of individuals, families and whole societies, and irreparably damage their natural and cultural heritage.

It is essential that policy decisions should be clearly and comprehensively communicated to those affected by them and those who have to implement them. In many cases they need to be expressed in detailed guidelines or instructions, but the drafting of such policy statements or guidelines should never be confused with the process of policy making itself.

The term 'policy management' refers to the management of the process by which policy is developed, decided and put into practice. A 'policy manager' is someone who has been given responsibility for ensuring that a policy problem is solved, or that an initiative is seen through all its stages to a satisfactory completion in an economical, efficient and effective manner. Managing the policy process is part of the job of being a senior manager in the public service, in the same way as managing financial and other resources, managing people, and managing processes like strategic planning and budgeting.

Identifying issues and setting the policy agenda

Any government will almost always be faced with many more issues than it can tackle at any one time. Not everything can be done at once. A key role for the political leadership is therefore determining which matters will find a place on the policy agenda, and in what sequence.

Sometimes a government will adopt a formal Policy Framework, or negotiate a Government Programme with coalition partners. In other cases, policy priorities will derive initially from the winning party's election manifesto and be developed incrementally after that. The policy agenda will also be shaped by the concerns that individual members of the government bring with them when they assume office, and by undertakings that they have made during the electoral process. Much activity will also be driven by emerging events: newly arising social, economic or environmental problems, requirements imposed by international agreements, or complaints about flawed or inconsistent policies or weaknesses in service delivery that are brought to the notice of government by the media or by members of the public.

While it will ultimately be for the political leadership to decide which of the many issues competing for attention and resources will be given priority, officials should not passively await direction: senior officials should be proactive in bringing policy issues to the attention of Ministers, and seeking agreement on which should be given active consideration. Conversely, significant resources should not be devoted to developing proposals on any policy issue without the consent of Ministers.

Box 3.1 Bermuda

A series of workshops was held with the Premier, Cabinet and Permanent Secretaries of the Government of Bermuda in 2003–4 as part of a process of clarifying the respective roles and responsibilities of the political leadership and the civil service. A policy cycle model provided the framework on which responsibilities for decision making and the development of policy proposals could be mapped. It also enabled the linkages between the policy process and strategic planning to be explored. The resulting agreed approach to improving policy making was subsequently rolled out to all senior officials at Director and Head of Department level.

It is important for both Ministers and senior officials to bear in mind the need to balance the achievement of 'quick wins' – which will reassure the public that the government is addressing matters of general concern – with the fact that it will take longer to develop and implement solutions for some more complex problems. Policy resources may need to be devoted from an early stage in a government's term of office to some work that may not bear fruit until near its end, or even after the next election.

The greater the clarity with which the problem or issue to be addressed can be identified at the outset, the greater the chances that there will be a successful outcome. Much effort can be wasted trying to solve non-existent or misunderstood problems: once an issue has been identified as demanding attention, officials should seek as much information as possible to corroborate or if necessary challenge initial assumptions.

Establishing policy aims

Once it is clear that a matter is on the government's policy agenda, whether as a proactive initiative or in reaction to events, it is important for policy managers to make sure they have agreed with Ministers what in general terms is being aimed at. What is it that the government really wants to achieve in this area? If necessary, officials should take the lead in proposing possible formulations of the aim for Ministers' agreement. Without clarity at this stage much effort may be wasted in developing policy options which do not reflect the intentions of the political leadership.

At this early stage it is likely to be possible to formulate aims only in very broad terms, reflecting a vision of the outcomes of government intervention (e.g. a more efficient road transport system, a more highly educated society). The development of specific and detailed objectives will have to await more work on possible options for action, and their cost and feasibility. It is an essential feature of good policy making that the development of solutions should begin with a view of the desired outcome, and then work back through the actions needed and obstacles to be overcome in order to achieve it.

It is also important to distinguish clearly between outcomes and outputs. Outcomes are the end result of a policy intervention, representing a change in society, the economy or environment (or the prevention of an undesirable change). Outputs are the products of the systems and processes operated by or on behalf of government (for example, the miles of road resurfaced, the numbers of people completing vocational training courses). Poor policy development often follows from confusing commitments regarding increases or changes in outputs with the final aim (outcome) to which they are intended to contribute.

Option generation and appraisal

Developing proposals about what government might do to achieve its desired aims requires both wide-ranging, imaginative and creative thinking about possible solutions, and rigorous analytic thinking which appraises the options in the light of the best available evidence and narrows down the possibilities to mutually exclusive alternative courses of action. Early in the policy process it is especially important to think widely and freely about possible options, as well as looking at what other countries have done in similar circumstances.

Policy managers should also be prepared to engage Ministers in (possibly quite informal) dialogue about possible options at an early stage, and not restrict discussion to the point at which a fully developed course of action required approval.

The next stage is to subject the options generated to a process of rigorous analysis, using the best available evidence about the nature of the problem and the likely effectiveness of the proposed solution. It is necessary to appraise options in terms both of their feasibility (financial, economic, administrative, legal, social, cultural and technological), and their relative desirability. The second criterion will include considerations of alignment with the broader policy intentions and preferences of the government and with other policy initiatives, likely effectiveness in achieving the desired outcomes, and possible unintended consequences under differing scenarios or in different combinations of circumstances.

The policy appraisal of any option that is given serious consideration should, as a minimum, include analysis of its:

- effectiveness
- acceptability
- affordability
- economic cost
- regulatory impact
- fit with other policies
- legal basis
- implementability
- time-scale
- consequences
- environmental impact
- social impact.

It is not expected that a policy manager will necessarily have the skills and knowledge to carry out all aspects of the appraisal in person. Full use should be made of the skills available within the department concerned, and if necessary information and advice sought from other departments. The involvement of the government's Law Officers is likely to be required for any option which appears to require new legislation or the amendment of existing legislation, and of the Finance department for any option which would entail additional expenditure or have revenue implications.

The policy appraisal process should culminate, wherever possible, in the formulation of two or more options – representing clearly distinct and mutually exclusive courses of action – for decision makers to choose between. They should be presented with a concise summary of the costs, consequences and other arguments for and against each one, with the opportunity to seek more comprehensive explanations if they so wish. The aim for policy managers is to present decision makers with everything they need to know to make an informed choice. The absence of adequate evidence and argument, or the provision of excessive and unnecessary detail, will serve equally to obstruct and undermine good decision making.

Box 3.2 St Helena

The December 2010 Memorandum of Understanding between the Government of St Helena (SHG) and the United Kingdom Government secured funding for the development of an airport for the island subject to a number of conditions. These included the requirement for SHG to establish an appropriate legislative and policy environment, particularly with regard to land use and disposal, immigration and investment. Policies were to be as simple as possible, transparent and predictable, non-discriminatory and compatible with other relevant policies and legislation. Progress in this direction was already being made through the Public Service Modernisation Programme of 2008–13, one component of which was concerned with the strengthening of governance and institutional arrangements for public sector management.

A Policy Handbook was produced, which was constructed around a policy cycle model and emphasised the concept of policy management, seen as the effective and proactive management of this cycle. From this basis other compatible guidance materials were developed – Policy Guidance for Government Departments, Policy Guidance for Councillors (elected members of the Legislative and Executive Councils), and a Policy Checklist for Councillors. Training and advisory support were also provided.

The final review of the modernisation programme in 2013 found that progress using this approach had exceeded expectations; in particular it had led to a tangible increase in demand for evidence as part of the policy making process, and a change in Councillors' understanding of their role in policy development and monitoring. The airport project has proceeded.

Objectives

Precise and quantified objectives cannot be established until detailed work has been done on the development and appraisal of options. Exactly what can be achieved, and by when, will depend to a large extent on which course of action is adopted. Difficulties can arise if governments become committed too early to very specific objectives before sufficient analytic work has been done on the means by which they might be delivered. Objectives may relate both to outcomes and to outputs, but in both cases should be specific, measurable and set a time-scale for achievement.

Consultation

Depending on the nature of the issue, consultation of various kinds is likely to take place at a number of points in the policy process. For all but the most minor issues, policy managers will need to take the advice and views of interested or expert bodies, inside and outside of government, in order to understand fully the nature of the problem. Moreover, for all significant policy initiatives it is important that – unless there are exceptional, overriding reasons for confidentiality – there has been an appropriate form of consultation, with the public at large or with the groups principally affected, on the most favoured or most feasible options before they are put to the government for decision.

A commitment to consultation is not simply a matter of democratic principle and open government; it is also the case that wide exposure of the government's thinking to a range of those likely to be affected by any intervention may well reveal misunderstandings or errors in analysis before irrevocable commitments are made. Participation makes for better or at least more acceptable policy, generally speaking. However, policy managers should not undertake public consultation without the express agreement of Ministers. The fact that the government is considering action on an issue, or the nature of the options it is examining, may themselves be a cause of controversy.

Policy decisions

Decisions on policy matters are by definition political. The role of policy managers is to put clearly and accurately articulated choices in front of those with authority to decide, with a firm recommendation as to the preferred course of action, and then to ensure that what emerges is implemented. They cannot determine the decisions that will be made. It is the duty of officials to bring to the attention of decision makers any matters they believe may have been overlooked which might render the decision ineffective or not implementable, or lead to undesirable consequences, but if the decision is confirmed officials must implement it, or resign.

It is the responsibility in the first instance of officials to determine which matters raise policy questions that need to be debated and decided at political level, and which are routine administrative issues that simply require the interpretation and application of existing policy. This is largely a question of professional judgement: officials must take a view as to whether novel or contentious issues or matters of wide public interest are being raised, and also to identify issues in which it would be improper for Ministers to intervene. If in doubt they should take an early opportunity to discuss the matter with Ministers.

Implementing policy decisions

Implementation refers to the act of putting a decision into practice, making the thing decided on happen. Once a decision has been reached by the appropriate authority it is the responsibility of the policy manager to ensure that it is implemented. The policy process is only complete when practical results have been delivered and evaluated. This does not mean that the work of implementation will necessarily be carried out by or even under the direct management control of the policy manager; other government departments and public bodies, organisations in civil society or private contractors may all be involved. The role is one of oversight, ownership and taking responsibility for delivery on behalf of the government.

Depending on the nature of the decision being put into effect, implementation may entail anything from large-scale construction projects to the passage of new legislation, the launch of a new public service or the initiation of a government publicity campaign. Implementation should always be regarded as a time-limited phase of activity, for which sufficient resources must be allocated and clear deadlines set. Project or programme management techniques will help to ensure that results are delivered within the time, cost and quality requirements of government. Implementation is also about making change happen, and policy managers need to be aware of the principles of good change management.

It is important that policy managers should not only maintain active oversight and ownership of policy implementation, but also take responsibility for keeping Ministers informed about progress. Ministers will be held accountable by the public for any actual or perceived delays in implementation, and must be kept in a position where they can answer for what is happening (and if necessary take action to expedite progress).

Implementation of policy may or may not involve preparation and passage of new primary or secondary legislation, depending on the nature of the policy decision, and whether adequate legal powers already exist to enable the government to achieve its desired outcomes. Effective publicity and public relations are also often an essential element of implementation, on which policy managers should be prepared to advise Ministers.

Box 3.3 Grenada

One component of the Public Service Management Improvement Project undertaken by the Government of Grenada in 2003–6 involved the development of more effective Cabinet systems. Points of weakness in the current arrangements included poor liaison between senior officials and Ministers and uncertainty about their respective roles in the development of policy proposals; lack of capacity amongst more junior officials to identify problems and support policy development; and failure to implement Cabinet decisions.

A policy cycle model was used in workshops with Permanent Secretaries and heads of department, as a means of identifying and focusing attention on weaknesses and securing agreement on solutions. A Policy Handbook was produced, based on the same model, and endorsed by Permanent Secretaries and Cabinet. The approach was widely disseminated through training in order to promote a common understanding and language in policy work across government. At the same time the required format for Cabinet Submissions was revised to sharpen the presentation of key arguments, evidence and recommendations, and to ensure that the costs and benefits of implementation had been properly assessed. New tracking systems were also introduced to ensure that progress in implementing decisions could be monitored by Cabinet.

Policy maintenance and monitoring

Once implementation is complete, and a new policy and any associated processes, systems or service are in place, the policy manager should maintain responsibility for ownership and oversight of the policy. Specific policy maintenance responsibilities include:

- oversight – verifying and providing assurance that all is going to according to plan;

- accountability – responding to queries from the legislature about what is being achieved and the use of public money, and supporting the Ministers in responding to questions;
- communication – responding to queries from the public or the media about the policy, and ensuring that relevant information is available;
- monitoring – ensuring the routine and systematic collection of information about performance against agreed indicators, reviewing the information gathered and proposing remedial action if necessary;
- resources – ensuring that a robust case is made in the annual strategic planning and budgeting process for adequate resources to support the continuation of the policy, if necessary;
- review – initiating regular periodical reviews of the policy to ensure that the conditions to which it was responding still hold good, that it is being administered as intended and that it is achieving the desired results;
- policy application and development – answering queries about the application of the policy and clarifying its intentions when necessary, taking decisions about how the policy applies in difficult cases or unforeseen circumstances, and proposing adjustments or refinements to Ministers as needed.

Evaluation

Evaluation refers here to the systematic and comprehensive retrospective examination of a policy initiative, after a period long enough for some evidence to be available as to the impact it has had on the problem it was intended to address. At its simplest, evaluation sets out to determine what has been achieved, by what means, at what cost and with what other consequences. Monitoring data will contribute evidence of the effectiveness of the policy and the efficiency of its implementation, but evaluation will also make a much more fundamental assessment of all aspects of the policy, including the underlying causal assumptions (i.e. the reasons for believing that the chosen course of action would deliver the desired outcomes), and the extent to which these have proved well-founded.

The fundamental framework for eventual evaluation of any policy should lie in the original submission on the basis of which agreement to proceed was given by Ministers. It is important for policy managers to think about the prospective evaluation framework at an early stage of policy formulation. The key question is "Could we ever tell whether this initiative had been successful?" If the answer is negative it may not be worth proceeding further.

Evaluation serves three important needs: it helps government to account to the electorate (and if relevant to international donors or financial institutions) for what it has done, it helps policy managers to identify where corrective action may be needed to make an existing policy or programme more efficient or effective, and it enables them to learn lessons about what kind of interventions actually work, which they can draw on when formulating new proposals. It is therefore part of the role of policy managers to ensure that evaluations of the policies for which they are responsible take place and that the findings are acted upon.

Evaluation studies can be technically complex, especially with regard to the assessment of impact and its attribution to specific policy interventions, which may require advanced statistical techniques to demonstrate conclusively. Specialist assistance to design and carry out evaluations may be available internally from within government, or may need to be commissioned from outside. Whoever actually conducts an evaluation, the important thing is that ownership of the process and the results should rest with the policy manager.

Conclusion

It should be evident from this demonstration that the policy cycle heuristic is capable of providing a simple robust framework within which policy managers can develop appropriate and flexible responses to a wide range of different policy problems, and deploy different sorts of evidence at different points in the cycle. Guidance based on the cycle, even in the abbreviated form reproduced here, is able to embrace many of the issues which its detractors often allege it ignores, from the complex and often iterative and incremental nature of the process, to the relationship between political and technocratic considerations, the importance of striking a balance between the programmatic or agenda-driven and the reactive and responsive aspects of policy making, and the need to be inclusive of as wide a range of stakeholders and interests as possible.

More speculatively, it might be the case that some of the deeper attraction of the cycle heuristic lies in the appeal that it implicitly makes to some fundamental human needs. Parallels can be drawn between the policy cycle, conceived in this way, and David McClelland's acquired need theory of motivation (McClelland 1988). McClelland seeks to universalise three needs: for achievement, for power and for affiliation. It could be said that the policy cycle accommodates all three, and privileges or prioritises each at different points in the cycle. The power aspect is uppermost at those points when the focus is primarily on political control and decision making; achievement is about delivering what has been decided, and making a difference to society; and affiliation relates to inclusiveness, co-production and social solidarity, particularly at those points in the cycle when consultation is essential.

There is nothing indispensable about the circular graphical representation of the process, though it helpfully emphasises the desirability of feeding learning from evaluation back into policy formulation. Much of the same benefit for policy management can be derived from a linear listing of the stages in the process, as in Brian Hogwood and Lewis Gunn's presentation of nine stages through which policy issues are likely to pass (Hogwood and Gunn 1984), or Eugene Bardach's eight-step approach to policy analysis (Bardach 2012). Alternatively, simple checklists of key questions can be developed as ready-reference guides both for policy officials and for politicians.

It is the underlying set of practical issues that is really important, not the convenient cyclical heuristic device. Yet the latter remains much more visually appealing and memorable than a simple list, and thus embodies considerably greater power to persuade. To lose this powerful and practical aid to action in the real world, in the interests of greater theoretical sophistication of analysis, would indeed be to throw baby out with the bath water.

References

Bardach, E 2012, *A practical guide for policy analysis: the eightfold path to more effective problem solving*, 4th edn, CQ Press, Thousand Oaks, CA.

Booth, D 2014, 'Applied political economy analysis and "working politically" in development work: *keeping it all together*', (forthcoming).

Bridgman, P and Davis, G 2003, 'What use is a policy cycle? Plenty, if the aim is clear', *Australian Journal of Public Administration*, vol. 62, no. 3, pp. 98–102.

Cabinet Office 1999, *Professional policy making for the twenty-first century*, Cabinet Office, London.

Hogwood, B and Gunn, L 1984, *Policy analysis for the real world*, Oxford University Press, Oxford.

Institute for Government 2011, *Policy making in the real world*, Institute for Government, London.

Jackson, P 2008, *Evidence-based policy-making: a PMPA/national school of government practitioner exchange report*, Public Management and Policy Association, London.

McClelland, D 1988, *Human motivation*, Cambridge University Press, Cambridge.

Sabatier, P (ed.) 2007, *Theories of the policy process*, Westview Press, Cambridge, MA.

Shaxson, L 2008, 'Who's sitting on Dalí's sofa', *Evidence-based policy-making: a PMPA/national school of government practitioner exchange report*, Public Management and Policy Association, London.

4   Influencing policy from inside and outside of government

John Chesterman

Introduction

The difference between seeking policy change from inside as opposed to outside government is less significant than many might think. Over the past 20 years I have worked as an academic, and then from inside government as it were, as a public servant, and along the way I have drawn upon research and practice experience in encouraging social policy reform.

Each perspective, from my experience, has one core advantage and one core disadvantage. As an academic, I was as free as one could imagine to draw from my research in arguing for policy developments. The core challenge in that role was to be heard. As a public servant, my ability to seek reform is appropriately constrained to areas within the legislative authority of the organisation for which I work. But, perhaps surprisingly, I have found far more engaged audiences in the public sector for that policy advocacy.

In this chapter I will detail my experiences in advocating for policy change from both outside and inside government, with a view I hope of informing readers about the challenges and possibilities presented by both perspectives. More than this, though, I want to move beyond this dichotomy to present some thoughts on when and how policy change occurs.

My academic past involved a lot of study of activism concerning the rights of Indigenous Australians, and, if I may segue for a moment into that field, there are plenty of examples there about the way policy reforms came about through processes both internal and external to government (see Chesterman 2005). Nor is it easy to attribute changes to one or the other. Even purely bureaucratically developed reform ideas can have greater urgency and success when 'external' activism is making governments reform minded. In the case of the rights of Indigenous peoples, protests about land and other culturally specific rights made the attainment of civil or equal rights for Indigenous people a far speedier process than it would otherwise have been.

I'll leave my academic research now to one side and concentrate on my own experiences of seeking reform both as an academic and now as a public servant. As an academic and an outsider to government I was free, for instance, to advocate for set parliamentary seats for Indigenous Australians

(Chesterman 2006), and to promote the idea of a new Indigenous elected body to replace the Aboriginal and Torres Strait Islander Commission (Chesterman 2008). The challenge, as I say, was to be heard, not by other academics, but by policymakers. My advocacy on these matters, it has to be said, was not wildly successful.

I write this chapter now as an insider, in that I work for a public sector organisation. The Office of the Public Advocate (OPA) is the guardian of last resort in Victoria for adults with decision-making incapacity, and so in many ways is an instrument of the state. At the same time, OPA has a systemic advocacy role which differentiates us from most government departments and instrumentalities, and we are in some ways therefore a reform-seeking government agency. (While all of Australia's states and territories have an adult guardian of last resort, only Western Australia, South Australia, Victoria and the Australian Capital Territory have this role played by an Office of the Public Advocate. Other states have an Office of the Public Guardian as guardian of last resort. Queensland is unique in having both an Office of the Public Guardian as last-resort adult guardian, and a separate Office of the Public Advocate, which conducts systemic advocacy).

A core part of the Victorian OPA's role is:

> to promote, facilitate and encourage the provision, development and co-ordination of services and facilities provided by government ... for persons with a disability with a view to ... promoting the development of the ability and capacity of persons with a disability to act independently ... and ... minimizing the restrictions on the rights of persons with a disability.
>
> (Guardianship and Administration Act 1986 (Vic), section 15)

Further to this, OPA coordinates five volunteer programs, and we have a staggering number of volunteers – around 900 – who exercise functions that in some ways monitor the treatment of vulnerable people by key agencies of the state. Our biggest volunteer program, Community Visitors, inspects a range of accommodation settings in which people with cognitive impairments and mental ill health reside, and the state government is ultimately responsible for many of these settings. Meanwhile our Independent Third Persons sit in on police interviews where police are interviewing a person with an apparent cognitive impairment (who can be an alleged offender, victim or witness). Both of these functions see OPA volunteers as monitors of state authority, and these roles contribute significantly to OPA's status as a state government instrumentality with a difference (see further Feigan 2011).

I was caused to reflect upon OPA's unusual status when I gave evidence in 2013 before a Senate Committee that was inquiring into the then-new National Disability Insurance Scheme legislation. Before I gave evidence, I was reminded, as were other public servants, that we were there to provide expert testimony, but that we were not there to comment on government policy. In my case, I felt this statement to be in need of fine-tuning, as sometimes it is appropriate, even obligatory, for OPA to comment on government policy where this affects the quality of service provision to, or the rights of, people with disability (as articulated in OPA's legislative remit).

Who is inside and who is outside?

The insider/outsider dichotomy is central to human psychology and it is no surprise that is should appear in the area of policy development as a core variable. At first glance, the line dividing insiders from outsides is easy to draw. Either you work with government, or you do not. On close inspection, and as my introductory comments suggest, the line does become a little less bright.

Many non-government organisations instinctively hold, as they should, to their status as being outside government, which frees them up to advocate fearlessly for changes to improve the wellbeing of their core constituents or users of their services. Yet if they receive government funding for specific projects and programs, as most seek to do, does that change their status? Our answer to that question will always tend to be 'it depends'. The mere fact of receiving some government funding does not necessarily mean the organisation will be more muted in its criticism of government, or more compromised in seeking its core objectives.

I wrote my PhD (published in 1996) on the history of one organisation, the Fitzroy Legal Service, which in the 1970s began as a volunteer organisation and then endured significant internal debate as it sought to balance longer-term survival with the compromises that receipt of government funding might entail (Chesterman 1996).

Whether the receipt of government funds by a social-change orientated organisation makes it an 'insider' or an 'outsider' is less important than answering the question: does it make the organisation compromised in the stances it takes with government?

And when it comes to asking how and why policy change occurs, the insider/outsider debate doesn't actually tell us a great deal. As I've already suggested, there are almost innumerable examples of insiders and outsiders bringing about policy change. The status is by no means irrelevant to the policy change process, but there are other significant variables at play (see, for instance, Dowding *et al.* 2013).

To my mind, there are two central variables that explain when and how policy change comes about, and these variables do not centre on one's status as an insider or outsider. They can be articulated in two core questions: Is the policy window open? And, are you credible?

Is the policy window open?

The most obvious time to make reform recommendations will be when government is asking for them. This happens when inquiries are held, which can be conducted by departments, parliamentary committees, independent commissions, consultants or other review bodies. Despite the popular belief that inquiries are a vehicle used by governments, at times, to side-step difficult decisions, my experience has been that inquiries – especially those conducted by parliamentary committees and independent commissions – constitute the best way to collect, and the most opportune moment to provide, frank and forthright reform suggestions. That is not to say that the conclusions made by bodies conducting inquiries are always without fault, and nor are good reform recommendations that emanate from inquiries always adopted by government. (Indeed the completion of an inquiry rarely signals the end of any need for advocacy. Well-made recommendations often need advocates to continue to promote them.) But inquiries present the best opportunity to address reform head on.

In my six years at OPA, the Policy and Research Unit I head has written more than 25 submissions to inquiries that have been conducted by state and federal parliamentary committees, and by state and federal law reform commissions, among other bodies. I have also been involved many times in giving formal oral evidence before review bodies, including parliamentary committees, and I have provided less formal information on request to bodies conducting inquiries. The challenge here, I have learnt, is to appreciate how the review body understands the problem it has been asked to address, and then to draw on evidence to provide possible solutions. If inquiries are treated simply as opportunities to repeat previously articulated broad reform strategies, then that can amount to a wasted opportunity (in addition to being quite indulgent).

Formal inquiries constitute the most obvious opening of the policy window. But less formal occasions also exist. When a politician, for instance, wants to know your thoughts about a policy area, then the opportunity exists for a strong idea to take hold. Usually the timing of such requests is quite unpredictable, and tends to follow the appearance of a difficult problem. Having said that, a political adviser once asked me 'what are the big social policy ideas at the moment?', and I confess I stumbled initially. I had (and have) in mind a number of smaller reform ideas, and was surprised to be presented, albeit momentarily, with so blank a canvas.

The challenge for any social reformer is not just to respond to invitations to present reform ideas, as happens when inquiries are held, but to encourage, where necessary, the recognition of a social problem that requires fixing. To use the policy window analogy, this amounts not just to waiting for the policy window to open, but to opening the window oneself.

This can occur, for instance, when a report, or an emblematic case study, arises and government is asked, or chooses, to respond.

An example of this occurred in early 2011 when OPA publicly released a report on *Violence against people with cognitive impairments* (Dillon 2010). The report showed an alarming rate of violence against represented persons (people under guardianship orders). This came on the back of a rising awareness generally in the community about violence against people with disability.

Partly in response to the public release of our report, the Baillieu state government announced that it would ask a parliamentary committee, the Law Reform Committee, to inquire into the 'access to and interaction with the justice system by people with an intellectual disability and their families and carers' (Parliament of Victoria Law Reform Committee 2013). The Committee (whose final report was released in 2013) then set about seeking submissions to the inquiry. OPA made a written (2011) and an oral submission to this committee (Bedson and Hartnett 2011), which drew heavily on much of our other recent work, including a large study that we were completing of our volunteer Independent Third Person program (McGuire 2012).

So on this occasion, we not only took the opportunity presented by the inquiry to make reform suggestions, but we in fact also helped to open the policy window.

Are you credible?

The second variable that is important to understanding when and how policy change comes about concerns the credibility of the reform advocate. By this I don't mean the truthfulness of what's being sought, but whether the advocate is convincing both in terms of the reform proposals being made and the evidence being drawn upon to support them. One might think that a good argument is a good argument regardless of who makes it. In the area of social reform, however, where there will inevitably exist far more reform ideas than any government's budget and preparedness to institute reform would permit, the credibility of the advocate becomes important in quantifying the problem and in prioritising a response. Oftentimes the unspoken but central questions that exist in response to reform advocacy will be: 'but how big a problem is this really?', and 'will your proposals fix, or at least address it?'

Some level of trust in the advocate's credibility is required for governments to act. This trust can be acquired through long and repeat involvement with government, especially when the advocate is proficient in being able to draw on real-life practice. Governments respect those who provide strong evidence-informed critiques far more than many might imagine. And the ability to draw on evidence is crucial.

That evidence can take the form of well-researched broad studies. But equally it's important not to underestimate how powerful well-chosen anecdotes can be. The delivery of a well-timed anecdote can very quickly draw non-experts into real life situations and focus the minds of listeners not on the solution to some abstract problem that they may not be wholly convinced exists, but instead turns the minds of listeners to solving a problem facing a particular person. A terrific quotation that I like to use, which is attributed to Martha Nussbaum, is that 'You can't really change the heart without telling a story'.

At the same time, it is now routine to talk about evidence-based policy (see Kay 2011). I must confess that I don't particularly like this phrase, as a lot of policy decisions in the end are values based rather than being based on evidence. For instance, when we as a society are determining health-spending priorities, how do we determine that one kind of medical intervention should be supported by government funds in preference to others? How do we work out where the cut-off line should be for support under the National Disability Insurance Scheme? These are questions that certainly can be informed by evidence, but are not strictly evidence based.

Returning to the topic of credibility, OPA is Victoria's guardian of last resort for adults with decision-making incapacity. As such OPA has credibility in advocating for changes to our guardianship system, something we did at length during a review of our guardianship laws and practices by the Victorian Law Reform Commission (Victorian Law Reform Commission 2012). We continue to advocate with government for change on this topic as it considers the Commission's 440 recommendations.

Credibility can be hard won and easily lost. One danger that exists for social reform advocates is the temptation to stray from one's brief to seek broader reform than is informed by evidence to hand.

Any of us with a social reform aspect to our work must be wary of posturing, which can happen when we make broad claims outside our area of knowledge and expertise that may look good to some in our sector, or even to the general public, but that aren't grounded. This can happen when we make recommendations for changes that are not feasible and that haven't been thought through.

Another danger to credibility concerns a person's ability to move from making a valid observation about the existence of a social problem, to proposing a workable solution.

The more I'm involved in doing it, the more I realise that the ability to write and articulate solid reform recommendations is quite a different skill to the ability to identify social problems. This is important not only for the obvious bigger picture reasons, but for purely instrumental reasons. If government can dismiss one recommendation as being ill thought out, it's far easier to dismiss others being made by the same person or organisation. Often a study will point to a very real social problem, but the ensuing recommendations can tend to be generic and not particularly helpful. Recommending that 'the government should provide more funding' to address a particular problem, while sometimes justified, is inevitably going to be less persuasive than arguing that a particular government department, or unit within a department, might make certain specified reforms. So I suggest that care in making workable recommendations, that address agreed-upon problems, will improve a social reform advocate's likelihood of being heard. One observation that draws from my own practice is that the reverse also applies. I have found that the more I am listened to, the more care I take with what I say.

An example of this comes from one piece of advocacy OPA engaged in during 2012. OPA put together a report (Bedson 2012) on four troubling instances of sexual assault in Supported Residential Services (private residences where many people with disabilities are supported to reside). In that report we were seeking a number of changes. Given our previous work in the broad area, the government was receptive to what we were doing, and we gave the relevant department an early draft of the report.

The department was very engaged with our concerns, and OPA suggested that the department could consider putting a response to the report as an appendix. OPA did this because we took the view that if this meant the government would listen and respond to our concerns and reform suggestions, then that was all that we wanted.

This then led to several discussions with departmental representatives about the wording, and practicality, of our recommendations. This was great access, in terms of being in a position to encourage policy change to occur. At the same time, we needed to stay focused on, and keep pressing, our core reform suggestions.

After some fine tuning by us, the government ended up agreeing with the substance of all our recommendations, and so when we publicly released the report, we did so with no fanfare, because the government was agreeing. There was no story. But that was fine because we wanted the change, not the story.

Taking care with the way reform recommendations are expressed can also be subtle. Governments of all persuasions want to institute positive reforms. The 'trenchant criticism' approach to achieving reform isn't always going to lead to the best results. If a government is convinced about the existence of a problem that it needs to address, then it will be open to possible solutions. Governments can be helped here, rather than badgered. Sometimes this is as simple as moving from saying 'we're falling behind world standards' to 'we could be leading world standards'.

I don't pretend to have the answers, in fact I don't think there are answers as such. For reform advocates there is a danger in being too reactive to inquiries or consultations that are going on, rather than concentrating on agenda setting. The only way to address this is to be clear about what the reform priorities are. For us at OPA there are a number of large reform topics on which we are trying to drive change and I thought it might be helpful to list them here. These include:

National Disability Insurance Scheme

We are concerned about how the consumer model is working for people with cognitive impairments and mental ill health (for whom this 'choice' model can be problematic if appropriate support is not given). The need to develop appropriate safeguards and protections is essential here.

Violence against people with cognitive impairments and mental illness

One concern we have in this field is the ability of people in the support system to know what actions they should take when violence against people with cognitive impairments or mental illness is witnessed or suspected. OPA took the initiative here in 2013 by drafting, with extensive consultation, an 'interagency guideline for addressing violence, neglect and abuse' (IGUANA). At its launch we had 28 agencies, including disability support providers, carers groups and advocacy agencies, sign up to IGUANA, and more have since added their names to this list.

OPA has recently partnered Women with Disabilities Victoria and the Domestic Violence Resource Centre Victoria in the 'Voices against Violence' project (Voices against Violence Research Project 2014), which resulted in the production of seven reports that in combination seek improvements to the way our society works to prevent and respond to violence against women with disabilities.

Better functioning adult protection system

I was fortunate to receive a Churchill Fellowship to investigate possible improvements to our adult protection system, and this took me to Washington State, Nova Scotia, Scotland and England to examine this topic. I have recommended (Chesterman 2013) that the Public Advocate be granted broader powers of investigation in relation to at-risk adults (consistent with recommendations to this effect made by the Victorian Law Reform Commission (Victorian Law Reform Commission 2012, p. 456). If this change occurred then OPA could set up a one-entry-point contact number where people could register concerns about at-risk adults in cases of financial abuse, neglect, and even physical abuse where evidence is minimal and where police are unwilling or unable to investigate.

Supported decision making

This is one of the most significant terms in international human rights law. The United Nations *Convention on the rights of persons with disabilities*, which Australia signed in 2007 and ratified in 2008, requires, among other things, people with even the most profound cognitive impairments or mental illnesses to be supported to make and implement their own decisions. This is a challenging area for many countries, and a number of supported decision-making initiatives were recommended by the Victorian Law Reform Commission (Victorian Law Reform Commission 2012) as part of its guardianship review. One of these concerned the possible establishment by OPA of a volunteer supported decision-making program. OPA was successful in attracting a grant from the Victoria Law Foundation to set up this small program – which is matching isolated people with cognitive impairments with volunteer supporters – and we will be very keen to see, among other things, how our guardianship practices might be informed by our experiences in running this program.

Advance planning

OPA wants more people to take charge of their own affairs to the extent that this is possible prior to any loss of decision-making capacity. We are working on ways to ensure this can happen, which has involved: advocating for better laws governing powers of attorney and advance statements; and the provision of information in this complex area in more readily accessible formats. OPA is redesigning the way we present information on these topics on our website and in related publications.

OPA is continuing to seek reform in all these areas.

Conclusion

I met some months ago with an academic friend who, unsurprisingly, has more time than me to research. But she wanted to know how to get 'policy people', rather than simply other academics, to engage with her important research. I recall experiencing similar frustrations as an academic, and there is no simple response. Research design and writing up are of course relevant. Does the research confront agreed-upon problems? Does it suggest manageable solutions? As a public servant, albeit one at a slightly unusual government instrumentality, I now find that 'policy people', including members of the government, are very prepared to listen. The challenge for me now is to ensure that what I say is drawn carefully from OPA's casework and expertise, and to ensure that our arguments exist within OPA's legislative remit. If I'm not cautious with this, I know that audience will not remain.

Acknowledgements

My thanks to Catherine Joyce, Phil Grano and Colleen Pearce, with each of whom I have had numerous discussions about policy change and systemic advocacy.

References

Bedson, L 2012, *Sexual assault in supported residential services: four case studies*, Office of the Public Advocate, Victoria.

Bedson, L and Hartnett, L 2011, *Submission to the inquiry into access to and interaction with the justice system by people with an intellectual disability and their families and carers*, Office of the Public Advocate, Victoria.

Chesterman, J 1996, *Poverty law and social change: the story of the Fitzroy Legal Service*, Melbourne University Press, Melbourne.

Chesterman, J 2005, *Civil rights: how Indigenous Australians won formal equality*, University of Queensland Press, Queensland.

Chesterman, J 2006, 'Chosen by the people? How federal parliamentary seats might be reserved for Indigenous Australians without changing the Constitution', *Federal Law Review*, vol. 34, pp. 261–285.

Chesterman, J 2008, 'National policy making in Indigenous affairs: blueprint for an Indigenous Review Council', *Australian Journal of Public Administration*, vol. 67, pp. 419–429.

Chesterman, J 2013, *Responding to violence, abuse, exploitation and neglect: improving our protection of at-risk adults*, Churchill Fellowship report, viewed 16 May 2015, www. churchilltrust.com.au/media/fellows/Chesterman_John_2012_Report.pdf.

Dillon, J 2010, *Violence against people with cognitive impairments*, Report from the Advocacy/Guardianship program at the Office of the Public Advocate, Office of the Public Advocate, Victoria.

Dowding, K, Hindmoor, A and Martin, A 2013, 'Australian public policy: attention, content and style', *Australian Journal of Public Administration*, vol. 72, pp. 82–88.

Feigan, M 2011, The Victorian Office of the Public Advocate: a first history 1986–2007, PhD thesis, La Trobe University, Melbourne.

Kay, A 2011, 'Evidence-based policy making: the elusive search for rational public administration', *Australian Journal of Public Administration*, vol. 70, pp. 236–245.

McGuire, M 2012, *Breaking the cycle: using advocacy-based referrals to assist people with disabilities in the criminal justice system*, Office of the Public Advocate, Victoria.

Parliament of Victoria Law Reform Committee 2013, *Inquiry into access to and interaction with the justice system by people with an intellectual disability and their families and carers*, Parliamentary Paper, No. 216, Session 2010–2013.

Victorian Law Reform Commission 2012, *Guardianship final report 24*, Victorian Law Reform Commission, Melbourne.

Voices against Violence Research Project 2014, *Research papers one to seven*, Women with Disabilities Victoria, OPA, Domestic Violence Resource Centre, Victoria, viewed 16 May 2015, http://wdv.org.au/voicesagainstviolence.html.

Legislation

Guardian and Administration Act 1986 (Vic).

Part II

Influencing policy

5 Influencing policy

Lessons from the health sector

Jennifer Doggett

Introduction

The teeth of Queensland's children can tell us a lot about the role and limitations of science and research in policy making. Children in Queensland have almost twice the rate of tooth decay than those in other states in Australia. In fact, the most recent national survey on children's oral health found that 63 per cent of Queensland children have tooth decay in their baby teeth, compared with 38 per cent of children in the Australian Capital Territory (ACT) (Ha *et al.* 2011). This has nothing to do with different physiologies, diets or teeth cleaning practices in the two regions but is due to a longstanding policy decision by successive Queensland Governments not to introduce state-wide fluoridation of the water supply.[1]

Unlike the other states and territories in Australia, Queensland has not a consistent policy of fluoridating the water supply. Compared with a 100 per cent fluoridation rate in the ACT, only 5 per cent of Queensland's water has been consistently fluoridated since the 1960s.[2] Despite overwhelming scientific evidence that fluoridation results in a reduction in tooth decay, politics and public opinion in Queensland have worked together to prevent the introduction of this cost-effective and low-risk preventive health strategy.

This is just one of many examples in the health sector where there is a gap between science and policy. In many cases, this gap exists not due to ignorance on the part of politicians and policy makers – the research on fluoridation is clear and easily accessible to all – but because of other, non-scientific interests, that have dominated the policy-making process.

Attempts to counter this influence have not had lasting success due, in part, to their failure to take into account some key aspects of the policy-making process. These are often not well understood by academics, non-government organisations and others who, despite their practical, well-supported and evidenced-based solutions to policy challenges, frequently find themselves frustrated by the lack of success of their lobbying efforts.

This chapter uses John Kingdon's model of policy making (Kingdon 1995) as a framework to explore the lobbying and advocacy process through which policy proposals gain political support. It explores how groups that are often under-represented in these processes, such as researchers and community groups, can exert more influence and shape the future of our health system. It covers key factors for successfully influencing governments and addresses some common advocacy myths, such as the importance of lobbying the health minister. It also explains why an understanding of the political processes is critical to successfully promoting a new policy idea and why academics, researchers and other experts should not be afraid to 'get their hands dirty' by engaging in the political sphere in order to achieve lasting policy changes.

Health policy – the context for reform

Like many areas of public policy, the health sector is heavily influenced by vested interests, including the medical profession, the pharmacy sector, the pharmaceutical industry and representatives of other industries, such as the tobacco, soft drink, and alcohol lobbies.

These interest groups have had a longstanding influence and impact on our health system. Even our constitution has been shaped by sectional medical profession interests, including the Australian chapter of the British Medical Association (later to become the Australian Medical Association), which was instrumental in including a clause prohibiting civil conscription in the 1946 Referendum. This clause has had a profound impact on the evolution of the Australian health system. For example, it is the primary reason why Medicare operates as an insurance scheme which rebates consumers a fixed amount of an uncapped doctor's fee and does not place any geographical restrictions on where doctors can practise (unlike in other countries such as Canada where there are restrictions on what doctors can charge for their services and where they can practise).

The fact that Australian consumers cannot buy prescription medicines, along with our groceries, at convenience stores or supermarkets (while pharmacies can sell everything from confectionary to sun glasses, along with medicines) is another example of the influence of vested interest groups on our health system. In this case it is the pharmacy lobby which has convinced successive governments to enforce anti-competitive practices which advantage pharmacists (particularly those who already own pharmacies) over the general community.

Groups such as the medical and pharmacy professions exert influence over policy-making processes not because they are intrinsically more powerful or more important than any other stakeholder group. They have the power they have because, over time, they have devoted significant efforts and resources into influencing political and policy decision-making processes.

The overall impact of the power exercised by a small number of powerful interest groups is a health system that reflects provider and industry rather than consumer interests. This may not always be obvious, as established practices come to be seen by stakeholders as inevitable and are therefore rarely questioned.

However, there is nothing inevitable about the current structure or organisation of our health system. Health systems worldwide vary significantly in their structures, funding mechanisms and the way in which they provide services to consumers. In Singapore, people are able to buy their prescription medication at the same time and place as they receive their medical consultations. In Canada, the Government can restrict the fees charged by doctors who receive public funding. In the UK, the Government can restrict doctors funded by the National Health Service from practising in areas of oversupply. None of these practices occur within the Australian health system, except for in very specific situations, although arguably all of them would improve the delivery of health care to consumers.

Changing longstanding practices in areas of public policy dominated by vested interests is a challenge. However, it is possible to combat the influence of interest groups in order to improve the system for consumers through sustained and targeted efforts. These require an agreed vision of the end goal, an understanding of the policy-making process and an ability to identify and take advantage of political and media opportunities.

The many text books written on public policy provide theories and models of how policies are developed and implemented in modern Western democracies. These can be useful in understanding the broad framework of policy making and the processes involved. The most useful, such as John Kingdon's model (Kingdon 1995), outlined below, take into account the dynamic relationship between the political environment and policy ideas. However, while models can provide a useful theoretical framework, in practice policy making is more art than science and even the best theories have their limitations. In 'real life' situations, policy making is a messy, complex and non-linear process which has as much (or more) to do with the personalities of the people involved (and their relationships with each other) than any theory or formula. This means that every policy-making and policy reform process is different and that past experiences can only provide a partial guide to future outcomes.

Achieving a healthy influence

For people who have worked in the health system outside of government and the public services, trying to achieve changes at a political and policy level can be extremely frustrating. It would be easier for those seeking influence if there were a formula or straightforward process to follow in order to have an effect rather than the variable and contextual processes by which stakeholder groups work to achieve influence. Also surprising for many people used to the worlds of academia or research is that there is generally no clear authorship for creating and influencing policies. Often those with minimal influence receive credit for a policy while those who had instrumental roles receive little recognition. Typically, there are so many isolated influences and such long and complex processes that identifying the specific influence of one individual or group is impossible. For those seeking policy change, this means that even when a desired outcome is achieved it is impossible to know whether and to what extent their efforts were responsible. While this may discourage researchers and academics from engaging in the policy-making process, the benefit of getting involved is that these efforts can make a difference to people's lives and shape the future of our country in a way that research on its own rarely does.

Additionally, while there are few rigid rules that will guarantee influence in the policy-making process, there are some general principles that can help maximise the opportunity for influence. These are outlined in more detail, below.

Find common ground

The single most important strategy for individuals and groups seeking to influence public policy is to find the intersection between what they want and what the government is trying to achieve. By focusing on solving the Government's problem (rather than their own) groups can target the objectives that they have in common. Finding the common ground between the policy objectives of the individual or group and the Government's sphere of influence is crucial and this is where policy pitches should be targeted.

This requires putting the issue in perspective, something that can be difficult to do for someone passionate about their work or cause. It is also important to be realistic about the aims and constraints of the Government, not simply identifying what an individual politician or Minister would like to achieve. Most Ministers in social policy areas, such as health, would love to achieve much more within their portfolios than they are able to given their limited time, budgets and political capital.

From the 'outside' of politics, it is easy to over-estimate the power of Governments and Ministers. Despite their high profiles, there are both formal and informal constraints on their power and in reality they may have less actual scope to make changes than is apparent to interest groups. These constraints may come from budgetary restrictions as well as real or perceived political realities, such as the need to keep a powerful interest group on side. Understanding the broader agenda of the Government and the political and media environment in which it operates will give those seeking influence a good sense of how far it is possible to shift the Government's position on a specific issue. For example, if the Government has made specific economic commitments, such as keeping the Budget in surplus, it will be very difficult to persuade a Minister to support a policy or program requiring a high level of spending. Or if a Government is relying on support from a specific lobby group, such as the AMA, to win the next election it will not want to do anything to put this support at risk (See Box 5.1).

Box 5.1 Power of lobby groups

Australia's health workforce is characterised by archaic workforce divisions and practices that no longer exist in many other countries. For example, doctors in Australia perform many lower-risk services (such as routine immunisations) that in other countries are safely and more cost-effectively provided by practice nurses or other health professionals. Increasing the flexibility of the health workforce to support greater substitution between professional roles (such as allowing nurse practitioners to take over some tasks currently only undertaken by doctors) would increase the productivity of the health workforce and may also lead to lower overall costs and increased consumer satisfaction. However, opposition to these changes by the doctors' peak[3] body the AMA has meant that successive governments have been reluctant to push for changes in this area.

Seeking a policy change that is outside the Government's actual 'sphere of influence' does not mean that the issue is not important or justified. But it might mean that practically it is not worth investing resources at that time to effect change. Other strategies, such as influencing public opinion via the media, may be more effective than direct lobbying of Government.

Advocates for workforce reform, such as nurse practitioners for example, could focus their arguments for change in a number of different areas. Increasing the scope of the role for nurses could deliver them greater professional satisfaction and increased remuneration, thus making nursing a more attractive and higher status profession. It could also give consumers greater choice of health care provider and therefore allow more diversity of health care provision. While all of these may be valid reasons to support increased workforce flexibility, they do not reflect the main policy interests of the current Government and so would be unlikely to have an impact. However, addressing the rising rates of chronic disease and strengthening the capacity of primary health care to undertake prevention and chronic disease management services are policy priorities stated by the Government which could be supported by workforce changes. Therefore, for maximum impact this is where advocates for change in this area should focus their efforts.

Just like campaign dollars or program budgets, the time and energy of people involved in influencing a policy agenda is a limited resource. By identifying the best possible opportunities for achieving success, they can ensure that these resources are used as efficiently as possible. This involves focusing on current or emerging windows of opportunity for policy change. These 'windows' are defined by John Kingdon as requiring at least two of the following three 'enabling' conditions: an identified problem, a workable solution and an appropriate political climate (Kingdon 1995). This does not mean that policy goals that do not meet these criteria should be abandoned but they may need to be seen as longer-term aims and not the main focus for an organisation's immediate or short-term time and energy. Rather than investing more resources into fine tuning the details of a policy that has little likelihood of being supported in the short term, organisations would be better of to put their efforts into identifying windows of opportunity as they arise and making the most of these to achieve other policy goals (even if these are lower order priorities). One example of how interest groups took advantage of the 'policy window' created by the introduction of the GST (goods and services tax) is provided in Box 5.2.

It is a key challenge for advocacy groups and others seeking changes to current policies to balance the allocation of their resources between achieving lower priority short-term changes and preparing to take advantage of windows of opportunity for higher-priority, longer-term changes. This is particularly the case as in the health sector opportunities can arise quickly and unexpectedly, for example as a result of a media story, change of Minister or emerging public health threat. Being on hand with a workable policy solution at the start of the process, i.e. when the Government is still in the process of identifying the problem, can put an organisation in prime position to play a key influencing role on that issue.

Kingdon (1995) also identifies 'policy entrepreneurs' as playing an important role in the policy-making process, in particular in developing and promoting a policy solution to governments. Policy entrepreneurs are defined by him as people who can introduce and promote their ideas in many different forms and invest time and energy to increase the chances for an idea to be placed on the decision agenda. Identifying and seeking to influence policy entrepreneurs (both within and outside of government) is one important strategy for promoting a specific policy solution.

Understand the politics

Politics is a very different world from that of academia, scientific research and the community sector. Every policy decision that is made by governments is played out against a backdrop of broader political and ideological agendas which largely differ from those influencing other sectors of society This creates a distinct political culture, with unique norms, values and constraints. Having a knowledge of these and the broader political landscape is important for individuals and groups trying to effect change.

In addition to the enabling conditions outlined above, Kingdon also describes the specific processes needed to get an issue on the 'policy agenda' as: 'problems, proposals and politics'. He argues that these three factors operate independently and that at least two need to be in place before an issue can be put on the Governments 'policy agenda'. Of these three conditions, academics, organisations and other advocates generally find the first the least challenging of the three and the third the most challenging. At any one time in the health sector there are a number of high quality, evidence-based and workable solutions being proposed by interest groups and experts to meet current policy challenges but there is a high failure rate in attempting to navigate the politics of policy change.

This does not mean that everyone needs to become an expert on the Westminster system or political campaigning in order to successfully influence politicians. However, a basic knowledge of politicians and their roles, the political landscape and the policy priorities of the Government is useful in order to achieve influence. The case of the introduction of the GST provides a useful example.

Box 5.2 Interest group and GST

When the GST was proposed by the Howard Government in the 1998 election, the Government required the Senate to pass the legislation in order for the policy to take effect. As the Labor party and independent Brian Harradine opposed the legislation, the Government needed the support of the Australian Democrats which at that time held the balance of power. This created an opportunity for interest groups and other stakeholders to lobby for changes to the proposed new tax. These efforts resulted in a package of exemptions, compensation packages and other changes agreed to by the Government in return for support for the relevant legislation by the Democrats. These changes have largely been retained in our tax system today, one of which is the exemption from the GST for fresh food.

Some researchers resist seeing themselves as 'political' while still seeking and working towards policy changes. However, opting out from the politics of an issue is not realistic for anyone working in a sector, such as health care, largely dependent on government funding. Currently, around 70 per cent of total health system funding in Australia comes directly from federal and state/territory governments and therefore no health system issue lies outside of politics, in its broadest sense. While individuals and groups seeking political changes may not want to be partisan, there is no way of influencing policy that is not 'political'.

Similarly, it is both disingenuous and counter-productive for individuals and groups engaging in political advocacy to claim that they are 'not ideological' when seeking policy changes. The way in which we care for people who are sick or have disabilities and the policies we develop to support this care are inherently ideological processes. Effective advocacy involves acknowledging and making explicit the relevant moral beliefs and principles that underlie the policy goals being sought. Removing them from this ethical context will only negate the importance of these changes and reduce the potential that they will be implemented. For example, policy responses to the rising rate of obesity in Australia involving restrictions on junk food advertising involve specific beliefs about the role of individual and parental responsibility and that of corporations and governments. Policy differences in these areas can often be traced back to fundamental ideological differences which should not be ignored.

Understanding the political process can also provide additional opportunities for achieving influence. For example, the role of the Senate is one area not well understood and exploited by those seeking change at the political level. The Senate in Australia has a number of powers, including amending legislation, holding inquiries, forcing the production of documents and blocking regulations. Where the Senate is not controlled by the Government (the most common electoral outcome in Australia), the Opposition, minor parties and independents can be lobbied in order to influence the political and legislative process. This can provide interest groups with opportunities to raise issues in Parliament, review Bills passed by the Lower House (where the dominance of the Government prohibits significant scrutiny), initiate Senate Committee Inquiries into key issues, change laws proposed and passed in the House of Representatives by the Government and, in doing so, influence both laws and policies in specific areas.

Understanding the role of technology and the media in the political process is also important. Email and the internet have made politicians much more accessible to constituents and provided useful lobbying and advocacy tools. However, the development of these technologies and new media platforms has also resulted in a much-crowded communications and information environment. Politicians and policymakers have more data available to them than ever before, which can distract from the key issues and make decision making more difficult. Politicians are also being put under greater scrutiny on a day-to-day basis by the 24-hour media cycle. This can create challenges to those wanting to influence the policy debate as the constant media attention results in pressures for short-term over long-term fixes and makes competing for influence via longer-term strategies more complex.

Perfect your pitch

Ministers in social policy areas such as health and their advisers spend a significant part of their working days meeting with individuals and groups with ideas about how to improve the health of the community. All of these people are convinced that they have a solution to the challenges facing the Government in areas such as health.

To some extent they are all correct. Every new treatment, each newly developed drug or successfully piloted program has some potential to increase health and wellbeing of the community. However, when resources are limited there are only a small number of these which can ultimately be supported by the Government. To be successful, a policy idea needs to compete against all the other options on the table.

This can have as much to do with the delivery as the substance of the policy idea. One of the scarcest resources in politics is face-to-face time with key people, such as Ministers and their advisers. Making the best use of this resource requires careful planning and attention to delivery. Just like an actor auditioning for a role, it is important for people seeking to influence governments to develop a routine or 'pitch' for their policy idea to make it stand out from the others. This needs to be succinct and to resonate with the target audience by addressing one or more of their key concerns.

A useful framework for developing a policy pitch is to answer the following three questions:

> What is the problem? What is my solution? Why is this solution the best one?

This framework will ensure that the pitch sets the scene by describing the issue being addressed, focuses on the policy solution being proposed and provides some broader context and justification for why it is better than any other options. Also useful to include are some brief but relevant supporting data and examples. A case study or real life example of the impact of the policy proposal usually makes a pitch more memorable.

An effective policy pitch inspires as well as informs by telling a story and painting a picture of success. It should not contain any complex detail, as its goal is just to gain a foot in the door which can then be followed up with any additional relevant data or facts.

Some key suggestions for a successful pitch are to avoid using technical language or discussing methodology in great detail. It is also important to be honest about limitations of the research, without dwelling on the constraints to the extent that it detracts from the main message.

Practising a policy pitch can help ensure it is polished and effective. Keeping pitches brief and free of academic jargon is a challenge for many academics, used to having more time to explain the details of their research and speaking to audiences familiar with the technical language of their field.

In the early stages of seeking political or bureaucratic support for a policy proposal it is also important not to get bogged down in detailed discussions about the complications arising from the possible implementation of the policy. While clearly these will need to be addressed at some stage, initially it is important to focus on gaining support for the broad policy idea with the necessarily messier 'real life' implementation processes deferred until a later date. This can run counter to the approach generally taken by academics in their main areas of expertise, which is to explore all possible problems and implementation challenges before commencing research. It can also be a challenge for people from the community-based and/or service delivery sector as their roles often involve identifying and addressing implementation problems.

Of course, implementation is a key stage in the policy reform process and any potential problems with the implementation of a specific policy should not be ignored. However, all complex policies and programs will present implementation challenges at some point and with sufficient resources, expertise and political support these can usually be addressed.

Tell a story

Story telling is deeply ingrained in our human psyche and one of the most powerful ways in which we communicate with others. Politicians are typically very responsive to individual anecdotes and stories as, due to the nature of their work, they spend a great deal of their time engaged and interacting with their constituents. Politicians often approach policy issues via individual stories and they remember key policy details through the people they meet and the stories they relate.[4] Politicians also often use stories to communicate and sell their policies to the community.

Of course, individual stories need to be supported by evidence and research but, at least initially, painting a picture of a policy goal through telling individual stories can help capture the imagination of politicians and assist them in recalling it at a later date.

To maximise impact, a policy story should engage with the values and rhetoric of the government of the day. Every government has a story that it tells about itself, via the media and other forms of communication. This story may be more about symbolism and image than substance, e.g. coalition governments frequently present themselves as 'economically tough' while providing widespread subsidies to some sectors of industry, such as private health insurance. However, recognising and reflecting this narrative back to the Government via an appropriate individual example can go a long way towards selling a policy to a politician.

However, this strategy can backfire if it is not credible or does not resonate well with the target audience. One example of a failed attempt at selling a policy via story telling is Health Minister Peter Dutton's attempt to promote the Government's proposed A\$7 co-payment for GP bulk billed services. In selling this policy to the community the Minister painted a picture of people 'taking advantage' of the bulk billing system by going to the GP unnecessarily and therefore 'freeloading' on other tax payers. However, this story did not resonate with many people in the community, who rejected the idea that people were taking advantage of Medicare and needed a price signal to make them value the service.

A more successful approach to influencing policy changes via narrative is the one taken by the consumer health sector. Health consumer groups use narratives describing the experiences of consumers in seeking health care to argue for changes to health policies and programs. These can be very effective communication tools, which have power because they are genuine, 'real life' examples that people can relate to. By demonstrating the impact of public policies in the context of an individual's life, rather than via an abstract set of facts and figures, advocacy groups can increase community support for their policy goals. While not generally sufficient on their own (they need to be supported by evidence and respond to an identified political need) stories can play a key role in promoting policy changes.

Make friends and neutralise enemies

As discussed above, politicians are bombarded with pitches from interest groups and others wanting to influence policy changes. Part of the role of politicians, in particular those with ministerial responsibilities, is to select which out of the number of competing proposals being suggested would be the best to address the challenges facing the Government. One factor influencing this decision-making process is the likely response of key interest groups and the broader community. Very often the response of these stakeholders will be mediated by the communication of the proposal via the media and, therefore, consideration of the media's likely response to a proposal is also important to take into account.

Almost all policy decisions require an assessment and trade off between risks and benefits. Often in this process risks can carry more weight than benefits as Governments increasingly become more risk averse, partly due to the emergence of the 24-hour media cycle. The round-the-clock reporting of politics and the need for media outlets to continually find new material to report mean that even relatively small blunders by politicians will be picked up and reported on extensively. This can create an environment in which governments can be reluctant to take on policies which are likely to result in negative media.

In this climate of risk aversion it is vital to develop allies and neutralise potential opposition when seeking policy changes. While gaining support for a specific policy from supportive groups is important, it is also at least as important to identify and neutralise enemies. If a policy idea has the support of key interest groups and there does not appear to be significant opposition from any major stakeholders, it will be considered 'low risk' by government and therefore be more likely to ultimately gain support.

Almost all major policy changes involve disadvantaging a specific group or sector, relative to the status quo, either through a loss of influence, power or financial advantage. Therefore, opposition to most policy proposals should be expected and addressed before pitching an idea to governments. Although this can take time, engaging with an alternative perspective can help clarify the arguments in favour of the proposed policy change, as well as assist in developing strategies to address any resistance.

Sometimes compromise on the detail of a policy position is required in order to neutralise opposition from a particular group. This can be frustrating but can be crucial in overcoming barriers to acceptance of the proposal by government. Nine times out of ten a mediocre policy with no opposition from powerful groups will win over a great policy fiercely opposed by a vested interest group.

A large part of the success of the campaign to establish a National Disability Insurance Scheme (NDIS) was the way in which it engaged with the community, gaining the support of people from all walks of life, including celebrities, football teams, local community members, role models and ordinary people. This created the impression that the NDIS had the support of all sectors of the community and was likely to be popular with voters, resulting in bi-partisan support for the scheme despite its high cost to the community. By drawing in people who were not usually politically engaged, the NDIS campaign demonstrated that everyone who supports a policy change can be involved in the political process of lobbying for change, regardless of whether or not they would see themselves as 'political'.

Be persistent and realistic

Policy making can be a very non-linear and complex process, involving multiple stakeholders throughout a number of different stages of development.[5] Often the evolution of a policy is only clear in retrospect, as at the time the people involved did not have the required perspective to see themselves as part of a larger process.

Being an intrinsically good idea is not enough to make a policy idea take hold in the political arena. There are more good policy ideas presented to Ministers and the bureaucracy than could ever be implemented by a single government. The crucial factor influencing success is how these ideas are communicated and promoted to governments and other stakeholders.

As discussed above, the broader political, community and media environment is also important in influencing policy changes. New policy proposals often need a 'perfect storm' of factors to fall into place before they are adopted by governments and many policies fail due primarily to poor timing or a mis-step in the selling process. However, the groundwork needs to be done first in order to take advantage of the perfect storm environment, whenever this occurs. This includes building a relationship with politicians and other key stakeholders around the policy idea. This does not necessarily require a large commitment of resources, although sometimes resources can help, but it does require a clear vision of how the policy would work in practice and persistence over time. The most effective policy influences are those who deliver a consistent message over time to the appropriate stakeholders, with an eye on the political landscape to know when there is a window of opportunity opening (as described by John Kingdon) for a more concerted effort.

This means that people seeking to influence policy often need to persist for long periods until they achieve success. This can be discouraging as it is not always clear whether or not any progress has been made towards influencing policy change. However, often initial 'failures' and set-backs end up as being important in the ultimate success of the policy. For example, the first attempt to introduce a national health insurance system was Medibank, implemented by the Whitlam Government in 1975. While it only lasted a few months before its repeal by the incoming Fraser Government, many of the learning and the infrastructure developed for the original Medibank proved crucial in the eventual success of Medicare in 1983.

Another example of the length of time it can take to achieve policy change is the campaign by a number of health advocates over the years to abolish tobacco advertising. This started in the 1960s, not long after the US Surgeon General published a report linking smoking to a range of diseases in 1964. However, it was not until 1991 that most forms of tobacco advertising were banned in Australia and branding on tobacco packaging was only banned in 2012. The message of the health advocates has essentially been the same throughout this period but changes in Australia's acceptance of tobacco advertising has been incremental to achieve the policy goal of a tobacco advertising-free Australia.

Don't be afraid to get your hands dirty

For many people, achieving policy influence means stepping outside of the worlds of academia or research and entering into another world with different norms, cultures, expectations and standards of excellence. This can be uncomfortable and difficult but it is often when the worlds of academia/research and politics/policy making interact that successful policy changes can be achieved.

One of the most challenging issues for people making the transition from academia to politics is the lack of authorship involved in policy making. Unlike in academia, those involved in developing policies rarely receive credit or acknowledgement for their work. Policy making is a complex process involving a large number of people and groups, often over long periods of time. It is difficult, if not impossible, to attribute policy influence to an individual or group and the politics around successful policy changes often mean that the relevant Minister is the only person directly associated with a specific policy.

One of the greatest policy success stories of Australia is the introduction of Medicare, Australia's universal health insurance system, in 1983. This policy has transformed Australia's health system and made a significant contribution to our increasing good health over this period (to the point where Australians enjoy one of the highest life expectancies of any nation in the world today). However, the establishment of Medicare would not have occurred if two academics, John Deeble and Dick Scotton, had not stepped outside of their academic comfort zones and become intimately involved with the policy making process (Boxall and Gillespie 2013). This was no doubt challenging for them as they had no background in politics or experience in working in a political environment. However, by taking on this challenge they achieved a high level of influence in shaping Australia's universal health insurance system, Medicare.

Conclusion

Challenging the dominance of established policy ideas and the accepted influence of high profile groups can be daunting to individuals and groups without experience in the areas of politics or policy making. However, despite the seemingly impermeable wall of influence built up by interest groups in specific areas, it is always possible to create opportunities to challenge the status quo. Politicians are often looking for new policy ideas and can welcome the opportunity to challenge the influence of interest groups in their portfolio area. Even when the political environment is not receptive to new ideas, it is important to persist and seek input into the policy debate. Policy making by a small and narrow group of sectional interests is generally not based on a broad evidence base and is not in the interests of the general community.

Many of the traditional barriers to communicating with governments and other stakeholders, such as the time and expense involved in sending hard copy correspondence, have been eroded by new technologies which allow for quick and easy communications. Technology and the growth of social media mean that geographical proximity and a high level of resources are not as important as they once were for engaging in public debate. New technologies are also providing greater openness and transparency in many areas of policy making and creating opportunities for a greater diversity of voices to influence this process.

Learning how to work within this political and media environment is important in order to achieve influence over policy making. This does not require a huge amount of resources but does require a clear vision of policy goals, persistence over time and a willingness to engage in the political process. With these, even individuals and small organisations can have influence over the policy-making process leading to policy decisions which reflect a broader range of interests and ultimately benefit a greater number of people in our community.

Notes

1 State-wide fluoridation was briefly introduced by the Labor Government in 2008 but overturned by the incoming Liberal Government in 2012.
2 While most of Queensland's water supply requires fluoridation in order to reach the levels needed to prevent tooth decay, there are some communities in Queensland which have this level of fluoride naturally occurring in their drinking water.
3 'Peak body' is an Australian term for an advocacy group or professional/trade association.
4 For more information on this, see Deborah Stone's *Policy Paradox* (Stone 2001), which explores the role of stories and the various types of stories/symbols employed in political contests.
5 For examples in the Australian context see Denniss and Maddison (2009).

References

Boxall, A and Gillespie, J 2013, *Making Medicare: the politics of universal health care in Australia*, UNSW Press, Sydney, NSW.

Ha D H, Roberts-Thomson K F and Armfield J M 2011, 'The child dental health surveys Australia, 2005 and 2006', *Dental Statistics and Research Series*, no. 54. Cat. no. DEN 213, AIHW, Canberra.

Denniss, R and Maddison, S 2009, *An introduction to Australian public policy: theory and practice*, Cambridge University Press, Cambridge.

Kingdon, J W 1995, *Agendas, alternatives, and public policies*, 2nd edn, Longman, New York.

Stone, D 2001, *Policy paradox: the art of political decision making*, W. W. Norton and Company, Inc., New York.

6 Using metrics for policy change

Shawn McMahon and Mary Gatta

Introduction

The United States Department of Labor created the nation's first official budget-based, market-basket measure of wellbeing in 1909, when it studied the conditions of women and children working in the Massachusetts mills. This early metric is predecessor to multiple generations of metrics produced by the United States federal government and, more recently, by members of academic and non-profit advocacy communities. These measures raise awareness of what it means to escape the shadow of poverty and financial instability, and influence public policy and social services provision. They are grounded in rigorous methodologies intended to minimize political bias and increase their acceptance and use. However, metrics which help define financial wellbeing cannot be fully separated from political beliefs, norms and messages, and those used to inform the role of government and public sector budgets can face opposition.

In this chapter we present an overview of wellbeing metrics developed by researchers both inside and outside of the US government. We then discuss, in relation to seminal theories of policy change, a specific measure which helped shift conversation away from a traditional poverty discourse and toward contemporary definitions of need and economic security messaging frameworks. We conclude with discussion of challenges to modern measures of wellbeing.

Background on wellbeing metrics in the United States

For centuries, researchers, advocates and policymakers have attempted to quantify poverty at the individual and household levels, to define basic needs and count 'the poor'. In 1776, Adam Smith, considered by many the world's first modern economist, defined the lack of 'necessaries' as the experience of being unable to consume "not only the commodities which are indispensably necessary for the support of life, but whatever the custom of the country renders it indecent for creditable people, even of the lowest order, to be without" (Rossi and Curtis 2013, p. 112). In the early nineteenth century,

American sociologists and economists measured poverty by developing family budget standards, and determined that families whose incomes did not allow them to buy budget items deemed necessities fell into the 'poor' category. The first official American federal budget standards were developed in 1909 by the United States Department of Labor's Bureau of Labor Statistics (BLS) as part of a larger study on the working conditions in mills in the American South and the state of Massachusetts. The market-based budgets determined the prices of goods and services that a family would need at both a 'minimum level of subsistence' and a 'fair level of subsistence' (Johnson *et al.* 2001, p. 30). BLS stressed that the budgets were grounded in the "standards found to be actually prevailing among cotton-mill families of the several communities studied, and are not standards fixed by the judgment of the investigators or the Bureau of Labor" (Johnson *et al.* 2001, p. 30). During World War I, Congress instructed BLS to prepare budgets for government workers in Washington, DC for a family of five, for single men and for single women. These types of budgets proliferated during the Great Depression as part of Works Progress Administration programs to determine pay for workers on large-scale public works projects. These budgets were calculated for 59 cities and at two levels – maintenance budgets and emergency budgets (Johnson *et al.* 2001).

Such budgets came with challenges. Concern was expressed by members of Congress that these 'relief budgets' were being used by employers to argue against wage rises for workers. This led Congress to request that BLS develop family budgets that reflected costs of living that were 'sufficient but adequate' (Johnson *et al.* 2001). BLS spent the next three decades developing family budgets for a family of four and retired couples in a variety of US cities. From the 1940s to the final BLS budget of 1981, debate focused on data sources and the BLS's normative judgments on adequate levels of consumption. These concerns – methodological and ideological – along with decreased funding to BLS, lead to the elimination of family budget standards in the early 1980s, during the Reagan Administration.[1]

Meanwhile, in 1963, at the Social Security Administration, research analyst Mollie Orshansky created a new measure of poverty, the federal poverty thresholds, as part of President Lyndon Johnson's War on Poverty (Orshansky 1965).[2] The 1955 Household Food Consumption Survey demonstrated that the average family of three or more spent one-third of their after-tax income on food. As a result, she calculated the poverty thresholds as three times the United States Department of Agriculture's Economy Food Plan, a food basket for "temporary or emergency use when funds are low" (Blank 2008, p. 235). This measure remains the dominant poverty metric in the United States today and is updated each year using only an inflation methodology based on the BLS Consumer Price Index. The release of nation- and state-level poverty rates based on the poverty thresholds captures headlines – primarily in difficult economic times – each autumn. Multiples of the poverty thresholds are still used as unofficial definitions of 'near-poor', and the derived federal poverty guidelines are used as the chief income eligibility criterion for federal and state anti-poverty assistance programs (e.g. nutrition assistance, medical assistance).[3]

Despite their endurance over the decades, the poverty thresholds are a controversial metric. As Rossi and Curtis (2013) note, in capturing only cash transfers as income, the poverty thresholds may both undercount poverty and fail to capture the success or failure of major anti-poverty policies involving both cash and in-kind assistance such as nutrition assistance, housing and medical assistance, and federal and state tax credits aimed at low-income families. Further, the poverty thresholds' assumption that food is the most significant budget item for families does not reflect current reality. As Rebecca Blank (2008) notes, "If one sticks with a threshold based only on food costs, the current multiplier [one-third] would be much higher because food has become relatively cheaper and food expenditures have declined precipitously as a share of overall expenditures" (Blank 2008, p. 237). The poverty thresholds also do not take into account geographic differences in costs, and vary only by family size. Over the decades critics have loudly denounced the flaws of the poverty thresholds, and yet no substantive official change has been made to the poverty thresholds since their creation.

Metrics and policy change

The federal poverty thresholds' longevity is not surprising, as they have been used constantly and consistently for decades, and are therefore entrenched. On the other hand, multiple theories of policy change suggest the strategic value, if not the inevitability, of data and newer, properly designed metrics that will help change the social norms and political will that obstruct anti-poverty policy changes.

Prospect theory (also known as messaging and frameworks theory) holds that individuals develop preferences based on how options are presented or framed, not simply through rational consideration of costs and benefits (Kahneman and Tversky 1979; Tversky and Kahneman 1992). Individuals often make choices that are higher risk or less beneficial for themselves based on how information is presented, in part because information consumers simplify decision making and evaluate options based too heavily on perceived direct consequences, or by default choose definitive options over ambiguity. As a result, while decisions are influenced by personal characteristics, beliefs and habits, decision making can be significantly influenced by an issue's definition and strategic presentation.

The power politics theory (also known as power elites theory) describes how public policy outcomes are affected by stratified power and class structures. The objective in power politics theory is to develop relationships with and influence decision makers directly on specific issues, or to influence them indirectly by influencing those around them (Wright 1956; Dormhoff 2013). Decision makers and influencers include legislators, senior members of the executive and their agents. Alternatively, the objective is to affect the opinions of decision makers' potential supporters or opponents – business leaders, grass roots and union leaders, advocacy organisations, academics, journalists and religious leaders.

According to coalition theory (also known as the advocacy coalition framework), successful coalitions are constructed around a limited number of stable shared core beliefs, which reduces intra-coalition transaction costs and allows coalitions to be broad and diverse (Sabatier and Jenkins-Smith 1996; Sabatier 1999). Defeat of the status quo is largely dependent on coalitions' winning support of leadership at higher levels of government. Support may be gained through positive or negative political incentives, including public opinion informed by media campaigns, popular protest or demonstrations. Multiple direct and indirect efforts to gain support may be pursued simultaneously. This theory suggests that research and information can gain decision maker support directly by changing decision makers' perspectives and incentives, or can lead to support by influencing public opinion.

Each of these theories of policy change shares the requirement that beliefs and/or social norms change, that political will on an issue increases, and that decision makers act to change policy. This process can occur in many forms, and may originate with: information and data sharing; targeted external messaging and/or mass media engagement (prospect theory and coalition theory); establishment of common core beliefs, potentially created or supported by information, data and/or measures (coalition theory); or improved political alignment among actors and leaders that is supported by commonly accepted measures (power politics theory).

Using modern metrics to change policy

The past two decades have seen the development of a new generation of more accurate measures of financial wellbeing. Demand for these metrics is broad-based, coming primarily from non-profit advocacy organisations and academia, which have recognised the growing effect of data on attitudes and political will, and the need for standards and measurement tools to support evidence-based policy. Data is becoming an important policy tool in the United States, and advocates of all ideological stripes contest to better use data and metrics to frame issues, gain access to political leaders, and build larger, stronger coalitions. Demand for measures has also come from those leaders and decision makers who believe in the importance of data, both in formulating policy and generating political support, and from a public increasingly expecting to see numbers which demonstrate the need for policy change and the impacts of policy choices. Both supply and demand of metrics have been further increased by the development of the internet and social media, which have created an expectation that pithy professional and political information will be regularly dispatched and received among political leaders, opinion leaders, advocates, academics and leaders' constituents.

In 1996, Dr Diana Pearce, former Director of the Women and Poverty Project at non-profit training and advocacy organization Wider Opportunities for Women (WOW), developed the Self-Sufficiency Standard, which was among the first wellbeing measures developed within the American non-profit sector (Center for Women's Welfare 2009). The Self-Sufficiency Standard is a budget standard created to answer the question, 'What are modern basic needs, and how much income does a contemporary family require to become genuinely "self-sufficient" (i.e. able to afford basic needs without public assistance, private gifts or loans)?' The Self-Sufficiency Standard enumerates and sums local costs faced by 70 family types, and expenses include rent, food prepared at home, auto expenses (or cost of public transportation where a viable substitute for car ownership), childcare, health care, clothing, basic household necessities included as 'miscellaneous', and income and sales taxes.[4] The sum of these expenses then becomes a 'self-sufficiency wage'. Because they represented a higher standard of living, the Self-Sufficiency Standard thresholds were generally two or three times higher than the poverty thresholds, depending on the state or county in question. Proportions of households lacking self-sufficiency wages were also much higher than official poverty rates. The calculation methodology was rigorous and public, and utilised publicly available source data. The Self-Sufficiency Standard distinguished itself from the poverty thresholds in its explication and more ambitious definition of basic needs, in providing expense values and thresholds at the state, county and major city levels, and in its direct addressing of liveable wage issues.

The Self-Sufficiency Standard's creation was timely. There is a long tradition in the United States of speaking about poverty and its eradication, but the fight against poverty has periodically suffered 'issue fatigue'. In a society still characterised by many political leaders as meritocratic, as the 'land of opportunity', additional references to poverty have largely failed to garner additional attention to, or empathy toward, low-income families. American research, advocacy and political communities have therefore periodically reworked messaging around issues of wellbeing to reinvigorate discussion and discussion participants. While data and messaging continuity is valuable, redefining and reframing social welfare issues such as poverty is of particular interest to political leaders, who understand that measurement and messaging are inseparable, and changes in messaging aimed at a majority of voters or stakeholders often precede changes in policy. New metrics can help advocates and policymakers compete for their colleagues' attention and the public spotlight, and can help media outlets compete for ears and eyeballs. Further, they allow non-profit organisations to gain attention for their political issues in a competitive landscape and to change attitudes and norms over longer periods by connecting data to the personal narratives of those who suffer insecurity and petition government for policy responses or assistance.

The term 'self-sufficiency' was an ascendant, more inclusive term of art when the Self-Sufficiency Standard was created, and is still used within US federal legislation and public assistance programs. (As recently as 2012, the US Department of Health and Human Services created the online Self-Sufficiency Research Clearinghouse to co-locate self-sufficiency-related research on a variety of policy and social welfare issues.) Its use catered to some advocates' desire to avoid the 'negativity' of the term 'poverty'; to criticise the government's lack of coherent, aspirational, long-term anti-poverty policy; and to disassociate themselves from the very modest successes suggested by largely static poverty statistics. The higher Self-Sufficiency Standard thresholds suggested a much wider swathe of the American public having difficulty making ends meet, and that public policy should respond to millions living above the official poverty thresholds. They reflected a wider 'circle of concern' and softened ossified notions of wellbeing.

The concept of self-sufficiency was front and centre during a period of contentious debate on welfare reform that would in 1996 culminate in the passage of the federal Personal Responsibility and Work Opportunity Act, which converted the Aid to Families with Dependent Children (AFDC) entitlement program to the Temporary Assistance for Needy Families (TANF) block grant program, through which control of federal funding is largely devolved to state governments.[5] The legislation created a 'WorkFirst' model of welfare which restricted access to education and skills training, decreased funding for the federal government's primary anti-poverty cash assistance program, and imposed new work, training and job search requirements on public assistance recipients. As a workforce-related advocacy organisation and a proponent and provider of training for women in non-traditional occupations – those with workforces of less than 25 per cent female – WOW foresaw public workforce development systems routinely placing women leaving welfare into low-wage jobs that did not offer advancement opportunities or adequate support for their families. For several years after the passage of the Act, WOW and Dr Pearce used the new measure and related policy modelling and analyses to gain access to and inform federal legislators and executives on the Act's potential impacts on families. A second goal was to replace the prevailing definition of self-sufficiency – no receipt of government assistance – with a definition centred on access to good jobs, good wages and truly making ends meet. As control over welfare funds was devolved to the states, WOW and their state partners spoke to or before state legislators, city councils, workforce investment boards and opinion leaders to argue the gross inadequacy of monthly TANF payments to impoverished families with children, and the urgency of public workforce development that stressed inclusion of women and middle-skill jobs paying higher wages. Appeals were sometimes made in cooperation with local self-sufficiency advocates and/or grass roots organisers.

Where a large bureaucracy was, intentionally or unintentionally, preserving the status quo, the Self-Sufficiency Standard was used to push incremental change in institutional norms and practices, often beginning with simple changes in messaging that could eventually result in changed social conditions (i.e. equal opportunity, employment and income). Changes to the workforce system begun with TANF were continued with the Workforce Investment Act (WIA) of 1998, which funded and helped define the US government's primary workforce development programs.[6] WIA-funded programs serve both unemployed job seekers and employed adults seeking different or better employment. WIA established approved and required training activities, which states and localities were required to provide with federal funds, and it proscribed participation eligibility criteria, overarching goals and performance measures. Wider Opportunities for Women and allies were able to introduce the self-sufficiency income standards and framework to Congressional law-makers and Department of Labor leadership prior to the WIA's passage. As a result of that advocacy, Title I and Title II of WIA included several references to self-sufficiency. Most significantly, the legislation required states to use a measure of self-sufficiency (as opposed to poverty) to define eligibility for intensive services such as job workshops and training.[7]

WIA employment standard setting was a responsibility largely devolved to the states, although the Department of Labor strongly recommended that local workforce investment boards considered defining self-sufficiency as the Self-Sufficiency Standard defined it (United States Federal Register 2000). In 2003, Wider Opportunities for Women and the National Association of Workforce Boards conducted a joint survey of over 100 local workforce boards and found that 46 per cent of responding workforce boards' defini-tions of self-sufficiency were higher than the federal default definition, and 36 per cent of those workforce boards were using the Self-Sufficiency Standard as their benchmark metric (Wider Opportunities for Women 2003). For example, the Chicago Workforce Board and the Illinois state Workforce Investment Board developed their own goals to increase clients' ability to achieve self-sufficiency incomes, and utilised a self-sufficiency-based income benchmarking and public assistance eligibility online calculator. One of the state-wide workforce reporting benchmarks in Illinois has been the percent-age of individuals and families living above and below self-sufficiency income thresholds (Wider Opportunities for Women 2003).

Several states have also used their state Self-Sufficiency Standards to better understand or improve social service provision. The states of Connecticut, Hawaii, Illinois and West Virginia, for example, adopted Self-Sufficiency Standards as an official cost of living measure (Wider Opportunities for Women 2003). In Wyoming, the measure was introduced directly to deci-sion makers at the Governor's planning office, which supported development of a Self-Sufficiency Standard for the state and subsequently created the online Wyoming Self-Sufficiency Calculator, one of several public lookup or public assistance eligibility calculators which were supported by state govern-ments and other organisations around the country. The Self-Sufficiency Standard has also been used by caseworkers, who help clients assess income needs; develop short- and long-term career plans; understand their eligibility for public assistance; and understand the impact of changes in wages and family composition on their self-sufficiency levels and eligibility for public assistance programs.

Much of the attitudinal, norm or legislative change achieved at the state level using the Self-Sufficiency Standard was achieved through coalitions comprised primarily of non-profit advocacy organisations, often supported by academics who performed or were affiliated with related research. In some cases a state organ, such as an economic development agency, a women's commission, or an asset building commission, was important to the process. Coalitions were often diverse in their policy interests, which included workforce development, economic development, education, domestic violence, food security, disability, women's rights, immigration and others. As coalition theory would suggest, many organised around self-sufficiency or economic security as a shared ethos, and around new and newly consistent shared messaging, which helped hold coalitions together. For instance, the former California Family Economic Self-Sufficiency Coalition, led by the Insight Center for Community Economic Development (then the National Economic Development and Law Center), utilized the California Self-Sufficiency Standard in designing and helping to pass the Education Works law in 2004 for improving access to higher education for low-income individuals, foster care children, and non-native speakers of English (Insight Center for Community Economic Development 2008). The legislation also contained intent language that included enabling students to reach self-sufficiency, building a Student Parent Scholar program and ensuring that programs operating with federal TANF funding promoted education and training for jobs that paid self-sufficiency wages. The novelty of self-sufficiency tools and language and the diversity of the legislation's intent enabled creation of a coalition large enough to obtain earned media (i.e. news stories and opinion pieces that are not part of a paid media campaign) and gain the attention of the public, opinion leaders and legislators.

Recent metrics

The past decade has seen the development of several modern measurements of need, income adequacy and financial stability that improve upon the official federal poverty thresholds. In 2006, WOW, working with the Gerontology Institute at the University of Massachusetts Boston, developed the Elder Economic Security Standard Index (Elder Index), a measure of the incomes older adults need to meet their basic needs, to better protect their health and insure themselves against the financial impacts of poor health, and to age in their own homes rather than in public institutions (Gerontology Institute University of Massachusetts Boston 2012). The Elder Index was, immediately after its development, connected to messages and advocacy efforts supporting seniors' ability to age in their own homes, and the need to preserve federal entitlement programs such as Medicare, the US national health insurance program for the aged, and Social Security, the US national payroll tax-funded retirement benefits system.

In 2010, WOW created the Basic Economic Security Tables Index (BEST Index) with researchers from the Center for Social Development at Washington University in St. Louis (McMahon *et al.* 2010). The BEST Index is another budget standard, a contemporary investigation of the annual income and *savings* workers require for economic security across the lifespan. The BEST Index was designed in response to WOW partner requests to create a contemporary budget standard that incorporated savings and asset development and calculated separately the expenses of those with and without access to health insurance, unemployment insurance and defined contribution retirement savings programs, which in the US system are provided most often by or through employers. Both the Elder Index and the BEST Index were explicitly designed to respond to and further develop new messaging around 'economic security', which addresses those millions in America unable to afford basic needs or respond to unforeseen events, such as unemployment, poor health or financial loss. These economic security measures have been used in much the same way as the Self-Sufficiency Standard, and to support discussions on policy issues affecting large proportions of American workers and families, such as the housing crisis that precipitated the 2007–2009 'Great Recession' in the US, and health care reform pursued more recently by President Barak Obama's Administration.

Over the past decade, several American researchers have created additional metrics that embody new definitions of need or security. Most measures are budget standards, multi-indicator indexes designed to track change in well-being over time, or scorecards which grade and rank state policies.[8] Several are not unlike indices, scorecards and dashboards that have been utilised by the international non-governmental and private sectors to monitor economies, financial markets and transparent or effective government. Several have defined/redefined economic security, and some have been used to calculate proportions of the US population, or of sub-populations, who lack one or more aspect of a new definition of security.

The federal government has also become a modern metrics supplier. In March 2010, the US Census Bureau announced plans, as part of the Obama Administration's 2011 budget, to develop and release the Supplemental Poverty Measure (SPM). Unlike the poverty thresholds, the SPM accounts for geographic differences in the costs of living, household groups that include non-members, medical expenses, work-related expenses, tax credits, and some forms of public assistance (Rossi and Curtis 2013). In addition to its methodology, the SPM is notable for its development path. The US federal government does not have a history of adopting measures developed outside of the government. However, the SPM was founded on a methodology described in a 1995 white paper produced by a non-profit research institution, the National Academy of Sciences (NAS).[9] The impetus to formalise and publish the official SPM was born, at least in part, of pressure from proposed Congressional legislation requiring the Census Bureau to develop such a measure, and from the attention such bills and the NAS methodology received from academics and advocacy organisations in the mid-2000s.[10] The SPM's methodology is a great improvement over the poverty thresholds' methodology, and has contributed to the field of poverty research, but it is yet a measure of abject deprivation. In addition, the SPM thresholds are not used, and will not be used, as public assistance eligibility criteria (Short 2013). As such, it has done little to inform policy.

The United States Department of Commerce (2010) also published the Office of the Vice President's Middle Class Task Force's *Middle class in America* report, which demonstrates how families with lower middle, middle and upper middle incomes can achieve similar lifestyles by consuming middle class staples (e.g. food, automobiles, higher education) of differing cost and quality. This report contrasts with the SPM's stringency and points to the Obama Administration's interest in messaging around a broad American middle class, and to the idea that there is a minimum income required to participate fully in the American economy. Like the SPM, *Middle class in America* calculations have not yet been directly used in policy change.

Challenges to the institutionalisation of metrics

While metrics have made headway in gaining acceptance and users among researchers, policymakers and advocates, several obstacles remain. Some are technical: local data collection, below the state level, is still insufficient to allow full understanding of local economic phenomena. Some are financial: data collection is expensive, and adding questions to a federal survey tool, such as the US Census Bureau's Current Population Survey, can cost the government millions of dollars. Others are political.

Most of the many wellbeing measures in use today in the US answer distinct research questions and/or have been created for distinct purposes. However, nearly all such measures use in their titles or messaging a limited number of popular terms that the measures define narrowly and quantify. Terms, and associated measurements, currently popular in the US include 'economic security', 'opportunity' and 'inequality'. This common use of terminology in titles and messaging to describe unique data and calculations can create quiet competition among researchers and organisations, and at once promotes and defeats the success and adoption of new measures. When WOW began using the concept and language of 'economic security' in 2008, the term was still novel. Today, the United States has achieved and surpassed a 'tipping point', and discussion of economic security has impacted institutional cultures and become a preferred term and objective both within and without government. This widespread use of common language increases the rate of diffusion and accommodation of new language and concepts among the media, the public and policymakers. On the other hand, widespread use of a term such as 'economic security' to refer to multiple operationalisations of being can cause confusion among casual observers and fatigue audiences. This can create indirect competition among non-profits and advocacy organisations to 'own' terms and discourse spaces, and more direct competition for funding and 'first-mover' and early adopter advantages.

Measures and measurements which help define financial wellbeing and its fundaments, such as good wages, good jobs and affordability, are unavoidably political if they gain media and public attention, or are used to inform the role of government, public sector budgets and expenditures. Contemporary measures of wellbeing that demonstrate that need is greater than popularly perceived and understood often earn the enmity of fiscal conservatives, who counter by emphasising consumption or the potential for consumption, rather than income, as a proper wellbeing metric, or by stressing the increasing affordability of basic goods such as food, electronics and appliances.[11] Metrics which expand the definition of insecurity and suggest additional government responsibility for welfare have not always been received by incumbent administrations and legislators, liberal or conservative, who, should they embrace the new research, would see public perception of insecurity and need expand on their watches. Such metrics are often ignored by governments, which already suffer budgetary pressures due to contraction of government revenues, or whose political philosophies and spending priorities do not include social welfare spending or economic development, which intentionally and directly assists low-income families.

Despite potential challenges, measures of wellbeing can be successfully inserted into nearly any stage of policy change processes. Given sufficient methodological rigour, accessibility and time, measures can be used to influence political decision makers, thought leaders and the public, and ultimately affect the social norms and political will required for lasting change. However, the greatest obstacle to institutionalisation of wellbeing metrics is their potential as transformative, if not disruptive, technologies. Metrics which define economic security or similar levels of wellbeing are by definition audacious aspirational goals, and full adoption of aspirational goals must entail systems change. Wellbeing metrics' institutionalisation will change mental models, social norms and political will, and should alter how organisations and governments think of themselves, communicate, design policies and programs, budget, and provide services. As a result, a metric's use and lifespan is not only dependent on methodological rigour and descriptive or prescriptive power, but on potential early adopters' and champions' ability to recognise and embrace the full implications of ambitious metrics, and lend others the political courage to advance genuine social change.

Notes

1 The US Department of Labor continues to publish the Lower Living Standard Income Level Guidelines budget standard, income thresholds used by state and local workforce investment areas to determine income eligibility for Workforce Investment Act-funded worker training.
2 The federal poverty thresholds, used by the US Census Bureau to calculate official poverty rates, are often confused with the federal poverty guidelines, commonly

referred to as the federal poverty line (FLP), which the US Department of Health and Human Services and others use to determine public assistance and program eligibility. The thresholds and the guidelines are quite similar, as the guidelines are derived from the thresholds, but they are nonetheless distinct.

3 The current poverty threshold is US$12,316 for an individual and US$19,074 for a family of three. The current poverty guideline is US$11,670 for an individual and US$19,790 for a family of three.

4 The 70 family types included in Self-Sufficiency Standard analyses consist of combinations of one or two adults and children in four different age categories. For more information: www.selfsufficiencystandard.org/about.html.

5 For a larger discussion on block grants, see Finegold *et al.* (2004).

6 US public workforce systems are currently being redeveloped to reflect the Workforce Innovation and Opportunity Act (WIOA), which was signed into law in July 2014.

7 The Code of Federal Regulations Title 20 Part 663.230 clarifies that State or Local Boards must define self-sufficiency:

> State Boards or Local Boards must set the criteria for determining whether employment leads to self-sufficiency. At a minimum, such criteria must provide that self-sufficiency means employment that pays at least the lower living standard income level, as defined in WIA section 101(24).

8 For additional examples of metrics, see: Insight Center for Community Economic Development (2013).

9 For the full report, see: www.census.gov/hhes/povmeas/methodology/nas/report.html.

10 The Measuring American Poverty Act of 2009 (HR 2909) was introduced by Representative Jim McDermott (D-WA), and a corresponding bill (S.1625) was introduced in the Senate by Senator Chris Dodd (D-CT); the legislation would have required the US Census Bureau to produce a budget-based poverty measure similar to the Supplemental Poverty Measure not long thereafter released as an official federal metric. For the legislation see: www.govtrack.us/congress/bills/111/s1625/text for the Senate bill and www.congress.gov/bill/111th-congress/house-bill/2909 for the House of Representatives bill.

11 For examples of measures based on consumption, see: Rector and Sheffield (2011) and Meyer and Sullivan (2012).

References

Blank, R M 2008. 'Presidential address: how to improve poverty measurements in the United States', *Journal of Policy Analysis and Management*, vol. 27, pp. 233–254.

Center for Women's Welfare 2009, *The self-sufficiency standard: what a difference a measure makes*, viewed 2 January 2015, www.selfsufficiencystandard.org/docs/SSS%20General%20Handout_061909.pdf.

Dormhoff, W G 2013, *Who rules America? The triumph of the corporate rich*, 7th edn, McGraw-Hill, New York.

Finegold, K, Wherry, L and Schardin, S 2004, *Block grants: historical overview and lessons learned*, New Federalism: Issues and Options for States A-63:1–8, viewed 13 August 2015, www.urban.org/publications/310991.html.

Gerontology Institute University of Massachusetts Boston 2012, *The national economic security standard index*, Gerontology Institute Publications, Paper 75, viewed 15 August 2015, http://scholarworks.umb.edu/gerontologyinstitute_pubs/75.

Insight Center for Community Economic Development 2008, *How to use the California family economic self-sufficiency standard*, viewed 20 January 2015, www.sdgrantmakers. org/Portals/0/PastPrograms/How%20Standard%20Used%20One-Pager%20FINAL. pdf.

Insight Center for Community Economic Development 2013, *Measuring up: aspirations for economic security in the 21st century*, viewed 22 January 2015, www.insightced.org/uploads/besa/Insight_MeasuringUp_FullReport_Web.pdf.

Johnson, D S, Rogers, J M and Tan, L 2001, 'A century of family budgets in the United States', *Monthly Labor Review*, May, pp. 28–45.

Kahneman, D and Tversky, A 1979, 'Prospect theory: an analysis of decision under risk', *Econometrica*, vol. 47, no. 2, p. 263.

McMahon, S, Nam, Y and Yung, S L 2010, *The basic economic security tables for the United States*, Wider Opportunities for Women, Washington DC, viewed 16 May 2015, www.wowonline.org/documents/BESTIndexforTheUnitedStates2010.pdf.

Meyer, B and Sullivan, J X 2012, 'Identifying the disadvantaged: official poverty, consumption poverty, and the new supplemental poverty measure', *Journal of Economic Perspectives*, vol. 26, no. 3, pp. 111–136.

Orshansky, M 1965, 'Counting the poor: another look at the poverty profile', *Social Security Bulletin*, vol. 28 no. 1, pp. 3–29.

Rector, R and Sheffield, R 2011, *Air conditioning, cable TV, and an Xbox: what is poverty in the United States today?* Heritage Foundation, viewed 29 December 2014, www.heritage.org/research/all-research.aspx?categories=report.

Rossi, M M and Curtis, K A 2013, 'Aiming at half of the target: an argument to replace poverty thresholds with self-sufficiency or "living wage" standards', *Journal of Poverty*, vol. 17, pp. 110–130.

Sabatier, P A, 1999, *Theories of the policy process*, Westview Press, Boulder, CO.

Sabatier, P and Jenkins-Smith, H 1996, *Policy change and learning: an advocacy coalition approach (theoretical lenses on public policy)*, Westview Press, Boulder, CO.

Short, K 2013, *The research supplemental poverty measure: 2012*, US Department of Commerce, Economics and Statistics Administration, US Census Bureau: Washington, DC, viewed 14 August 2014, www.census.gov/prod/2013pubs/p60-247. pdf.

Tversky, A and Kahneman, D 1992, 'Advances in prospect theory: cumulative representation of uncertainty', *Journal of Risk and Uncertainty*, vol. 5, no. 4, pp. 297–323.

United States Department of Commerce 2010, *Middle class in America task force report*, viewed 13 August 2010 www.commerce.gov/news/fact-sheets/2010/01/25/middle-class-america-task-force-report-pdf.

United States Federal Register 2000, *Workforce investment act: final rule*, Code of Federal Regulations 20 CFR Part 652 and Parts 660 to 671, viewed 29 January 2015, www.doleta.gov/usworkforce/wia/finalrule.txt.

Wider Opportunities for Women 2003, 'Reality check: promoting self-sufficiency in the public workforce system', available on request from Wider Opportunities for Women, Washington DC.

Wright, M C 1956, *The power elite*, Oxford University Press, New York.

7 Evidence-based policy
Why and how?

Rachel Clark and Michelle Haby

Introduction

> good intentions and plausible theories alone are an insufficient basis for decisions about public programmes that affect the lives of others.
>
> (Oxman *et al.* 2010, p. 428)

In contemporary public health practice, it is widely accepted that interventions underpinned by research evidence will be more effective than those that are not; they also offer better value for money, transparency in decision making and accountability. As such, public health policymakers and practitioners are challenged to make their decisions based on the best available evidence. As simple as that might sound, the practice is inherent with challenges and complexities. Public health decisions (for both policy and practice) are made in a highly complex, politically charged environment, where other factors such as community and stakeholder preferences, availability of resources (financial and workforce) and political views are often competing with the findings from research. Relevant research evidence may not be readily available, accessible or considered viable at a local level, or key decisions may be made before the research is consulted.

A multitude of barriers exist for decision makers in using research evidence, yet little is known about how such barriers might be overcome. Significant progress has been made in theorising the use of research evidence; however, little evidence has been gathered about how best to support its uptake and most efforts have focused on individuals – often recognising, but seldom addressing, the organisational-, political-, and system-level influences and interactions that prevail. In addition, the focus of researchers on supporting the use of research evidence outweighs any kind of efforts to understand, document or support the process or practice of making evidence-informed decisions and the ways in which research is used alongside other important, and often competing, forms of evidence.

These concepts are described and discussed here. We begin with an overview of the notion of evidence-informed public health – its origins and established definitions. We then describe the typologies of research evidence and research use that exist, before introducing the field of knowledge translation, born out of efforts to enhance the uptake of research evidence in public health (and other fields of) decision making. Finally we consider the practice of evidence-informed decision making, thus far relatively unexplored, surfacing tensions between the theoretical foundations and the practices of being evidence informed.

The emergence of evidence-informed public health

Origins of evidence-informed public health

For the purpose of this chapter 'public health' refers to all planned efforts to "prevent disease, promote health, and prolong life among the population as a whole", focusing on populations as opposed to individual patients (World Health Organisation 2014).

The concept of 'evidence-based practice' within public health has its origins in the 'evidence-based medicine' movement which, despite its long history, gained momentum during the early- to mid-1990s when the term 'evidence-based medicine' was first documented in the medical literature (Ciliska *et al.* 2008). Evidence-based medicine (EBM) has been defined as "the conscientious, explicit, and judicious use of current best evidence in making decisions about the care of individual patients" (Sackett *et al.* 1996, p. 71) and within this, the integration of clinical expertise is said to be key (Sackett *et al.* 1996). 'Evidence-based public health' (EBPH) expands this to encompass its population focus and three definitions dominate the literature (see Box 7.1). Two draw directly on the accepted definition of EBM, (although Kotatsu and colleagues (2004) choose to highlight the importance of community preferences). The third acknowledges that EBPH encompasses the development, implementation and evaluation of interventions and involves different types of information.

Box 7.1 Key definitions of evidence-based public health

the conscientious, explicit, and judicious use of current best evidence in making decisions about the care of communities and populations.

(Jenicek 1997, p. 190)

the process of integrating science-based interventions with community preferences to improve the health of populations.

(Kohatsu *et al.* 2004, p. 419)

the development, implementation, and evaluation of effective programs and policies in public health through application of principles of scientific reasoning, including systematic uses of data and information systems and appropriate use of behavioural science theory and program planning models.

(Brownson *et al.* 1999)

Early on, concerns were raised around the connotations associated with the term *evidence-based*, said to imply that decisions should be based entirely on research evidence (Hammersley 2005). A misconception – since those advancing EBPH were doing so in recognition that evidence could not provide the sole foundations for a decision (Chalmers 2005) – however the notion of 'evidence-informed' public health emerged in recognition of this, and is the focus of this chapter.

Evidence-informed public health (EIPH) emphasises that decisions should be *informed by* evidence from research, while recognising that other factors such as context, public opinion and feasibility of implementation will also be important; research evidence is viewed as part of a mix of factors informing decisions (see Figure 7.1). The Canadian National Collaborating Centre for Methods and Tools (NCCMT) has defined evidence-informed decision making (EIDM) as "the process of distilling and disseminating the best available evidence from research, context and experience, and using that evidence to inform and improve public health practice and policy" (National Collaborating Centre for Methods and Tools 2014), again recognising the combined importance of integrating research with contextual and experiential evidence.

The value of evidence in decision making

Prior to the advancement of EIDM it had been suggested that public health decisions were too frequently driven by public and professional opinion,

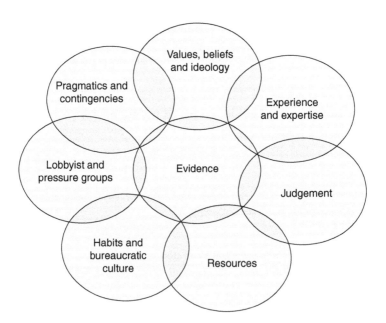

Figure 7.1 Factors influencing evidence-informed decision making (Davies 2013).

political perspectives and in response to issues or emergencies as and when they emerged (Greenberg 1992; Kohatsu *et al.* 2004). This was considered insufficient (Greenberg 1992) and it was recognised that (good intentions aside) interventions could on occasion do more harm than good (Macintyre and Petticrew 2000; Chalmers 2005).

Many well-intentioned public health programs were implemented for long periods before evaluation found them to be ineffective (Vaughan 2004). One example is the 'Scared Straight' program. 'Scared Straight' and similar programs were implemented over many years in a number of countries (including Australia, the United Kingdom and the United States), with a view to deterring juvenile delinquents (or those at risk of becoming such) from future offending by taking them on prison visits to meet current inmates. This 'deterrent' approach was based on the rationale that interaction with inmates and first-hand experience of prison life would discourage young people from offending. However, when research was conducted to examine the effectiveness of the programs it was observed that criminal behaviour either didn't change or increased after participation and it is now recommended that such programs should not be implemented (Petrosino *et al.* 2013).

Similarly, Fielding and Briss (2006) describe the example of the implementation of the Drug Abuse Resistance Education program (DARE), said to cost around three-quarters of a billion US dollars annually for implementation in the USA, and for which evidence suggests there to be little effect on the use of drugs (Fielding and Briss 2006). While implementation of this kind has no direct harmful effect, the implementation of an ineffective intervention uses scarce resources that could be better spent on an alternative that is known to lead to lifestyle or health improvements. Another important concern within public health is health inequalities, with efforts to improve health having been criticised for predominantly reaching those from higher socioeconomic groups (Acheson 1998). For example, in a recent review of obesity prevention interventions, 11 were found to be effective but only five of these were effective for low socioeconomic groups (Beauchamp *et al.* 2014). Hence, there is a need to consider effectiveness from an equity perspective in order to ensure that an 'effective' intervention is reaching those who need it most and not widening inequalities.

Evidence is thus deemed important: (1) to ensure that no harm will come from the implementation of an intervention; (2) to ensure that an intervention is effective in achieving intended outcomes; (3) to maximise use of resources and ensure the highest return on investment; and (4) to help minimise health inequalities.

Describing an evidence-informed approach

The NCCMT has developed a model of EIDM (see Figure 7.2), depicting (again) research evidence as one of many forms of evidence that public health decision makers can come into contact with but this time depicting all forms

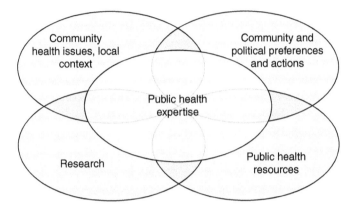

Figure 7.2 A model of evidence-informed decision making (Ciliska *et al.* 2008).

as equal. Integration of all of these forms of evidence is considered key, and public health expertise is highlighted as being central (Ciliska *et al.* 2008).

Efforts have also been made (by researchers) to describe the process involved in making an evidence-informed decision, the rationale being that the use of a systematic and transparent process will be more likely to yield an effective decision and ensure that evidence is used appropriately (Oxman *et al.*, 2009a). A number of key steps have been proposed, based again on EBM, and are displayed in Box 7.2 (Ciliska *et al.* 2008). The steps, while presented in a linear manner, are viewed cyclically and the cycle can be entered at any stage.

Box 7.2 The process of evidence-informed decision making (Ciliska *et al.* 2008)

Step 1: Define	Clearly define the question or issue
Step 2: Search	Search efficiently for research evidence
Step 3: Appraise	Critically appraise the research evidence
Step 4: Synthesise	Interpret research evidence and form recommendations
Step 5: Adapt	Adapt information to local context
Step 6: Implement	Decide whether (and plan how) to implement adapted evidence
Step 7: Evaluate	Evaluate the effectiveness of implementation efforts

---

A useful starting point for understanding what an evidence-informed decision should involve, this depicts an 'ideal' whilst also focusing on individual decision makers. The implications of this will be raised later in this chapter.

Challenges and complexities of making evidence-informed decisions

Despite accumulating support, there are a multitude of barriers involved in making evidence-informed decisions. Inherent complexities associated with contemporary public health practice, which involves whole communities as opposed to individuals, present the most obvious challenge (Orton *et al.* 2011). Many public health interventions need to operate at the population level – within and across communities, working at multiple levels, and involving a wide variety of stakeholders – and this is challenging both to implement and evaluate (Rychetnik *et al.* 2002). Understanding of evidence varies and does not always encompass the many types of evidence (from research or otherwise) that exist, and the notion of 'best available evidence' is fluid, highly dependent on the availability of evidence and the nature of the question being asked (Oxman *et al.* 2006).

In addition, decision-making processes are typically 'messy'. While 'ideal' processes can exist (see Figure 7.3) in reality, policy and practice decisions are likely to be driven by opportunities and conditions that present themselves as opposed to any kind of logical explicit process (Colebatch 2002). This presents a misalignment between the reality of decision making, and the types of models and structures that have been theorised from an EIPH perspective.

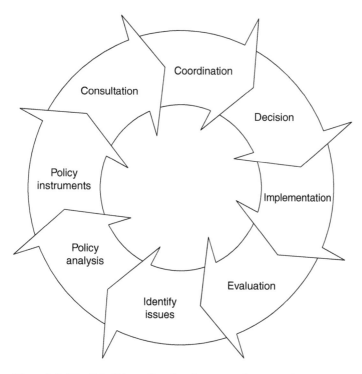

Figure 7.3 The 'ideal' in policy development: the Australian policy cycle (Bridgman and Davis 2004).

While the EIDM model displayed in Box 7.2 might work well in an ideal situation, as yet there is no alternative for the more reactive style of decision making.

Understanding research evidence and how it is used

While the concept of evidence in evidence-informed public health does comprise many forms of evidence, evidence derived from research is central. It is typically considered more trustworthy (Fielding and Briss 2006) and convincing, having been generated through systematic methods as opposed to (more arbitrary) observations (Oxman *et al.* 2009a). For this reason, it is necessary to explore the different types of research and ways in which it can be used.

Types of research evidence

Three types of research evidence have been documented in the literature: data from descriptive and analytical epidemiological research, for example describing the magnitude, prevalence or determinants of an issue (Type 1); research relating to the effectiveness of an intervention, for example from randomised controlled trials or observational studies (Type 2); and research describing the processes or circumstances in which an intervention was conducted, for example qualitative studies (Type 3) (Rychetnik *et al.* 2002; Brownson *et al.* 2009; Fielding and Briss 2006). Research from economic evaluations, for example describing the cost-effectiveness of an intervention or comparing the cost-effectiveness of a suite of interventions, present an additional category (Swinburn *et al.* 2005; Fielding and Briss, 2006).

All types of research are valuable, typically at different stages of decision making. For example, observational studies (such as cross-sectional surveys) are useful for identifying problems, effectiveness evidence for finding possible solutions for implementation, qualitative and descriptive evidence to determine how an intervention should be implemented, and economic evidence to set priorities for implementation (Swinburn *et al.* 2005; Lavis 2009). Any one, or any combination, of these types of research evidence may well be used to inform any one decision and, while this typology could be applied to any type of evidence, it is most commonly applied to research evidence (Fielding and Briss, 2006). Systematic reviews also warrant mention as an important source of information for decision makers. Having searched for, assessed and synthesised research evidence on a defined topic, systematic reviews are often considered to represent the best available evidence, providing information from multiple studies or identifying gaps in research. They have a valuable role in evidence-informed decision making because they save time, make it easier for decision makers to use the best available research evidence and help to prevent the selective use of research (Lavis *et al.* 2005).

Types of research use

There is broad acceptance that research can be utilised in three different ways. Instrumental research use is direct, specific use of research evidence and likely to be linked directly to a policy or practice decision or, perhaps, the development of a protocol. Conceptual use is an indirect use, less easy to observe or define, whereby research is used for general enlightenment. Symbolic research use resembles instrumental use, but involves the legitimisation of an action that already exists or a policy decision that has already been made (Beyer 1997; Estabrooks 1999). The defining principles of instrumental use align most with a 'rational' approach to decision making (Estabrooks 1999), which implies that research will be methodically collected and applied as part of a decision-making process (although this is not commonly the manner in which policy and practice decisions occur). It has also been observed that research is most often used in a conceptual manner (Amara *et al.* 2004) and that predicting factors vary for each type of use (Amara *et al.* 2004; Milner *et al.* 2005). There has been little inquiry into the nature of research use in public health decision making, and this may well be central to understanding how better to support use, particularly given the different types of decision making that exist (Bowen and Zwi 2005). If decisions are typically non-rational and research use is typically conceptual, the uptake or integration of systematic EIDM processes may be limited.

Supporting the use of research evidence – a focus on knowledge translation

> Accelerating the integration of scientific discovery into routine public health practice and policy deserves priority attention.
>
> (Fielding and Briss 2006, p. 970)

In recognition of the important role of research evidence in EIDM, considerable attention has been given to understanding the barriers and facilitators to the use of research evidence and strategies to support the use of research evidence. An overview of this field – commonly referred to as knowledge translation – is provided here.

Advancements in knowledge translation – processes, models and strategies to support the use of evidence

Numerous terms exist to describe the efforts to support or accelerate the uptake of research, for example knowledge transfer, 'knowledge-to-action', diffusion of innovations and knowledge exchange (Graham *et al.* 2006). Knowledge translation (KT) is utilised for the purpose of this chapter, defined by the World Health Organisation as "the synthesis, exchange, and application of knowledge by relevant stakeholders to accelerate the benefits of global and local innovation in strengthening health systems and improving peoples' health" (Pablos-Mendez and Shademani 2006; World Health Organisation 2012).

Substantial effort has also been put into conceptualising the KT process; a number of models and frameworks have been developed and synthesised or collated by several leading organisations seeking to provide an overview of the KT literature (Sudsawad 2007; Moore *et al.* 2009; World Health Organisation 2012), although admittedly none have originated with a public health focus (Moore *et al.* 2009). For example, the 'Knowledge-to-Action' framework is commonly referred to in the literature and encompasses 'creation' and 'action' as two core components, each comprising a number of phases (Graham *et al.* 2006). Knowledge creation is portrayed as a funnel, whereby knowledge becomes more refined as it moves down to its narrowest point. The wide top of the funnel represents a large number of studies from primary research, narrowing to syntheses of this research (for example, systematic reviews) then products or tools informed by syntheses of research that directly support a decision (for example, reviews of systematic reviews). The action cycle reflects key stages to be undertaken to support the use of research findings in the decision-making process.

The 'linking research to action' framework was developed with health policy making in mind, to assist in country-level efforts to link research and decision making (Lavis *et al.* 2006). The framework consists of four components: (1) climate for research use; (2) research production and appropriate synthesis; (3) efforts to link research and action; and (4) evaluation. 'Push' and 'pull' efforts are introduced here as sub-components of efforts to link research to action, whereby researchers 'push' their findings out to decision makers (for example, via tailored messages), facilitate a 'pull' from decision makers to access research findings (for example, via a knowledge broker available to provide relevant research findings on request), create 'user pull', where end users are supported to gather research as needed (perhaps via training to better understand how to access research) and participate in 'exchange' efforts, where partnerships are formed between researchers and decision makers (for example, in the design and conduct of a piece of research) (Lavis *et al.* 2006; Oxman *et al.* 2009b).

Greenhalgh and colleagues (2004) developed a model depicting "the diffusion, dissemination and implementation of innovations in health service delivery and organisation", based on an extensive systematic review of empirical literature combined with expert consultation (Greenhalgh *et al.* 2004, p. 595). The model provides a comprehensive overview of key drivers of evidence uptake at multiple levels, both internal and external to an organisation; for example, individual knowledge and motivation, the relative advantage of an innovation (as compared with what already exists or alternative options) and the level of risk that may be associated with adopting a new idea. It highlights the true complexity involved in the transfer of an innovation (i.e. research findings) into decision making.

It is worth noting that these models are yet to be tested empirically as a KT strategy, a line of inquiry that is now warranted in order to progress the field.

Barriers and facilitators to the use of research evidence

There is a growing literature describing the barriers to the use of research evidence in public health decision making, documented in numerous systematic reviews, based on the presumption that for the most part there is a disconnect between what is known from science and what is actually being implemented in policy and practice (World Health Organisation 2004). Barriers include a lack of knowledge and skills among individual decision makers for finding, assessing and applying research (Lavis *et al.* 2005), negative attitudes towards research evidence (Lavis *et al.* 2005), a perceived lack of research evidence (Orton *et al.* 2011), negative perceptions of available research evidence (such as the degree of uncertainty in findings) (Orton *et al.* 2011), poor timeliness or relevance of research (Lavis *et al.* 2005), mutual mistrust between researchers and decision makers (Innvaer *et al.* 2002; Lavis *et al.* 2005), and power and budget struggles (Innvaer *et al.* 2002). Among managers, lack of support from those driving implementation has also been acknowledged as a barrier (Lavis *et al.* 2005). While little attention has been given to the organisational, institutional and political factors that shape how evidence is used (Orton *et al.* 2011), a recent review suggests all of these factors to be influential (Liverani *et al.* 2013).

On the other hand, a range of facilitators and possible solutions to these challenges has also been generated. Facilitators include timely and relevant research, decision maker involvement in the research process and interactions with researchers (Innvaer *et al.* 2002; Lavis *et al.* 2005); organisational readiness to use research; and availability of/access to specialist advice (Moore *et al.* 2009). The need for evidence to be 'flexible' has also been emphasised as an important precursor to use (Liverani *et al.* 2013). Possible solutions synthesised by Moore and colleagues (2009) are displayed in Box 7.3.

Box 7.3 Possible strategies to support the use of research (Moore *et al.* 2009)

- repositories of evidence
- knowledge brokers to facilitate access to research and interactions between researchers and decision makers
- agreement (between researchers and decision makers) on research priorities
- partnership research programs, involving decision makers in the research cycle
- co-funded research projects
- supporting use of local data
- integration of research into roll out of policies and programs

---

The evidence underpinning knowledge translation and effective strategies

Some studies (and systematic reviews of studies) have examined the effectiveness of particular strategies to support the uptake of research evidence (Mitton et al. 2007; Moore et al. 2009; LaRocca et al. 2012) although few empirical studies exist and typically those identified have targeted individuals, focused on individual level strategies, and perhaps with the exception of one knowledge brokering intervention (Dobbins et al. 2009), have proven to be relatively unsuccessful in achieving enhanced evidence use. Examples of strategies include training for individual decision makers (in accessing, assessing, adapting and applying evidence), evidence summaries, tailored messaging, and sessions to allow researchers and decision makers to interact. Often the complex political system (Bowen and Zwi 2005) or even the organisational system surrounding their decisions is acknowledged in KT studies as being key, but not addressed in intervention design and, overall, the level of evidence around collective-level KT is weak (Contandriopoulos et al. 2010). Given the influence of such factors, the development and testing of interventions designed to operate at this level deserves priority attention.

An emphasis on 'evidence-informed' and progressing the practice

The rhetoric around EIDM in public health is unmistakably strong, and the concept has been much theorised, yet little attention has been given to defining or describing the processes involved with making an evidence-informed decision or how it occurs in practice. Efforts to improve EIDM have centred on supporting or accelerating the use of research evidence – despite much recognition that other forms of evidence are important. Often in public health it is necessary to make decisions about where and how to intervene in the absence of evidence of effectiveness, or based on poor quality, inconclusive and inconsistent evidence (Anderson et al. 2005). There are tools to work through this and program planning models that can be followed – but even such tools suggest the use of other forms of research evidence (such as theory and data to develop and evaluate new interventions) rather than political imperative, local context and history of local practice, for example.

For interventions that are evidence based, there is a growing recognition of the importance of adaptation. It is unrealistic to consider that all interventions will be directly relevant under differing localised conditions and in future it will be important to understand how best to weigh up adaptation (to local context) against fidelity (to an evidence-based intervention design); what parts of an intervention can be altered to better fit with local context; and what needs to be kept the same to maintain an intervention effect (Hawe et al. 2004).

The focus on KT as a support for EIDM sees research evidence as central to decision making and seeks to strengthen its use; however, it has been acknowledged that KT theory can only offer part of the solution for EIDM (Bowen and Zwi, 2005). The prevailing drive to increase use of research evidence does not wholly align with the underlying principles of EIDM, which view all forms of evidence as being important. Efforts to combine and/ or give weighting to different forms of evidence could be documented and examined as a foundation for articulating an evidence-informed approach.

Concluding comments and future directions

The evidence-based movement in public health has made considerable advances in the last two decades; however, there is still a long way to go. Progression in KT will aid this, but further exploration of mechanisms for combining different forms of evidence and adaptation of research evidence would also benefit the field. It is increasingly recognised that public health decisions are complex, evidence is lacking, and adaptation to context where evidence exists is vital: these factors need to be recognised and overcome. Complexity may well be a deterrent to using evidence, but this also needs to be dealt with. Researchers and decision makers need to work together to achieve this and a positive culture around using evidence needs to be fostered. There is clearly much to be gained by using evidence from research, but the value of other forms of evidence should continue to be recognised. Efforts to document and evaluate the 'evidence-informed' process will be a worthy next step for the progression of EIPH.

While the focus of this chapter is on public health, its application is broader and, given the inherent social and political nature of public health, many of the discussion points will be directly relevant to social policy where the importance of making 'evidence-influenced' decisions has already been raised (Nutley *et al.* 2002), and the challenges discussed and documented (Wiseman 2010). The learnings of public health, and its effort to apply the principles of EBM, will provide a useful platform for those interested in understanding and progressing the use of evidence in their own field.

References

Acheson, D 1998, *Report of the independent inquiry into inequalities in health*, HMS Stationery Office, London, UK.

Amara, N, Ouimet, M and Landry, R 2004, 'New evidence on instrumental, conceptual and symbolic utilization of university research in government agencies', *Science Communication*, vol. 26, pp. 75–106.

Anderson, L M, Brownson, R C, and Fullilove, M T 2005, 'Evidence-based public health policy and practice: promises and limits', *American Journal of Preventive Medicine*, vol. 28, no. 5, pp. 226–230.

Beauchamp, A, Backholer, K, Magliano, D and Peeters, A 2014, 'The effect of obesity prevention interventions according to socio–economic position: a systematic review', *Obesity Reviews*, vol. 15, pp. 541–554.

Beyer, J M 1997, 'Research utilization: bridging the gap between communities', *Journal of Management Inquiry*, vol. 6. pp. 17–22.

Bowen, S and Zwi, A B 2005, 'Pathways to "evidence-informed" policy and practice: a framework for action', *PLoS Med*, vol. 2, e166.

Bridgman, P and Davis, G 2004, *The Australian Policy Handbook*, 3rd edn, Allen & Unwin, New South Wales, Australia.

Brownson, R C, Gurney, J G and Land, G H 1999, 'Evidence-based decision making in public health', *Journal of Public Health Management Practice*, vol. 5. pp. 86–97.

Brownson, R C, Fielding, J E and Maylahn, C M 2009, 'Evidence-based public health: a fundamental concept for public health practice', *Annual Review of Public Health*, vol. 30. pp. 175–201.

Chalmers, I 2005, 'If evidence-informed policy works in practice, does it matter if it doesn't work in theory?', *Evidence and Policy*, vol. 1. pp. 227–242.

Ciliska, D, Thomas, S and Buffet, C 2008, *An introduction to evidence-informed public health and a compendium of critical appraisal tools for public health practice*, National Collaborating Centre for Methods and Tools, Canada.

Colebatch, H 2002, *Policy*, 2nd edn, Oxford University Press, England.

Contandriopoulos, D, Lemire, M, Denis, J L and Tremblay, E 2010, 'Knowledge exchange processes in organizations and policy arenas: a narrative systematic review of the literature', *Millbank Quarterly*, vol. 88, pp. 444–483.

Davies, P 2013, *Getting evidence into policy*. [PowerPoint slides]. Presented at the 3ie-LIDC Seminar Series at London School of Hygiene and Tropical Medicine, 20 February.

Dobbins, M, Hanna, S, Ciliska, D, Manske, S, Cameron, R, Mercer, S, O'Mara, L, DeCorby, K and Robeson, P 2009, 'A randomized controlled trial evaluating the impact of knowledge translation and exchange strategies', *Implementation Science*, vol. 4. p. 61.

Estabrooks, C A 1999 'The conceptual structure of research utilization', *Research in Nursing and Health*, vol. 22. pp. 203–216.

Fielding, J E and Briss, P A 2006, 'Promoting evidence-based public health policy: can we have better evidence and more action?', *Health Affairs*, vol. 25. pp. 969–978.

Graham, I D, Logan, J, Harrison, M B, Strauss, S E, Tetroe, J, Caswell, A and Robinson, N 2006, 'Lost in knowledge translation: time for a map?', *The Journal of Continuing Education in the Health Professions*, vol. 26, no. 1, pp. 13–24.

Greenberg, M 1992, 'Impediments to basing government health policies on science in the United States', *Social Science and Medicine*, vol. 35. pp. 531–540.

Greenhalgh, T, Robert, G, Macfarlane, F, Bate, P and Kyriakidou, O 2004, 'Diffusion of innovations in service organisations: systematic review and recommendations', *Millbank Quarterly*, vol. 82. pp. 581–629.

Hammersley, M 2005, 'Is the evidence-based practice movement doing more good than harm? Reflections on Iain Chalmers' case for research-based policy making and practice', *Evidence and Policy*, vol. 1. pp. 85–100.

Hawe, P, Shiell, A and Riley, T 2004, 'Complex interventions: how "out of control" can a randomised controlled trial be?', *BMJ*, vol. 328, pp. 1561–1563.

Innvaer, S, Vist, G, Trommald, M and Oxman, A 2002, 'Health policy-makers' perceptions of their use of evidence: a systematic review', *Journal of Health Services Research and Policy*, vol. 7, no. 4, pp. 239–244.

Jenicek, M 1997, 'Epidemiology, evidence-based medicine, and evidence-based public health', *Journal of Epidemiology*, vol. 7. pp. 187–197.

Kohatsu, N D, Robinson, J G and Torner, J C 2004, 'Evidence-based public health: an evolving concept', *American Journal of Preventive Medicine*, vol. 27, pp. 417–421.

LaRocca, R, Yost, J, Dobbins, M, Ciliska, D and Butt, M 2012, 'The effectiveness of knowledge translation strategies used in public health: a systematic review', *BMC Public Health*, vol. 12, pp. 751–751.

Lavis, J N, Davies, H, Oxman, A, Denis, L J, Golden-Biddle, K and Ferlie, E 2005, 'Towards systematic reviews that inform health care management and policy-making', *Journal of Health Services Research and Policy*, vol. 10, supp. 11, pp. 35–48.

Lavis, J N 2009, 'How can we support the use of systematic reviews in policy making', *PLoS Medicine*, vol. 6, no. 11, e1000141. doi:10.1371/journal.pmed.1000141.

Lavis, J N, Lomas, J, Hamid, M and Sewankambo, N K 2006, 'Assessing country-level efforts to link research to action', *Bulletin of the World Health Organisation*, vol. 84. pp. 620–628.

Liverani, M, Benjamin, H and Parkhurst, J O 2013, 'Political and institutional influ-ences on the use of evidence in public health policy. A systematic review', *PLoS ONE*, vol. 8, no. 10, e77404. doi:10.1371/journal.pone.0077404.

Macintyre, S and Petticrew, M 2000, 'Good intentions and received wisdom are not enough', *Journal of Epidemiology and Community Health*, vol. 54, pp. 802–803.

Milner, F M, Estabrooks, C A and Humphrey, C 2005, 'Clinical nurse educators as agents for change: increasing research utilisation', *International Journal of Nursing Studies*, vol. 42, pp. 899–914.

Mitton, C, Adair, C E, McKenzie, E, Patten, S B and Perry, B W 2007, 'Knowledge transfer and exchange: review and synthesis of the literature', *Millbank Quarterly*, vol. 85, pp. 729–768.

Moore, G, Todd, A and Redman, S 2009, 'Strategies to increase the use of evidence from research in population health policy and programs: a rapid review', *Evidence Check rapid reviews brokered by the SAX Institute*, Primary Health and Community Partnerships Unit, NSW Department of Health, New South Wales, Australia.

National Collaborating Centre for Methods and Tools 2014 *Evidence-Informed Public Health*, 2 July, viewed 14 November, 2014, www.nccmt.ca/eiph/index-eng.html.

Nutley, S, Davies, H and Walter, I 2002, *Evidence based policy and practice: cross-sector lessons from the UK*, ESRC UK Centre for Evidence Based Policy and Practice: Working Paper 9, viewed 16 May 2015, www.kcl.ac.uk/sspp/departments/politi-caleconomy/research/cep/pubs/papers/assets/wp9b.pdf.

Orton, L, Lloyd-Williams, F, Taylor Robinson, D, O'Flaherty, M and Capewell, S 2011, 'The use of research evidence in public health decision making processes: systematic review', *PLoS ONE*, vol. 6, no. 7, e21704. doi:10.1371/journal.pone.0021704.

Oxman, A, Bjorndalm A, Becerra-Posada, F, Gibson, M, Block, M A G, Haines, A, Hamid, M, Odom, C H, Lei, H, Levin, B and Lipsey, M W 2010, 'A framework for mandatory impact evaluation to ensure well informed public policy decisions', *The Lancet*, vol. 375, pp. 427–431.

Oxman, A, Fretheim, A and Schuneman, H J 2006, 'Improving the use of research evidence in guideline development: 7. Deciding what evidence to include', *Health Research Policy and Systems*, vol. 4, no. 19. doi:10.1186/1478–4505–4–19.

Oxman, A D, Lavis, J N, Lewin, S and Fretheim, A 2009a, 'SUPPORT Tools for evidence-informed health Policymaking (STP)', *Health Research Policy and Systems*, vol. 7, supp. 11, I1.

Oxman, A D, Vandvik, P O, Lavis J N, Fretheim, A and Lewin, S 2009b, 'SUPPORT Tools for evidence-informed health policymaking (STP) 2: improving how your organisation supports the use of research evidence to inform policymaking', *Health Research Policy and Systems*, no. 7, supp. 11, S2.

Pablos-Mendez, A and Shademani, R 2006, 'Knowledge translation in global health', *Continuing Educations in the Health Professions*, vol. 26, pp. 81–86.

Petrosino, A, Buehler, J and Turpin-Petrosino, C 2013, 'Scared straight and other juvenile awareness programs for preventing juvenile delinquency: a systematic review', *Campbell Systematic Reviews*, vol. 5, doi: 10.4073/csr.2013.5.

Rychetnik, L, Frommer, M, Hawe, P and Shiell, A 2002, 'Criteria for evaluating evidence on public health interventions', *Journal of Epidemiology and Community Health*, vol. 56, pp. 119–127.

Sackett, D L, Rosenburg, W M C, Gray, M J A, Haynes, R B and Richardson, W S 1996, 'Evidence based medicine: what it is and what it isn't', *BMJ*, vol. 312, p. 71.

Sudsawad, P, 2007, *Knowledge translation: introduction to models, strategies, and measures*, Southwest Educational Development Laboratory, National Center for the Dissemination of Disability Research, Austin, TX.

Swinburn, B, Gill, T and Kumanyika, S 2005, 'Obesity prevention: a proposed framework for translating evidence into action', *Obesity Reviews*, vol. 6. pp. 23–33.

Vaughan, R 2004, 'Evaluation and public health', *American Journal of Public Health*, vol. 94, pp. 360.

Wiseman, J 2010, *Occasional paper no. 11. Dancing with strangers: understanding the parallel universes of academic researchers and public sector policy makers*, Australian School of Government and State Services Authority, Australia.

World Health Organisation 2004, *World report on knowledge for better health*, World Health Organisation, Geneva.

World Health Organisation 2012, *Knowledge translation framework for ageing and health*, World Health Organisation, Geneva.

World Health Organisation 2014, *Public Health*, World Health Organisation, viewed 16 May 2015, www.who.int/trade/glossary/story076/en/.

8 Using a randomised trial to evaluate an innovative homelessness intervention

The J2SI pilot

Guy Johnson, Sue Grigg and Yi-Ping Tseng

> One cannot improve unless one evaluates.
>
> (Boruch *et al.* 2000, p. 341)

Introduction

In 2009 Sacred Heart Mission (SHM) launched the Journey to Social Inclusion (J2SI) pilot program in inner city Melbourne. The aim of the pilot was to assist 40 long-term homeless people to make a permanent transition out of homelessness. The central premise of the J2SI program was that people who are homeless for a long time need different kinds of assistance to those who have been homeless for a short period.

Nine philanthropic organisations[1] and the Department of Human Services (Vic) committed $3.4 million over three years to fund J2SI, a substantial sum for an innovative but untested approach to resolving long-term homelessness. Resolving long-term homelessness has posed an enduring challenge for both policymakers and practitioners, and a key aspect of SHM's bid to secure philanthropic funding was a commitment to undertake a rigorous evaluation of the J2SI program.

When the pilot finished, a randomised controlled trial (RCT) found that after three years J2SI had indeed made a significant and positive impact on the participants' housing stability, emotional wellbeing, and service use patterns. However, the evaluation also found a number of areas where there was little change. Most notably, there was little observed change in the substance use behaviour of the participants. Similarly, the extent to which the participants felt connected to, and supported by, the community did not change a great deal over the three years.

Unlike in the US, RCTs are rarely used to evaluate welfare service interventions in Australia (Roberts *et al.* 2012), and, in the area of homelessness, a RCT has never been successfully undertaken. Critics maintain that experimental studies are "inapplicable to the social field" (Oakley 2000, p. 315), arguing that, along with serious ethical issues, there are problems with "cost, public and professional acceptability and generalizability" (Roberts *et al.* 2012,

p. 1025). This chapter examines why the evaluation of the J2SI program succeeded and how it overcame concerns about its feasibility, as well as the
ethical issues associated with RCTs. We start by describing the context in
which SHM developed J2SI, as well as the J2SI model. The next part of the
chapter explains why a RCT was selected and describes the initial stages in
designing the evaluation. The chapter then discusses some of the challenges
associated with running a RCT with the long-term homeless. Some outcomes of the J2SI pilot are then presented. In the final section, we identify
the factors that were critical in enabling us to successfully implement a RCT
with a disadvantaged population in a resource-constrained environment.

Developing the J2SI model

Research shows that the long-term homeless have very different needs from
individuals whose experience of homelessness is short (Chamberlain and
Johnson 2013). Studies show that most of the long-term homeless are single
and that their physical and mental health is extremely poor (Calsyn and Morse
1991). Many have experienced childhood trauma and almost all have had
traumatic experiences as adults (Taylor and Sharpe 2008). The prevalence of
chronic substance misuse among the long-term homeless is high (Johnson and
Chamberlain 2008b; Sadowski *et al.* 2009). Although this group is relatively
small, research from overseas indicates they consume a disproportionate
amount of health, justice and welfare resources (Culhane and Metraux 2008;
Rosenheck 2000, 2010).

In Australia, responses to homelessness are typically based on relatively
brief interventions. While this can help the short-term homeless to regain
their housing, it struggles to meet the more complex needs of the long-term
homeless. We know this because most of the long-term homeless have been
supported and accommodated by existing specialist homelessness services,
often on numerous occasions, but their problems generally remain unresolved
(Johnson and Chamberlain 2008a; Johnson *et al.* 2008).

The J2SI model was born out of the recognition by SHM that new types
of services were necessary to break the cycle of long-term homelessness. The
J2SI service model differed significantly from existing approaches in five
important ways. First, J2SI provided long-term support. The median length
of support provided by specialist homelessness services in 2007–8 was ten days
(Australian Institute of Health and Welfare 2009, p. 39). When long-term
support is available, it is generally limited to six months. J2SI supported each
client for three years. Second, J2SI provided intensive support. Existing
caseloads in specialist homelessness services are typically between 1:24 to
1:48 over a 12-month period. The J2SI client caseload was 1:4 for the three-
year period. Third, J2SI focused on the rapid re-housing of participants in
safe, secure, affordable, long-term housing. Fourth, J2SI responded to the
mental health and psychological needs of participants, with a specific focus on
the impact that trauma had played in peoples' lives. Finally, J2SI included an

integrated training and development component that aimed to provide participants with interpersonal, practical, tenancy and vocational skills.

Both SHM and the philanthropic partners who funded the pilot were particularly interested in establishing which aspects of J2SI worked and which did not, with the explicit intention of influencing policy and program development.

Designing the evaluation

In 2008 when SHM began developing the framework for the J2SI model, they initially drew on their practice experience. However, SHM also recognised the importance of drawing on the latest empirical evidence. At this point SHM involved researchers from RMIT University and the University of Melbourne to discuss various aspects of the J2SI model and to consider the most effective way to evaluate the pilot.

In Australia, the quality of homelessness service evaluations is uneven – samples are often very small, sources of selection bias are commonly ignored, comparison groups are rarely used, and only recently have longitudinal approaches become more common (Johnson and Chamberlain 2013; Mission Australia 2012; Parsell *et al.* 2013a, 2013b). Thus, extant evidence on the effectiveness of existing interventions is equivocal and often difficult to defend. The lack of rigour is not altogether surprising – in a competitive funding environment, resources are tight and services are often cautious about exposing their practices to independent scrutiny.

Nonetheless, at about the same time as the J2SI model was being developed two significant changes in the policy environment occurred. First, there was an explicit move towards 'evidence based policy'. Second, the then Prime Minister Kevin Rudd took a great deal of interest in homelessness and identified it as a policy priority (FaHCSIA 2008). In his key note speech at the National Homelessness Conference, the Prime Minister put the two together when he outlined a vision to "draw out bold new ideas and to identify evidence based approaches to reduce homelessness" (Rudd 2008).

Although 'evidence-based' policy is a difficult idea to define, SHM, the philanthropic partners, and the research team all agreed that if J2SI was going to have any policy impact, the evaluation had to provide defensible evidence that demonstrated how the J2SI program affected the participants' housing stability, mental and physical wellbeing, and social and economic participation over time. Thus, it was clear from the onset that the evaluation would need to be longitudinal. Our first decision was to follow participants over the three years of the pilot, and then for one year after the pilot ended.[2] Quantitative data was collected every six months in seven rounds of interviews over the three-year period.

Although quantitative data formed the backbone of the evaluation, we recognised that evaluations of social programs can be enhanced through "well-constructed qualitative research" (Gray *et al.* 2009, p. 41). Qualitative material offers researchers the opportunity to explore in greater depth complex social processes. A qualitative component that involved three in-depth qualitative interviews with half of the trial participants was subsequently included. The three interviews coincided with the baseline survey and the 18 and 36-month follow-up (FU) surveys. The qualitative material proved to be crucial in making sense of many of the survey results.

While a longitudinal approach offered many benefits, observing how participants' lives changed over time would not tell us whether changes were the result of the J2SI intervention, changes that would have occurred anyway, or a combination of both. The most rigorous way of testing the impact of the J2SI program was to compare the participants in the program with those in a control group whose characteristics were similar to J2SI participants when the pilot commenced. With a control group, stronger causal inferences about the impact of J2SI could be made. Therefore, our second decision was to include a control group.

There are many ways of selecting a control group but most methods assume that all of the factors that influence an individual's circumstances are known to the researchers. This is rarely the case, perhaps even more so with the chronically homeless. To address this issue we selected a randomised controlled trial (RCT) approach. While not without their critics, RCTs are considered by many as the 'gold standard' in program evaluation.

Finally, as interested as we were in the impact/outcomes of the J2SI pilot, we wanted to know what inputs (works practices, resources, program logic) contributed to various outcomes. Thus, we agreed to undertake a process evaluation alongside the RCT to make a connection between inputs and outcomes. The information generated in a process evaluation can play a crucial role with respect to developing evidence-based best practice (McGraw *et al.* 2009; Parkinson 2012). The process evaluation involved extensive trawling of the J2SI client management system, policies, meeting minutes, as well as interviews with staff, and external agencies (see Parkinson and Johnson 2015).

This approach appealed to all stakeholders (researchers, funders and SHM) because it was robust, could link inputs with outcomes, provide both social and economic data, and was unique, not just in the context of Australian evaluations of homelessness service interventions, but internationally as well.

With the design of the evaluation determined, the next step involved formulating working hypotheses that aligned with the key objectives of the J2SI model. Five working hypotheses were developed:

- that J2SI participants would exhibit lower rates of homelessness than those receiving existing services;
- that J2SI participants would achieve and sustain greater residential stability than those receiving existing services;
- that J2SI participants would exhibit greater improvements in the physical and psychological health than those receiving existing services;
- that J2SI participants would exhibit a greater reduction in rates of alcohol and drug abuse than those receiving existing services; and,

- that J2SI participants would exhibit higher rates of social and economic participation than those receiving existing services.

It is important to note that RCTs pose significant risks for agencies and Government – it is not uncommon to find that RCTs either fail to produce statistically significant results or indeed demonstrate that well meaning programs are in fact harmful (Petrosino *et al.* 2000, p. 358). Indeed, despite the potential value of RCTs, public administrators are often "unsympathetic ... if not downright hostile to, randomised trials" (Roberts *et al.* 2012, p. 1026). This is a sobering reminder that the relationship between research and policy development is complex and "rarely linear or logical" (Macintyre 2012, p. 218). Yet, despite the potential risks, SHM agreed to publish all findings, both positive and negative, and agreed to make the data publicly available at the end of the evaluation. At this point we applied for and received ethics approval from RMIT University to conduct the study.[3]

Challenges

Despite the obvious strengths of the evaluation methodology, three issues were foremost in our minds before we started – ethics, recruitment and participant attrition. We deal with each issue below.

Ethics

As noted, ethics approval was sought and received from RMIT University. This was important but it did not necessarily address concerns held by some people in the community sector and some people in the policy community. While even the strongest critics of RCTs generally acknowledge that they are a powerful method of enquiry, the use of RCTs to evaluate social programs has been characterised as 'inappropriate' and 'unethical'. Two arguments are used to support this position. First, that it is unethical to treat humans as subjects of a social experiment. Second, that it is unethical to deny people access to a service (Flatau and Zaretzky 2008). We were sympathetic to these concerns but were not convinced by them for two reasons.

With respect to the argument that it is unethical to treat humans as subjects of social experiments, we shared the view that all social interventions "constitute a form of (usually uncontrolled) experimentation" (Oakley 2000, p. 318) and that governments are "constantly engaged in experimentation" (Oakley 2000, p. 323). Despite a great deal of public money spent on homelessness programs each year, there is little evidence they work. More than any other method, RCTs can identify programs that have the greatest social and economic impact.

The second issue relates to the mechanisms used to decide who is admitted to a program. In the homelessness service, system demand exceeds supply, which means that people are commonly denied a service they require. Services have developed a range of allocation procedures to ration services. Among homelessness services, allocation procedures generally fit under the rubric of 'needs-based assessment'. Theoretically, 'needs based' allocation procedures are a transparent and an objective way of allocating resources in an environment characterised by scarcity. Policymakers, far removed from the service delivery environment, often place a great deal of faith in needs-based assessments but there are numerous systemic, organisational and individual channels that can introduce bias into the assessment process. This means that those with the highest needs are not necessarily guaranteed a place. For example, some agencies cherry pick clients, sometimes people are excluded due to previous 'problems' with a service, and sometimes people with complex needs are unable to even access the system to be assessed (Busch-Geertsema *et al.* 2010; Evans *et al.* 2011). The random allocation of places into the J2SI pilot meant that once a person had satisfied a broad set of criteria they had the same chance of getting into J2SI as anyone else. In short, rather than being cruel and unjust, we felt that randomisation was the most fair, equitable and transparent means of allocating places in, and evaluating the impact of, social welfare programs (see also Boruch *et al.* 2000).

The importance of clearly considering the ethical aspects of the RCT and articulating our reasons for selecting the approach was evident during the initial referral stages of the program. A small number of referring workers viewed the evaluation with suspicion, expressing concern about language such as 'experimental design' and 'treatment group'. These concerns were addressed by openly discussing the strengths and benefits of the RCT, as well as acknowledging the limitations of RCTs.

Recruitment and randomisation

The second challenge was recruiting participants for the pilot. Potential participants were referred by SHM, with a small number from other homelessness agencies in inner city Melbourne. Of the 99 people initially referred, 88 people satisfied the following admission criteria:

- had slept rough continuously for more than 12 months; and/or
- had been in and out of homelessness for at least three years (including people who have been housed in the last six months and are at risk of further homelessness); and
- were aged between 25 and 50 (within 12 months of their 25th birthday or 50th birthday at commencement of the program).

The 88 individuals were told about the evaluation and gave informed consent to participate. They were then randomly assigned to two groups: 40 people were assigned to the treatment group (receiving J2SI services). The remaining 48 were assigned to the control group, which received existing services. We decided to increase the size of the control group to mitigate against potential attrition. T-test and Pearson's chi-squared test were used to test the independence of treatment assignment based on variables drawn from the referral data. We found no statistically significant differences between the control and treatment groups.

Although the referral process was generally effective, some referrals did not commence J2SI, some dropped out of the program early ($n = 5$) and some temporarily exited the program ($n = 3$). This required the recruitment of 16 additional people and the subsequent random allocation of eight to the treatment group.

Attrition

The third issue was retaining participants. One of the biggest challenges for any longitudinal study is reducing attrition. Among hard to reach and chronically disadvantaged populations, this can be particularly challenging. Longitudinal studies involving homeless participants have reported attrition rates as high as 60 per cent over the course of 12 months (Mission Australia 2012; Mission Australia and Murdoch University 2010, 2011). We developed a number of strategies to reduce attrition, focusing particular attention on the control group as we assumed the treatment group would be more straightforward to retain due to their relationship with the J2SI program.

To start with a number of procedures basic to any longitudinal study were put in place. At the baseline survey and at each subsequent interview, information on key contacts (or anchor points) was collected. Participants were paid $30 per interview, and interviews were conducted at a location and time nominated by the participants. We stressed the importance of face-to-face interviews as a means of building rapport with the participants, and approximately 90 per cent of the 494 surveys conducted during the trial were face-to-face. The research team had considerable expertise in the area of homelessness and were aware that if the survey was too long we risked participants becoming uninterested. If the survey was too short, we risked having insufficient data. Although we were reasonably confident that we had struck the right balance, we nonetheless piloted the survey tool, and sought advice from a homeless peer support program.[4] This resulted in some minor changes to the survey tool.

Perhaps the single most important strategy was employing two research assistants who had years of experience working with homeless people, strong knowledge of the homelessness service system, and existing relationships with workers in that system. The research assistants were skilled in building rapport with disadvantaged people, had the experience to judge when participants were stressed or experiencing any form of emotional discomfort, and had relationships with other services which significantly enhanced collaboration.

The success of these strategies is illustrated in Table 8.1, which shows that after three years just over 80 per cent of the original participants remained involved in the evaluation. Table 8.1 also shows that retention rates were reasonably consistent throughout the project.

Table 8.1 Retention rates

	Survey participants	Base Line	6mFU	12mFU	18mFU	24mFU	30mFU	36mFU
Group E	44	$n=42$ (95.5%)	$n=35$ (79.5%)	$n=34$ (77.3%)	$n=31$ (70.5%)	$n=32$ (72.7%)	$n=36$ (81.8%)	$n=34$ (77.3%)
Group J	40	$n=33$ (82.5%)	$n=37$ (92.5%)	$n=36$ (90.0%)	$n=36$ (90.0%)	$n=36$ (90.0%)	$n=38$ (95.0%)	$n=34$ (85.0%)
TOTAL	84	$n=75$ (89.3%)	$n=72$ (85.7%)	$n=70$ (82.1%)	$n=67$ (79.8%)	$n=68$ (81.0%)	$n=74$ (88.1%)	$n=68$ (80.9%)

Findings

The evaluation results suggest that J2SI had a significant impact on the lives of most participants (Johnson *et al.* 2014). After three years 85 per cent of J2SI participants were housed, compared with 41 per cent of those who were receiving existing services. Over the course of the trial J2SI participants were housed for 67 per cent of the time, or nearly twice as much time as those in the control group (35 per cent).

The outcomes data revealed ongoing improvements in other areas as well. The emotional health of the J2SI participants improved and they reported lower levels of stress, anxiety and depression after three years compared with where they were at the start of the trial, and also compared with the control group. The physical health of the J2SI participants improved with the proportion reporting no bodily pain increasing from 27 per cent to 41 per cent over the three-year period.

Although there was some variation in the use of health services, the most important empirical finding was that the treatment group's average use of emergency psychiatric services and their average number of days hospitalised in both a general hospital and a psychiatric unit declined both over time and relative to the control group. More specifically the evaluation showed that the average number of days the treatment group were hospitalised in the six months prior to each survey declined from 4.4 days at baseline to 1.4 days at the 36 month survey; the average number of times the treatment group used emergency psychiatric services declined from 1.5 times at baseline to 0.1 times at the 36 month survey. There was no material change in the control group's use of either system throughout the trial. This translates into a substantial health care cost impact and suggests that an intervention comprising of stable housing and intensive case management can reduce the public burden associated with the over-utilisation of expensive health services.

With respect to employment, few people in either group were employed at the end of the trial and the number of J2SI participants looking for work declined in the last 12 months. Nonetheless, twice as many J2SI participants were looking for work compared to the control group. The evaluation also found improvements over time and relative to the control group in the use of welfare and homelessness services, and the amount of time incarcerated.

As noted earlier, using RCTs can be risky as they often produce findings that are neither hoped for nor anticipated (Oakley 2000). We found a number of areas where there was little change. We observed little change in the substance use behaviour of the participants, and little improvement in the participants' sense of community connection over the three years. However, the most unanticipated finding related to the economic analysis of the J2SI intervention. In setting up the J2SI pilot, SHM had emphasised the potential economic benefits of investing in an intensive, long-term intervention. SHM's argument was based, in part, on the findings of a number of studies that indicate providing the long-term homeless with housing and support can generate significant costs savings. Despite questions about the methods and reliability of some of these studies (Johnson *et al.* 2012), SHM positioned potential cost savings, along with housing retention, as the 'killer facts' it intended to use to influence government policy. However, the results were not what we expected. We found the short-term economic benefit to be modest, with a return of between 0.15 and 0.22 for every dollar invested. Taking into account lives saved over a 10 year time frame the economic benefit was more substantial, with a $1.30 return for every dollar invested.

In summary, the evaluation found that J2SI had a positive impact on the lives of many participants. While it challenged the view that chronically homeless individuals cannot maintain independent housing, given the right level of support, the evaluation also found that the difficulties of addressing long-term substance addiction and social exclusion had been under-estimated, and that the short term cost offsets were not as large as anticipated. Finally, while the evaluation provided strong evidence of the social and economic impact of the J2SI pilot, little was learnt about the 'treatment as usual' services delivered to the control group – what the services were, their duration, intensity and focus. A lack of attention to what activities make up 'treatment as usual' has been noted elsewhere (Boruch *et al.* 2000, p. 334). Future RCTs should consider more closely what constitutes 'treatment as usual' services, as such information would be of great value to both program designers and service providers.

Factors that contributed to the success of the J2SI evaluation

In reflecting on the J2SI evaluation, it is difficult to reduce it to a prescriptive set of 'must-do' factors – many aspects of the evaluation overlapped and interacted, and both the service delivery and policy environments were dynamic and, at times, quite volatile. Nonetheless, a number of factors critical to the success of the evaluation stand out.

Having the evaluation embedded in the J2SI pilot prior to it starting was important for three key reasons. First, from the moment J2SI staff were employed they were aware of, informed about, and expected to engage with the evaluation. Staff support was crucial. Second, fully briefing referral and external support workers about the scope and intent of the evaluation reduced normative concerns and encouraged collaboration. Finally, having a clear set of research questions explicitly tied to the aims and objectives of the program meant that staff and management at J2SI were continually reflecting on the progress of the pilot and the evaluation throughout the three-year period.

The evaluation also benefitted from a sound understanding of the target population and the inclusion of multiple strategies to mitigate the risk of attrition. Employing research assistants with the appropriate skills and refining the survey tool to collect key information within short timelines were crucial in this respect. In addition, the evaluation sought to resolve ethical considerations prior to commencement of the pilot, openly discussing real and perceived issues with all stakeholders.

Another factor that assisted the evaluation was the robust governance structure developed by SHM. A Steering Group oversaw the project and an Evaluation Reference Group focused specifically on the RCT. Each of these groups benefitted from stable membership, committed attendance and active participation throughout the project. Both groups contained senior representatives from a range of stakeholders and they were aware of the risks associated with undertaking a RCT. Nonetheless, they pushed the research team throughout the project – problems were openly discussed and strategies to address them actively sought. The Steering Group carefully monitored the evaluation via detailed quarterly reports that outlined progress and identified successes and challenges across key domains.

Strong leadership from senior management and the board at SHM also assisted the evaluation in two specific ways. First, SHM's leadership committed to open dissemination of findings (both positive and negative) throughout the pilot. Second, the SHM leadership team provided clear direction to the J2SI staff team regarding their expected engagement in the evaluation and monitored the data collection process. This was crucial to participant engagement and retention.

Finally, philanthropic funding was also crucial for two reasons. First, in seeking and securing philanthropic funding the J2SI pilot and the evaluation enjoyed more operational and intellectual freedom than if J2SI had been funded by government. Second, the philanthropic agencies' commitment to the pilot and evaluation was reflected in the allocation of sufficient funding for both.

Conclusion

The evaluation of the J2SI pilot had two broad goals. The first goal was to generate defensible evidence of what worked, what did not, and for whom in terms of addressing long-term homelessness. The second goal was to influence policy design and program development. In terms of the first goal, the evaluation provided strong evidence that a well-resourced, long-term and intensive service model can end homelessness, achieve greater residential stability, improve physical and psychological health and reduce the burden on expensive health services for most participants. Reducing alcohol and drug abuse and enhancing social and economic participation, however, proved more difficult, as did generating cost offsets that matched the cost of delivering the pilot. The latter findings are consistent with overseas literature and serve as a timely reminder for policymakers that they need to be realistic about what programs working with the long-term homeless can achieve.

In terms of the second goal of 'policy impact', from the outset SHM understood that the evaluation was just one, albeit important, element in their strategy of influencing policy. Policymakers were engaged in the project through participation in the Steering Group and awareness of the pilot was maintained by the release of four annual 'outcome' reports. J2SI received a number of awards for innovation and excellence and both the pilot and the evaluation results have been cited in a number of important policy documents. SHM worked closely with the Victorian government throughout the pilot and in the last 18 months commenced negotiations with the Mental Health Drugs and Regions Division of the Victorian Department of Health regarding expanding the pilot across several sites in Victoria. The Minister's office and the Department were receptive to the approach and submitted to the Federal government for funds to deliver a program designed to end long-term homelessness called Breaking the Cycle (BTC). BTC drew extensively on the J2SI model, with only minor differences. The Government's bid was successful and submissions were called for in August 2012. However, the Department of Health subsequently provided BTC resources only to existing mental health services, despite general agreement that the long-term homeless require a more integrated, cross program approach. So, while there is some evidence that J2SI had an impact on the policy agenda, it is also the case that the evaluation had little success in breaking down a lack of cooperation between Government departments, which hinder systems integration and service development.

Nonetheless, the J2SI evaluation demonstrated that "random methods are a feasible and efficient way of evaluating social interventions" (Oakley 2000, p. 324) and RCTs have a legitimate place in evaluating homelessness programs. While we are not suggesting that RCTs should be applied to all social welfare evaluation, we feel that many of the concerns expressed about RCTs are misplaced, and in some instance demonstrably wrong. In advocating for the increased use of RCTs we are conscious that many people are uncomfortable thinking about the long-term homeless as subjects in an experiment. However, these normative concerns have to be balanced against the capacity of RCTs to tell us whether a program has a positive or negative impact. Although some service providers and policymakers will remain resistant to RCTs, both groups nonetheless have an "ethical responsibility to rigorously evaluate, on a continual basis, the policies, practices, and programs" they implement (Petrosino *et al.* 2000, p. 371). The failure to rigorously evaluate means that the very people charged with assisting the community's most vulnerable individuals wilfully ignore the possibility that social welfare programs might be ineffective or even harmful (Petrosino *et al.* 2000). For the long-term homeless, who often find themselves in arbitrarily administered, evidence-free programs, the J2SI pilot has demonstrated that the use of a RCTs is both a fair approach, but also one that provides defensible evidence about what sorts of programs are needed to resolve long-term homelessness permanently.

Notes

1 Lord Mayors Charitable Foundation, The Peter and Lyndy White Foundation, RE Ross Trust, William Buckland Foundation, St Mary's Parish, Andy Inc. Foundation, Limb Family Foundation, Carbini Health, Orcadia Foundation.
2 In 2014 Johnson and Tseng were awarded an ARC linkage grant to extend the project to six years.
3 Ethics register number HRESC B-2000197–07/09.
4 The Peer Education Support Program, managed by the Council to Homeless Persons (Vic).

References

Australian Institute of Health and Welfare 2009, *Homeless people in SAAP: SAAP national data collection annual report 2007–2008 Australia*, AIHW (cat. no. Hou 191), Canberra.

Boruch, R, Victor, T and Cecil, J 2000, 'Resolving ethical and legal problems in randomized trials', *Crime and Delinquency*, vol. 46, no. 3, pp. 330–353.

Busch-Geertsema, V, Edgar, W, O'Sullivan, E and Pleace, N 2010, *Homelessness and homeless policies in Europe: lessons from research*, European Consensus Conference on Homelessness, FEANTSA.

Calsyn, R and Morse, G 1991, 'Predicting chronic homelessness', *Urban Affairs Quarterly*, vol. 27, no. 1, pp. 155–164.

Chamberlain, C and Johnson, G 2013, 'Pathways into adult homelessness', *Journal of Sociology*, vol. 49, no. 1, pp. 60–77.

Culhane, D and Metraux, S 2008, 'Rearranging the deck chairs or reallocating the lifeboats', *Journal of the American Planning Association*, vol. 74, no. 1 pp. 111–121.

Evans, T, Neale, K, Buultjens, J and Davies, T 2011, *Service integration in a regional homelessness service system*, Department of Families, Housing, Community Services and Indigenous Affairs, Canberra.

FaHCSIA 2008, *The road home: a national approach to reducing homelessness*, Department of Families, Housing, Community Services and Indigenous Affairs, Canberra.

Flatau, P and Zaretzky, K 2008, 'The economic evaluation of homelessness programs', *European Journal of Homelessness*, vol. 2, pp. 305–320.

Gray, M, Plath, D and Webb, S A 2009, *Evidence-based social work: a critical stance*, Routledge, New York.

Johnson, G and Chamberlain, C 2008a, 'From youth to adult homelessness', *Australian Journal of Social Issues*, no. 4, pp. 563–582.

Johnson, G and Chamberlain, C 2008b, 'Homelessness and substance abuse: which comes first?', *Australian Social Work*, vol. 61, no. 4, pp. 342–356.

Johnson, G and Chamberlain, C 2013, *Evaluation of the Melbourne Street to Home program: 12 month outcomes*, Department of Families, Housing, Community Services and Indigenous Affairs, Canberra.

Johnson, G, Gronda, H and Coutts, S 2008, *On the Outside: Pathways in and out of homelessness*, Australian Scholarly Press, Melbourne.

Johnson, G, Kuehnle, D, Parkinson, S, Sesa, S and Tseng, Y 2014, *Resolving long-term homelessness: a randomised controlled trial examining the 36 month costs, benefits and social outcomes from the journey to social inclusion pilot program*, Sacred Heart Mission, St. Kilda, VIC, Australia.

Johnson, G, Parkinson, S and Parsell, C 2012, *Policy shift or program drift: implementing housing first in Australia*, Australian Institute of Housing and Urban Research, Melbourne.

Macintyre, S 2012, Evidence in the development of health policy, *Public Health* vol. 126: 217–219.

McGraw, S, Larson, M, Foster, S, Kresky-Wolff, M, Botelho E, Elstad, E, Stefancic, A and Tsemberis, S 2009, 'Adopting best practices: lessons learned in the collaborative initiative to help end chronic homelessness', *Journal of Behavioral Health Services and Research*, vol. 37, no. 2, pp. 197–212.

Mission Australia 2012, *The Michael Project, 2007–2010: new perspectives and possibilities for homeless men*, Mission Australia, Sydney.

Mission Australia and Murdoch University 2010, *Increasing our understanding of homeless men: the Michael project*, Mission Australia, Sydney.

Mission Australia and Murdoch University 2011, *How homeless men are faring: some initial outcomes from the Michael project*, Mission Australia, Sydney.

Oakley, A 2000, 'A historical perspective on the use of randomized trials in social science setting', *Crime and Delinquency*, vol. 46, no. 3, pp. 315–329.

Parkinson, S 2012, *The Journey to social inclusion in practice: a process evaluation of the first 18 months*, Sacred Heart Mission, St. Kilda.

Parkinson, S and Johnson, G 2015, *Integrated case management in practice: final process evaluation of the journey to social inclusion*, Sacred Heart Mission, St Kilda.

Parsell, C, Tomaszewski, T and Jones, A 2013a, *An evaluation of Brisbane Street to home: final report*, Department for Families, Housing, Community Services and Indigenous Affairs, Canberra.

Parsell, C, Tomaszewski, T and Jones, A 2013b, *An evaluation of Sydney way2home: final report*, Department for Families, Housing, Community Services and Indigenous Affairs, Canberra.

Petrosino, A, Turpin-Petrosino, C and Finckenauer, J 2000, 'Well-meaning programs can have harmful effects! Lessons from experiments of programs such as Scared Straight', *Crime and Delinquency*, vol. 46, no. 3, pp. 354–379.

Roberts, H, Petticrew, M, Liabo, K and Macintyre, S 2012, 'The 'Anglo-Saxon' disease: a pilot study of the barriers to and facilitators of the use of randomised controlled trials of social programmes in an international context', *Journal of Epidemiology and Community Health*, vol. 66, pp. 1025–1029.

Rosenheck, R 2000, 'Cost-effectiveness of services for mentally ill homeless people: the application of research to policy and practice', *American Journal of Psychiatry*, vol. 157, pp. 1563–1570.

Rosenheck, R 2010, 'Service models and mental health problems: cost-effectiveness and policy relevance', in I Ellen and B O'Flaherty (eds), *How to house the homeless*, Russell Sage Foundation, New York, pp. 17–36.

Rudd, K 2008, 'Prime Ministers key note speech', transcript, viewed 1 August 2014, http://pmtranscripts.dpmc.gov.au/preview.php?did=15924.

Sadowski, L, Kee, R, Vanderweele, T and Buchanan, D 2009, 'Effect of a housing and case management program on emergency department visits and hospitalizations among chronically ill homeless adults: a randomized trial', *Journal of the American Medical Association*, vol. 301, no. 17, pp. 1771–1778.

Taylor, K and Sharpe, L 2008, 'Trauma and post-traumatic stress disorder among homeless adults in Sydney', *Australian and New Zealand Journal of Psychiatry*, vol. 42, pp. 206–213.

9 Producing change

An integrated model of social services, research and public policy advocacy

Ruth Liberman and Deborah Connolly Youngblood

Introduction

Julia is a poor single mother. She is, she told us, living in "one of *those* households." By this she means, one of those households that everyone stereotypes. A household with a single mother and multiple children, striving to make ends meet. Her story is complex; full of struggles, mistakes, hopes, obstacles, joy, short-term survival strategies and long-term exhaustion from trying so hard and not getting enough traction. Her story is complicated in the same the way that every poor person's story is complicated. This is not to say that these stories are all the same – indeed nothing could be farther from the truth. However, a common thread ties together the stories of many single mothers working to overcome poverty; that thread *is* complexity. There is never one discrete cause of hardships and never one solution that will fix it all. Behind the sobering statistics of growing numbers of single parent-headed households living in poverty are the intricate histories and present of people living their lives, trying to, as Julia put it, "Be heard, understood and supported in my plan to lift my boys and myself out of poverty – from a life of mere survival, into the realm of achievement, the realization of our potential and self-sufficiency."

So the burning question is how? And not just how economic mobility can happen for Julia and her family, because stories of the lucky ones who beat the odds have always over-populated anti-poverty dialogues. Instead, how can we develop widespread, sustainable, replicable models that promote economic independence and have demonstrable results for many? And how can we use those models to inform and change public policy to pave the way for even more?

Crittenton Women's Union (CWU), a US organisation based in Boston, Massachusetts, has developed an innovative action tank model combining direct service delivery, original research and public policy advocacy to produce more effective economic mobility programming and generate more favourable policies for low income families. This chapter focuses on how CWU's integrative approach, the architecture of the action tank, has provided the foundation for developing innovative programs that successfully promote economic mobility while engaging in research and advocacy initiatives to influence the broader landscape of how economic mobility is understood and promoted. The CWU action tank model of integrating direct service, research and advocacy under one umbrella provides a potential model for other organisations committed to producing change at multiple levels. We will first outline the action tank architecture of CWU and then illustrate how it works through some examples of the programs, research and advocacy approaches CWU has developed and/or deployed.

What is an action tank?

CWU coined the term 'action tank' to refer to the unusual organisational model that combines direct service programs with think tank-like research and informed public policy advocacy. These three elements – direct services, research, and advocacy – make up what CWU sometimes refers to as the three-legged stool approach. Each one of these areas represents a leg of the stool, essential for balance and mutually supportive of each other in creating the stool seat (the organisation). In other words, CWU operates these three areas so that they continually inform and build upon the others. Direct services are both the object of CWU's research and they provide the impetus and focus for research questions explored outside of programming. At the same time, CWU uses the learning from both original research and relevant external studies to innovate better program models, program tools and approaches. Lastly, CWU public policy advocacy is directly rooted in the testimonies of the people CWU serves and is supported by the findings from the CWU research team. In turn, the advocacy work promotes better public understandings of key issues and better policies to pave the way for economic mobility. Each leg requires the other to stand. Thus, the action tank model refers to an organisational approach where research is consistently applied, direct services are designed and implemented based on research and data, and advocacy is rooted in both research and service experience developed into positive anti-poverty policies. In what follows, we will describe the Mobility Mentoring® services, a CWU designed self-sufficiency program model, in order to illuminate how the action tank approach works in practice.

Mobility mentoring: a new service approach to promote economic mobility

Since 2006, CWU has been designing and testing new program models for assisting low-income families to reach economic independence. This process led to the creation and implementation of an economic mobility strategy called Mobility Mentoring®. Mobility Mentoring services uses the Bridge to Self-Sufficiency® (the Bridge) as its central framework and theory of change which posits that becoming economically stable requires most people to optimise their lives in five key areas:

- family stability
- wellbeing (physical, mental, and social)
- education and training
- financial management
- employment and career management

If a family struggles significantly in any of these key areas, it is virtually impossible for the head(s) of household to attain and keep a family-sustaining job. The Bridge is a tool for assessment, goal setting and outcomes measurement designed to help low-income parents attain and preserve economic security. CWU has used the Bridge as the framework for services delivered over the past five years to hundreds of families who come to the organisation for family shelter, job readiness, adult education and teen-parenting supports. Mobility Mentoring® services partners each client with a mobility mentor (coach) who, over time, helps the client acquire the resources, skills, and sustained behaviour changes for self-sufficiency. The role of mobility mentors who staff the program is different from traditional case management. Mobility mentors help participants move from consistently operating in a crisis-response mode to addressing issues with a more planned and reasoned approach through which they can set longer-term goals. Mobility mentors help participants gain the skills needed to maintain the forward momentum that can lead to economic security.

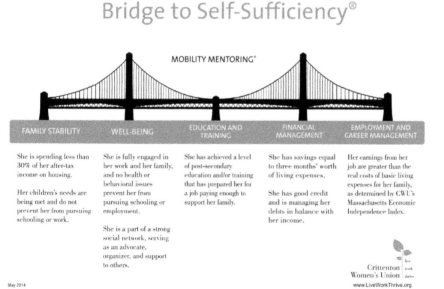

Figure 9.1 Bridge to self-sufficiency (Crittenton Women's Union 2015).

CWU's Mobility Mentoring services offer a social laboratory to better understand what works and what does not to promote economic independence. The program model was based on extensive poverty alleviation research as well as the program development team's decades of experience in social services. First deployed as a small pilot and now a rapidly expanding initiative, Mobility Mentoring services and client outcomes are carefully documented and rigorously tracked, allowing CWU to use the outcomes data to make changes and improvements to the model as needed. This also provides CWU with strong evidence-based results to grow and scale the model and to promote the work with external audiences and current and potential stakeholders.

Using research to produce positive change

The implementation of Mobility Mentoring is an example of CWU's impact at the individual, direct service level. Program participants are offered high quality economic mobility services, and it is gratifying to see many of them make significant self-sufficiency gains. However, the CWU action tank model is to increase the total impact that can be obtained at the individual service level by improving program designs and then using the data that comes out of its programs to inform and strengthen advocacy efforts and generate more widespread change. In this way CWU research plays a key role in the development and improvement of programs and advocacy for public policies.

For example, several years ago CWU improved its services by integrating new learning about developments in brain science research into its Mobility Mentoring services. Brain science literature illuminates the difficult challenges faced by low-income parents who must navigate the complex strategic decision making required to map and maintain a course toward economic security. Each step along the journey requires critical and strategic thinking and constant juggling and multi-tasking. Families need to figure out how to stretch limited resources to cover rent, transportation and other daily needs, while at the same time keep up with the paperwork and appointments necessary to remain in compliance with critical benefit programs. Simultaneously, they are trying to sort through often conflicting information about training and education programs that will lead to family-sustaining wages, and how to finance and succeed in them. This balancing act becomes a high-stakes exercise because there is no room for error in investing their time and limited resources for families who have no personal safety net.

Importantly, supporting participants in decision making is very different from merely making decisions for them. In the supportive approach, CWU mobility mentors coach people on how to weigh their options and make the most productive decisions for themselves and their families. In the latter scenario, service providers dictate a course of action (often based on their own criteria) sometimes without fully understanding the individual's situation or gaining their buy in. This latter scenario is common in the social service arena but often falls short of producing the substantive gains social service agencies seek. The mobility mentoring model relies on external support designed to build those skills in participants themselves, thus creating long-term sustainable change.

What CWU staff are learning from brain science is that the stress of living in poverty impacts optimal decision making. Situational stress caused by constant preoccupation with financial, safety, relationship or other worries can negatively impact the decision processes involved in problem solving, goal setting and goal attainment – the very skills and strengths required to navigate out of poverty (Babcock 2014). These skills are often broadly grouped together and described as executive functioning. Executive function challenges can be magnified for those who experience significant trauma and chronic poverty from an early age. Ample medical research confirms that environmental risk factors prevalent in low-income households, such as stress, poor nutrition and environmental toxins, have direct impacts on the development of parts of the brain that are crucial to optimal executive functioning (Harvard Center on the Developing Child 2011).

While the field is nascent, some social service organisations and even state governments are beginning to develop brain science-informed services and some promising early outcomes are linked to programs and tools designed to address executive function challenges in low-income adults (Babcock 2014). By developing services that combine concrete resources, specific and informed guidance on what is really required to sustain a family, along with coaching on how to sort through complex information, establish priorities, set goals and maintain focus on goal attainment even in the face of crisis, families are provided with key skills needed for long-term success.

This new approach has led to outcomes that outperform more traditional poverty alleviation programs. Below are some examples of CWU's participant outcomes relative to national or regional benchmarks.

Exploring and incorporating brain science research into programs is an example of how CWU utilises external research. Internally, CWU both produces original research and tracks client outcomes for continuous performance improvement and for developing an evidence-base for program scaling and replication. CWU conducts original research on topics that span many areas pertaining to economic mobility. For example, they produce a triennial labour market analysis called 'Hot jobs: promoting economic independence through informed career decisions' (Youngblood *et al.* 2013) that reports on the availability and accessibility of employment that pays family-sustaining wages for job seekers with less than a bachelor's degree. This widely cited regional report serves both as a concrete tool for low-income job seekers and an advocacy vehicle informing the public and policymakers about this issue. CWU has produced many such research pieces over the past six years or so on topics ranging from the role of social networks in economic mobility, for-profit schools, the binds that safety net-program policies place recipients in, and a forthcoming study on consumer debt.[1]

Table 9.1 Mobility Mentoring® outcomes for adults served in fy2013 (1 July, 2012–30 June, 2013)[1]

Bridge to Self-Sufficiency® Pillar	At Mobility Mentoring® program entry	As of last FY13 outcome measurement	Comparison to community benchmarks
FAMILY STABILITY	100% of participants in CWU's Career Family Opportunity (CFO) program were residing in subsidised housing.	89% of CFO participants resided in subsidised housing • 9% have purchased homes • 2% have moved to market-rate rental.	Nationally, 6% of homebuyers are single mothers and 4% of homebuyers are single mothers with an income of 0–80% of area median income (AMI).
	CWU served 158 families in housing stabilisation, all of whom originated from emergency family shelter.	100% of CWU families in stabilisation maintained permanent housing 12+ months after exiting shelter.	75–91% of families participating in three Mass. Homelessness prevention efforts maintained housing stability after 12 months.
WELL-BEING	20.3 Overall Quality of Life Score[2] for CFO participants 66% of CFOs scored above 19.	21.5 Overall Quality of Life Score for CFO participants 89% of CFOs scored above 19.	Scores below 19 indicate a poor quality of life. A difference in two to three points in the overall score has been found to be clinically meaningful.
EDUCATION AND TRAINING	32% of CFO participants had an AA degree or higher broken down as follows: • 14% Associates; • 14% Bachelors; • 4% Masters.	52% of CFO participants have an AA degree or higher broken down as follows: • 27% Associates; • 14% Bachelors; • 2% graduate certificate; • 9% Masters.	Six-year college completion rate for low-income students is approximately 11% 46% of adults of any income level in Mass. have an Associate's degree or higher.

	FINANCIAL MANAGEMENT		
	$0 saved into matched savings account.	$1,528 average saved into matched savings account.	76% of families in the bottom quintile have bank accounts. Of those with bank account, the median balance is $600.
	21% of adults entering shelter had any money saved.	40% of adults in shelter saved at least $150 or contributed at least $150 towards debt.	

	EMPLOYMENT AND CAREER MANAGEMENT		
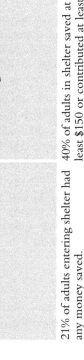	59% of CFO participants were employed: average wage $14.82/hr.	68% of CFOs are employed; average wage $20.18/hr.	The median income for single mothers in Mass. is $13.13/hr.
	0% of CFOs were earning a family-sustaining wage[3] at entry.	30% of CFOs are earning a family-sustaining wage.	
	45% of adults were either enrolled in school OR employed at program entry.	80% of adults were either enrolled in school OR employed in FY13.	64% of low-income families in Mass. are employed; 53% of the non-elderly, non-disabled HUD public housing authority-assisted households are employed.

Notes
1 Results in black are for short-term program delivery in CWU shelters in Boston and Cambridge with average participation of 12–18 months. Participation numbers (N) vary based on program type. Shaded results are for multi-year program delivery through a Mobility Mentoring® program called Career Family Opportunity. Participants enter this program on a rolling basis after an application process, and had achieved 2.5 years average program participation at the time these data were gathered.
2 The Ferrans and Powers Quality of Life Score measures both satisfaction and importance of various aspects of life. Scores are weighted in order to reflect an individual's satisfaction with areas of her life that she values most. Scores are calculated for psychological, social, economic and family satisfaction, as well as life satisfaction overall.
3 CWU publishes a cost of living measure called the Massachusetts Economic Independence Index (Mass. Index) which reports exactly how much income it takes for a family to make ends meet in Massachusetts without relying on public assistance. We use this data to determine family specific self-sufficiency wage goals in CWU programs. For more information go to www.liveworkthrive.org.

In addition to original research, CWU tracks participant status within key self-sufficiency domains over time to chart progress toward self-sufficiency. After establishing concrete benchmarks for economic independence,[2] a rigorous data collection and analysis framework is deployed to track outcomes. Additionally, CWU researchers gather relevant national and/or regional benchmarks against which to measure CWU outcomes, enabling a more accurate reflection of where CWU stands out successfully and where there are shortcomings that need to be improved.

CWU in the public policy arena

The third key strategy of the action tank is to increase the impact of CWU's work through development of a public policy presence. City, state and federal government officials are instrumental in determining funding priorities as well as passing legislation that significantly alters the landscape and opportunities for the people CWU serves. Thus, designing and implementing an advocacy strategy to influence government initiatives is a powerful way to increase impact. The main tools for achieving this are: (1) policy briefs, (2) advocacy, and (3) leveraging the media to educate wider audiences on issues and potential solutions. Importantly, these efforts are done in partnership with program participants. For example, CWU features participant stories in published briefs and elicits participant feedback on how government services could better support their journey out of poverty. Additionally, participants regularly join CWU staff in legislative visits to inform lawmakers of their realities and testify at hearings and are often featured in relevant news stories. CWU also works closely with coalition partners in the non-profit sector, labour unions, social justice organisations, business leaders and academics. In what follows we describe various advocacy approaches in some detail.

Policy briefs

As mentioned earlier, CWU publishes briefs to illuminate key issues and provide an evidence-based foundation to promote positive economic mobility policies. In addition to the briefs already outlined, in recent years CWU has also released three briefs that illuminate various aspects of Mobility Mentoring® and the Bridge to Self-Sufficiency®. The first brief, *Mobility mentoring* (Babcock 2013) provides the scientific and sociological underpinnings of the Mobility Mentoring approach. The second, *Using brain science to design new pathways out of poverty*, (Babcock 2014) offers concrete ideas on how findings from brain science can inform the design of safety net and other programs to improve outcomes for low-income populations. The third brief, *A plan for building skilled workers and strong families through the Massachusetts transitional aid to families with dependent children program* (Liberman 2013) provides specific recommendations on how mobility mentoring concepts could be incorporated into an on-going effort to reform the state's cash assistance program for low-income families. These briefs, like all of those produced by CWU, are targeted to an audience of service providers, law-makers, philanthropists and researchers with the goal of building public support for CWU's approach to economic mobility work. These publications also provide CWU's policy advocates with opportunities to reach out to policy and thought leaders in the state, share CWU's work and experience, and establish CWU as a leader in this field. Writing comprehensive briefs that delve into the issues, provide original analysis and illuminate potential solutions is a long-standing approach in CWU's policy work.

Advocacy

CWU regularly engages in legislative, budget and administrative advocacy, employing two full-time staff members in this capacity. Legislative advocacy includes both supporting (and opposing) bills and filing CWU written bills as a vehicle for advancing our policy recommendations. For example, in January 2013, CWU worked with many state senators and representatives to file the *Pathways to Family Economic Self-Sufficiency* bill. The bill would enable low-income adults and teens with dependent children to attain education and/or skills training for jobs in high-demand occupations. Participants would receive vocational assessment, pre-employment training, remedial education, college navigation, opportunity for work-study jobs, internships or on-the-job training, and case management support to ensure successful job placement and retention. The bill called for $2 million in new funding promoted through a coordinated budget campaign. Unfortunately the effort did not pass in the first legislative session it was filed, which is true for the majority of bills filed in the Massachusetts legislature. And those that do pass often need multiple attempts to become law. However, even without becoming a law, the bill provided CWU and its coalition partners with a platform to share recommendations, hence educating lawmakers and promoting positive change. These opportunities included legislative briefings on the bill, distribution of fact sheets and emails/calls requesting co-sponsors and support of the effort, organising individuals (including board members who are business leaders in the community and clients) as well as other organisations (both service and advocacy) to testify at hearings and meetings with legislators.

Moreover, even though the bill did not pass, the push by CWU and its partners to educate legislators on how best to help low-income families nevertheless proved effective. In July 2014, Massachusetts Governor Deval Patrick signed a major welfare reform bill which included provisions in line with CWU's advocacy efforts, such as allowing education and training to count towards the welfare work requirement for two years, enabling welfare recipients to save money beyond the $2,500 asset limit, and investing $11 million to provide job placement support as well as education and training programs. It is critical not to underestimate the power that informing legislators about issues on which one is well versed and thus persuasive can have over the long term.

CWU staff simultaneously engage in budget advocacy to promote changes or enhancements to budget line items which impact important services accessed by CWU clients. For example, CWU advocates for the protection of state funding for services that CWU provides, such as family emergency shelter, and also for critical resources that clients require after transitioning from CWU programs, such as subsidised child care vouchers or free workforce training opportunities. The budget process also provides opportunities to test new ideas such as seeking funding for a mobility mentoring pilot program or to revise current program administration by permitting or limiting certain uses of funding. In 2014–15, CWU successfully advocated for increased education and training resources for low-income parents in Massachusetts.

Ultimately, this process of developing and moving a bill or a budget priority through the legislature is a significant CWU strategy to influence public policy. Involving the families CWU serves in this process is part of what makes CWU's advocacy unique and effective, as does the basis in original research.

Administrative advocacy

Most of the attention around policy advocacy tends to be focused on elected officials. Yet, much of the real change in the public sphere happens at the agency level as a result of administrative rule making, regulatory policy or the development of internal agency budgets or procurement opportunities. CWU develops relationships with the leaders of the state's executive offices such as Labor and Workforce Development and Housing and Economic Development. CWU staff meets at least annually with the cabinet secretaries and relevant undersecretaries to share recommendations related to the departments under their leadership. Here again, CWU staff often share research briefs or involve clients who share their experiences of striving to rise out of poverty.

CWU also seeks opportunities to participate on task forces convened to advise the state on issues related to economic mobility. Task force participation has led to important and tangible opportunities to incorporate CWU's recommendations into new program models. For example, CWU's participation in a work group on services for residents in state public housing led to the creation of a new comprehensive five-year economic mobility program funding stream that incorporates many elements of CWU's Mobility Mentoring.

Media

CWU works to develop a relationship with local media to gain coverage of relevant issues. The organisation sends out press advisories for CWU events such as legislative briefings, presentation of new research, program openings, conferences and fund raising events. CWU often incorporates client speakers at these events and has found that reporters are very interested in incorporating family stories into their work. Highlighting clients' stories in the media is a powerful tool that puts a human face on an issue for the public in general and also pushes lawmakers to take action. By raising awareness about an issue through media coverage, CWU motivates lawmakers to create policies and make funding decisions that help not only its clients but other low-income families as well.

This was the case when CWU tackled the issue of unmanageable student debt related to for-profit post-secondary school enrolment by CWU clients. Through internal data collection CWU found that a high percentage of clients who were over-burdened by student debt had attended one or more for-profit vocational schools. Through working with these former students, CWU researchers collected stories of egregious school practices such as false promises to non-English speaking students that translation services are available, and instances where schools provided answer sheets to prospective students who were incapable of passing entrance exams on their own. Staff knew that these stories had the potential to draw media attention and thus raise the likelihood that legislators would take interest and action. Indeed, multiple CWU clients ultimately testified at a Massachusetts legislative hearing on the for-profit school issue and some were also interviewed by reporters. CWU publicised the hearing and received coverage that helped educate the public on this issue. Ultimately, CWU was able to influence the enactment of substantial changes in Massachusetts to better regulate and oversee for-profit post-secondary schools.

Media coverage also boosts CWU's standing as a non-profit thought leader. CWU aims to release research and policy reports to maximise media coverage, thinking carefully about timing and the right spokespersons. For instance, CWU's triennial *Massachusetts Economic Independence (Mass Index)* report was released at the beginning of the calendar year when there is widespread focus on cost of living and employment. The *Mass. Index* report outlines salary requirements to make ends meet in Massachusetts without reliance on public or private assistance. It helps families determine how much they need to earn in order to cover their basic needs, such as housing, transportation, healthcare and food. CWU engaged non-traditional partners such as important business leaders to speak at the *Mass Index* press event because they are more likely to be covered in the news. As a result of these strategies, and the compelling research content, the report received significant media coverage and has been cited regularly by legislators, most recently in the successful campaign to raise the state's minimum wage. It is through on-going media outreach that CWU has become a go-to organisation for poverty and economic mobility issues.

Conclusion

The action tank model is CWU's approach to realising its mission, a mission to transform low-income women's lives through innovative social service programs, applied research, and effective advocacy so they and their families can attain economic independence. It is an approach designed to stay close to the individual, to keep women like Julia directly in focus, valuing the importance of each family and wanting them to succeed. The approach then expands that focus on the individual so that the millions of women like Julia who are over-burdened by poverty and unable to reach their potentials are also recognised. Thus, the work begins to make inroads in promoting economic independence for ever greater numbers through the further reaching approaches of published research informing scholarly and public thought and public policy advocacy influencing legislation and opportunities. By providing direct services, conduct-ing innovative research, and promoting a public policy agenda, CWU tackles poverty alleviation from a variety of angles. Each of these arenas mutually sup-ports the organisation and contributes to economic mobility efforts. CWU's strength and outcomes ultimately rest on the interconnectivity of services, research, and advocacy – three areas that continuously build upon and inform each other. The sum is truly greater than its parts.

Julia summed it up this way, "My story and my family's experiences are not unique. While no story is exactly like ours, there are many women with similar stories who all want their families to thrive. We are entirely capable of making that happen. We simply need the opportunity and long-term support to do it. We just need a chance. We need Crittenton Women's Union to hear us and to partner with us. And I'm thankful that CWU stands at the ready."

Notes

1 All of these research briefs are available free of cost for download at CWU's website, www.liveworkthrive.org.
2 CWU produced the Massachusetts Economic Independence Index (most recent update 2013) to quantify precisely what it costs for individualised families to make ends meet (Ames *et al.* 2013). By engaging in this analysis, CWU was both able to educate and lobby around the issue and to provide program participants with con-crete, evidence-based targets for self-sufficiency. The report and corollary calculator can be found at CWU's website, www.liveworkthrive.org.

References

Ames, M Lowe, J, Dowd, K, Liberman, R and Youngblood, D C 2013, *Massachusetts economic independence index 2013*, Crittenton Women's Union, Boston, MA.

Babcock, E 2013, *Mobility mentoring*, Crittenton Women's Union, Boston, MA.

Babcock, E 2014, *Using brain science to improve policies and programs for low-income fam-ilies*, Crittenton Women's Union, Boston, MA.

Crittenton Women's Union 2015, *Bridge to self-sufficiency*, Crittenton Women's Union, Boston, MA, viewed 19 May 2015, www.liveworkthrive.org/research_and_tools/bridge_to_self_sufficiency.

Harvard Center on the Developing Child 2011, *'Air traffic control' system: how early experiences shape the development of executive function*, Harvard Center on the Develop-ing Child, Working Paper #11, Cambridge, MA.

Liberman, R 2013, *A plan for building skilled workers and strong families through the Massachusetts transitional aid to families with dependent children program*, Crittenton Women's Union Working Paper, Boston, MA.

Youngblood, D C, Dowd, K, Morgera, M, Melnik, M and Liberman, R 2013, *Hot jobs 2013: promoting economic independence through informed career decisions*, Crittenton Women's Union, Boston, MA.

Part III

Disrupting business as usual

10 The effects of hybridity on local governance

The case of social enterprise

Jo Barraket, Verity Archer and Chris Mason

Introduction

Social enterprise as a vehicle for service delivery and social inclusion has gained prominence in public policy frameworks in a number of world regions (Barraket and Archer 2010; Teasdale 2010). Early policy approaches to social enterprise development were linked in a number of jurisdictions with a place-based focus on responding to socio-economic disadvantage (Reid and Griffith 2006). This is consistent with a Third Way policy agenda, which views 'community' as a site in which failures of the market and the state will be redressed (Reddel 2004). Also consistent with the Third Way agenda, governmental investment in social enterprise was broadly positioned within a discourse of 'network governance' (Considine 2005; Rhodes 1997), whereby effective local responses to disadvantage are purportedly enabled by access to the embedded resources of multiple sectors through 'partnerships' and coordinated cross-sectoral endeavours. As other writers have observed, networked approaches to mobilising resources and governing organisational activity are not unfamiliar to social enterprise. (Gardin 2006, p. 112) suggests that, as well as being 'multi-goal' and 'multi-ownership' organisations, social enterprises are themselves 'multi-resource' organisations that mobilise a range of market and non-market resources to meet their objectives. The hybridity of emergent forms of social enterprise – as multi-stakeholder entities that explicitly inhabit both social and economic domains (Battilana and Dorado 2010; Battilana and Lee 2014) – suggests some congruence with the logic of network governance (Barraket 2008).

Despite shifts in political regimes away from Third Way logics in recent years, social enterprise has continued to attract some public policy attention. Recast within discourses of community self-reliance, the assumed value of social enterprise as a vehicle for efficiently delivering social goods and services *in situ* has been invoked in policy regimes, such as Big Society in the UK (Thompson 2011). Within both earlier and more recent policy approaches, local government has been a locus for various policy interventions designed to stimulate social enterprise activity.

The contextual focus for the research reported in this chapter is the Australian state of Victoria. Consistent with networked approaches to governing and resource mobilisation, a range of relationships – from ad hoc funding support through to contractual and highly formalised partnership arrangements – has emerged between some social enterprises and local governments in Victoria. These relationships are located within a wider discourse of new approaches to local governance (Røiseland 2011), with local governments increasingly examining their role as network brokers in the coordination of community planning. This includes a trend within local government toward facilitating both internally 'joined up' work and external 'partnerships' to support the design and implementation of community development policy initiatives.

In this chapter, we draw on neo-institutional theory to examine the impacts on local governance of relationships between social enterprise and local government in the Victorian context. Much of neo-institutional theory has focused on tracing the ways in which institutions reproduce themselves through processes of isomorphism (DiMaggio and Powell 1983), emphasising variously the structural dimensions of isomorphism (Meyer and Rowan 1977; Tolbert and Zucker 1983; Zucker 1977) and the processes by which this occurs (Deephouse 1996; Haveman 1993). In the social enterprise literature, neo-institutionalism has been invoked by writers exploring the ways in which social enterprise practice is shaped by dominant – governmental and market – institutional logics within different settings (Aiken 2006; Dart 2004; Nicholls 2010a).

While neo-institutional theory has often been used to explain the similarity or stability of organisational arrangements within a given organisational field, some writers have considered the potential of neo-institutionalism to provide an explanatory framework for the transformative effects of the internal dynamics of organisations (Greenwood *et al.* 2011; McDonald and Warburton 2003; Greenwood and Hinings 1996). They have also sought to contest and extend neo-institutional theory through examinations of the causes of radical organisational change (Kraatz and Zajac 1996). These studies question the neo-institutional presumption of inevitable isomorphism at the level of the organisation. Yet, there has been relatively little examination within the neo-institutional framework of how *institutions* themselves change. In the last decade, some writers deploying neo-institutional frames in the analysis of governance have examined processes of institutional change that occur when governmental path dependencies are disrupted by the presence and interactions of multiple policy actors (Crouch and Farrell 2004; Lowndes 2005). This analytical approach has particular resonance in light of theories and practices of network governance, where governing is understood as processes of co-production of policy by a diversity of state and non-state actors.

In this chapter, we consider the ways in which locally focused social enterprises participate in and influence the institutions of local governance. Rather than focusing on the more commonly investigated question, 'how does the state shape social enterprise?', our inquiry examines whether, and how, social enterprise informs institutions of governance – and particularly the state – at the local level. Based on interview data from 24 people involved with 11 social enterprise–local government relationships in Victoria, we seek to explicate the ways in which some of the social enterprises in our sample have disrupted institutional norms, reframing dominant responses to governing through dialogic processes that unsettle day-to-day practice of local government staff and other institutional actors.

Definitions of social enterprise have been widely debated (Spear *et al.* 2009). For the purposes of analytic precision, we define social enterprises in this chapter as not-for-personal-profit organisations that exist to produce public benefits and trade in the market place in order to fulfil their mission (Barraket and Archer 2010). This definition is empirically derived from Australian experience and utilised by a number of Australian governments in operationalising their investment into social enterprise development. The social enterprises examined in this study operated in a number of industries and had diverse governance structures. However, all of them focused on producing benefits for a specific local population and did so by trading in local and regional markets.

Understanding the institutional context: social enterprise and public policy in Australia

Australia has a tradition of social enterprise and non-profit business ventures. Consumer and producer cooperatives have played a significant role in rural development, and friendly societies and credit unions have been a long-term part of the financial institutional landscape (Lyons 2001). In comparative terms, Australia has a highly enterprising non-profit-sector ranking ahead of both the US and the UK – although recent data suggest that its enterprising activity has fallen in relative terms in recent years (Salamon *et al.* 2013).

Since the introduction of the concept of social enterprise in the 1990s, there has been increased debate amongst Australian third sector practitioners and emergent social entrepreneurs about the nature of social enterprise, its potential value and implications for re-imagining civil society in a network era. Similarly to the experience in other countries (Defourny and Nyssens 2010; Kerlin 2006) this debate has often blurred the concepts of social enterprise, social entrepreneurship, social innovation and corporate social responsibility (Defourny and Nyssens 2010; Kerlin 2006).

While there is growing interest in social enterprise as a form of social innovation in Australia, there is no coherent movement or publicly recognisable social enterprise sector in the country. Australia is governed by three levels of government – federal, state and local. Across all levels of government, public policy support for social enterprise development has been relatively limited (Lyons and Passey 2006). The Victorian state Labor government was the first Australian government to invest in dedicated support for social enterprise development in 2004, and this investment has continued, albeit at reduced levels, under the successive conservative government. At the federal government level, social enterprise was valorised as a vehicle for employment creation in the Australian Federal Government's response to the 2008–9 global financial crisis and subsequent investments under the then Labor government included the establishment of a $40 million social enterprise development and investment fund to leverage private capital in support of social investment.

Local government interest in social enterprise development is variable. There are many cases of one-off support provided to social enterprise through standard community funding streams. A small number of metropolitan councils have partnered with a second-tier third sector organisation, Social Ventures Australia, to develop virtual social enterprise 'hubs' that provide business development services, networking opportunities and access to social venture capital to some social enterprises operating in or servicing their local government areas. In some small rural and remote towns, local governments have played a role in leveraging investment in support of community buyouts of various services, including service stations, convenience stores, cinemas, pubs and hospitals. Local government support for social enterprise appears to be growing, and reflects a general shift away from the 'rates, rubbish and roads' characterisation of Australian local governments of the past, toward an increased role in community development and social planning.

Conceptual approach

In this chapter, we emphasise the concept of new public governance, as well as new institutional theory, to examine the ways relationships among social enterprise, local governments and other policy actors reframe or disrupt normative practices.

A shift in language from 'government' to 'governance' has appeared in policy studies over the last 15 years (Considine 2001; Kooiman 2003; Rhodes 1997, 2007). This shift denotes a (not universally) recognised interpretive shift in the nature of policy making in a network era (Hajer and Wagenaar 2003). In broad terms, governance connotes a blurring of the traditional roles of governments, private sector and third sector actors and may be viewed as a combination of governing efforts by this range of public and private actors (Kooiman 2003).

New public governance includes market models of service provision, as well as more recent emphases on partnership and collaboration between sectors, often referred to as 'network governance' (Osborne 2006). The presumed virtue of these arrangements is that they

> provide hope for variety in organisation type to stimulate innovation, for private participation to shift capital costs off the public budget, to compel competitors to regulate one another, or to generate forms of non-profit service delivery that is voluntary and responsive to local needs.
>
> (Considine 2005, p. 166)

While not all forms of social enterprise are explicitly engaged in collaborative governance with state actors, the idea of social enterprise has clearly become instated in dominant narratives of governing as part of discursive trends toward shaping the 'governable terrain' (Carmel and Harlock 2008) of the third sector within a range of public policy regimes. Indeed an emergent trend in third sector discourse is to question the co-optation of third sector organisations into network collaborations, without a full understanding of the implications (Eikenberry and Kluver 2004; Eikenberry 2009). This raises questions about the influence of institutional norms on these processes of so-called co-production. In developing our analysis, we draw on neo-institutional theory to examine the effects on institutional arrangements of growing relationships between social enterprises and local governments within our research context. This, we hope, builds on existing analyses of social enterprise that utilise new institutional lenses (Aiken 2006; Dart 2004; Mason 2012; Nicholls 2010a, 2010b), but contrasts with it by examining the disruptive institutional work of social enterprise actors within governance networks.

Organisations are not institutions but, rather, are constituted in and by institutions, where we understand institutions to be the broader 'rules of the game' (Lowndes *et al.* 2006; Lowndes 2005). In these terms, to examine local governance "is to expand beyond technical processes and material requirements and explore informal aspects. These include aspects such as cultural norms and symbolic rituals…" (Mason *et al.* 2007, p. 292). While formal organisational structures may be useful guides to the hierarchy and authority embedded within institutions, neo-institutionalism allows that these can be eclipsed or subverted by competing 'informal systems' (Mason *et al.* 2007, p. 292). As Lowndes (2005) citing (Ostrom 1999) observes, a new institutional approach requires us not just to examine the 'rules in form' – or the stated practices of policy documented in organisational plans, policy framework etc. – but also the informal or unwritten customs and codes, the 'rules in use', enacted by policy actors within an institution.

Those examinations of social enterprise that draw on neo-institutional theoretical frames have tended toward an analysis of the isomorphic pressures brought to bear on social enterprises by dominant institutions (Desa 2012). For example, Dart (2004) suggests that social enterprise in post-industrial countries will increasingly command moral legitimacy – that is, normative legitimacy based on dominant political ideology – by emphasising its commercial and business-like characteristics over its capacity to create social value. He accounts for the recent popularity of social enterprises by suggesting that their practical legitimacy – that is, whether they produce any better social outcomes than other forms of social service delivery or community development activity – is less significant than their capacity to embody dominant values of commercial enterprise. Aiken (2006) also examines isomorphic pressures on social enterprise, although recognising, differently to Dart (2004), that social enterprises typically operate in both commercial markets and quasi-markets stimulated by governments. Aiken finds that the isomorphic pressures social enterprises face differ according to the markets in which they operate. For enterprises operating in a social welfare market, there is the danger of becoming passive agents of state programs, while for those operating in commercial markets, organisational values and social purpose may be too easily sacrificed in favour of commercialised private-sector business models (Aiken 2006, p. 268).

The focus of most writers in the neo-institutional tradition is on the homogenising effects of institutional fields. This ostensibly constructs institutional power as unidirectional, impersonal and inexorable. This rather centralised conception is curiously at odds with the simultaneous account of institutions as relational and multifarious systems of informal and formal rules of the game. The early literature on network governance was similarly concerned with the ways in which stability and the privilege of elite policy actors were sustained in policy networks (Rhodes 1997). More recently, however, Rhodes (2007) has suggested that explaining shifts from old forms of government to new systems of governance requires a decentred account of change. Specifically, (Rhodes 2007, pp. 1253–1254) argues that explaining changing conceptions of the state and governance requires us to simultaneously examine traditions – which explain how power, norms and order are instated and sustained – and dilemmas, which, he suggests, push people to reconsider their beliefs and the traditions that inform them, leading to reform through the contestation of meanings in action.

Methodology

Our research investigated the relationships between local social enterprise and local government in responding to community health and wellbeing. The project utilised a mixed-methods design (Creswell 2003), which involved an online survey of staff in all 79 Victorian councils, content analysis of municipal health and economic development plans, and in-depth interviewing of social enterprise managers, directors and local government staff or councillors involved in cases where local government–social enterprise relationships had been established.

We conducted in-depth interviews with 24 people. This included staff and members/participants of 11 locally focused social enterprises throughout Victoria, and local government staff and political leaders active in supporting social enterprise development. A snowball sampling approach was adopted, starting with contacts of social enterprise practitioners working with local government who were known to the researchers and the project advisory group. Our sample included representatives from regional, metropolitan and metropolitan fringe enterprises and covered three social enterprise models: intermediate labour market models – which provide training and employment opportunities in active industry contexts combined with strong social support; service models – which maintain or create new services in direct response to community needs, often in response to market and/or government failure; and income generation models – which generate surplus to support other public benefit activities. Interview data were analysed thematically, to identify commonalities and contradictions in respondents' experiences of working across social enterprise and local government in response to local residents' needs.

In order to further test and verify our analyses, we conducted two workshops: one with local government staff, which was attended by 14 people; and one with social enterprise practitioners, which was attended by eight people. These workshops were designed as discussion-based forums where we sought input and tested assumptions – both our participants and our own – through broad-based discussion of participants' experiences of working in both social enterprise and local government.

This chapter focuses on the case study aspect of the research, with a particular focus on deviant cases that illustrate the nature of unexpected outcomes relative to existing knowledge. A major advantage of deviant case studies is exploring the limits of a theory, by unmasking flaws previously concealed, e.g. through accommodative research designs or prevailing institutional norms of practice (Odell 2001). Thus a deviant case seeks to disrupt such patterns of concealment, portraying a version of social reality breaking from received wisdom. Three such cases presented in the research and their characteristics are summarised in Table 10.1.

Table 10.1 Summary of social enterprises and their local government relationships

Social enterprise type	Nature of local government relationship	Geographic location
Community-owned business, providing a revitalised entertainment venue of heritage significance	Initiated by the community; local government provided seed funding to support further fundraising to acquire the site, and access to a liaison officer to help coordinate the building redevelopment project	Rural
Work Integration Social Enterprise owned by a large non-profit, providing street cleaning services	Contracting of the social enterprise by council; initiated by the social enterprise based on past experience of working together between the parties	Inner Metropolitan
Work Integration Social Enterprise and community space owned by consortium of small non-profit agencies, providing food, retail and hospitality services	Lease tendered to the social enterprise by council; relationship initiated by council to improve amenities within the local community centre.	Outer Metropolitan

Our focus in this chapter is on the 'stories less told' in our interview data, augmented by workshop reflections. Our purpose is to examine examples where our participating social enterprises posed challenges or disruption to the rules in use through their interactions with local governance institutions. We are not seeking to present these findings as representative of the wider experience of Australian social enterprise, but to examine the particular and the irreducible in the grounded experience of the people and organisations with whom we conducted this research.

Social enterprises disrupting institutional norms

As organisations that explicitly bridge both social and economic domains, social enterprises potentially pose challenges to the traditional siloes of government. Below, we draw on two specific examples drawn from our interview data of how small institutional ruptures to local governance were effected through the activities of social enterprises that were working with or through local government in our sample.

Within a wider set of narratives about the isomorphic effects of working with local government, a number of our social enterprise respondents related stories of reconfiguring institutional practices to accord with their own organisational needs and social objectives. In a small number of instances, it appears that the iterative effects of local government relationships with social enterprise led to examples of local councils 'doing government differently'. Two themes of institutional disruption – or, at least, irritation – emerged within our sample. The first constellation of stories emphasised the combined social and economic imperatives of social enterprise forcing integrated or 'joined up' practice across functional areas of local government. The second, and prominent, theme related to the reconfiguration of institutional space produced by certain types and locations of social enterprise.

Compelling joining up

As discussed earlier, social enterprise operates purposefully and simultaneously within social and economic domains. As businesses with a social purpose, they combine the imperatives of business management with social, environmental, economic or cultural development goals. Their purpose and processes consequently transcend traditional divisions between social and economic domains enacted in governmental institutions. While the majority of social enterprise respondents related experiences of frustration and dysfunction in working across functional areas of local government, we heard several stories where the needs of social enterprise had, either purposefully or incidentally, forced the 'joining up' of different areas of local government. In one case, a nascent social enterprise group described the difficulties of, and their response to, working across functional divisions of local government that talked different languages and did not understand the integration of business and social principles embedded in social enterprise.

> but then [our idea went] into a part of council that – that was really hard because we ended up being in the sort of business, or the business part of council, the bean counters and the people who actually need to make sure – property management; people who know how to write up a good lease, had no concept whatsoever for what we were – we'd sit down and have meetings and it was like all the different species. We'd be going on about the vision and all that sort of stuff, and they'd be going "Well where's your business plan?" "Okay, that will come, but we want to talk about vision". That was very frustrating. So in the end, we circumvented that a little bit by saying "We think it's time to get the visionary back to the table, so we kind of called and asked them to have a meeting back with the [staff from the community and health services division of Council] who had the sort of foresight, and that kind of – we got around it. But I think that is an issue, not just with this but with lots of projects with council. They're such big organisations, they have so many layers to them that if you could cut through some of that red tape – it's just I don't know how you overcome that.

In this case, social enterprise practitioners deployed their experiential knowledge of institutional practice to circumvent local government's disparate community development and business development norms. By bringing all parties to the table, they forced a negotiation around the start-up of the social enterprise that was competent to meet both its social and business objectives. A subsequent interview with one council staff member involved in this process indicated that this had had a small flow-on effect to other council processes, by encouraging further coordination amongst the participating staff on other unrelated projects.

While this example illustrates a purposeful negotiation by social enterprise practitioners, other stories emphasised the role of 'institutional entrepreneurs' (Tracey *et al.* 2011) within local government working to join up internal council processes in support of social enterprise objectives. In these cases, council staff, or in one case a local councillor, acted as network brokers, working across functional areas of local government to facilitate the planning or start-up of a social enterprise. Qualitative accounts suggested that staff from social and health divisions of council were more frequently described as network brokers than those from economic development divisions.

While our focus in this research was on the integration of social and economic domains, our findings suggested that the industry orientation of social enterprise could also facilitate incidental joining up across other domains of local government. In the case of one enterprise in our sample – a street cleaning business owned by a local welfare agency – the council's involvement stimulated a new relationship between its engineering and facilities department and the community services unit. At the time of conducting the research, interviewees indicated that involvement with the social enterprise had facilitated a preliminary discussion within council about how it might better support both resident employment and service delivery through utilising some aspects of its facilities provision as intermediate labour market programs to train and employ local residents. It is unlikely that this conversation about how to 'do government differently' would have been initiated across these government divisions without the imperative to engage around the procurement of services from the social enterprise concerned.

Reconfiguring institutional space

Following Lefebvre's (1991) work on the social production of space, we can understand local civic spaces as being institutionally configured. Space is both materially shaped by institutional actors – for example, through planning and design – and shaped by the interactions of those institutional actors who use it. A dominant theme in our research was the role of social enterprises in the reshaping of civic and commercial spaces. This included common stories of social enterprises taking over and revamping disused council premises, including leveraging significant external finance to rehabilitate civic buildings – such as disused theatres and offices – for the purposes of public benefit.

Beyond physical improvements, the sociality of 'doing social enterprise' also involved the reinvigoration of social activity within given spaces, as people from across a locale become involved in the start up, management and use of social enterprise. In some cases, these were stand-alone activities independent of local government beyond the use or takeover of council premises. In others, they involved local government investment in accessing premises and/or supporting enterprise start up, for example the development of a community-owned cinema and theatre space in rural Victoria reshaped a disused civic space into a leisure space for the local residents. In this case, the local council provided $25,000 seeding money to assist with internal redesign of the space and the services of a local government community liaison officer to assist the auspicing group with the planning and paperwork associated with establishing the enterprise. (Auspicing is an arrangement where one organisation agrees to receive project funds on behalf of another group which is running the project.) Prior to its establishment, the nearest cinema was 90 minutes' drive away by car and could not be easily accessed by public transport. Apart from producing a new service, the planning and design of the space was explicitly concerned with meeting the leisure needs of different groups within the local area by seeking involvement from these groups in the establishment of the enterprise. The design and building processes themselves fostered relationships amongst local residents, as one person who was involved in the start-up of the enterprise described:

> There has been a whole lot of social benefit out of it from a whole series
> of people involved; there has been a series of networks developed

between young people and older people. We had secondary college students involved in building a part of the project, so that they had some real ownership. We had a lot of; we were fortunate in that some of the people who originally worked at [the theatre], which closed in 1972, were still around, so we could talk directly with them and get the oral history of the people who participated. So, we had a number of working bees where people; the kids who worked on their part of the project and the people who had worked [in the theatre] 30 years ago, were in the same place at the same time, so that interaction was really good.

These interactions fostered a strong sense of local ownership of the enterprise and the space it inhabits:

The kids will come down and say "yeah, well I built that, that was me". So they have a connection with it, and I think that connection will add to the long-term sustainability, because they have some real owner-ship of it.

The story presented by interviewees involved in this social enterprise was one of both local economic and social regeneration, where these two processes are explicitly interlinked; that is, supporting local economic development by building a community-owned enterprise was experienced as a distinctly social experience. In terms of local governance, the story was one of local and dis-persed civic ownership producing a wide commitment amongst residents to the use and sustainability of the enterprise. What was previously a disused council space had become, at the time of conducting the research, a site for connecting residents in positive ways to their built environment, each other, and their local economic destiny.

In a different example of a purposeful partnership between local govern-ment and social enterprise, a social enterprise training cafe provided a leisure space for community members to interact while using the wider facilities and services deliberately co-located by the local council. It provided the first point of contact with this service space, with the cafe acting as an entry and information point. A member of staff at the local council articulated the role of the social enterprise as providing a gateway to engagement between local residents and the various services available, as well as providing a point of connection between residents and the voluntary sector and training organisa-tions that are partners to the social enterprise:

The role that we saw the community cafe playing was to provide a sense of community activity and welcoming for people who were coming to use various parts of the community centre ... [T]he cafe runs as an integral part of a much larger community centre dealing with population groups that come through the centre...

In this case, the social enterprise provided an accessible 'community site' within a space dominated by governmental services. Interviewees from both local government and social enterprise sides of this initiative saw a major value of the social enterprise as being its role as a 'bridge' for residents into the unfamiliar institutional spaces of local government and other service providers.

Discussion and conclusion

New institutional approaches to local governance enable us to examine the ways in which institutions both change and stay the same through dialogic and contested processes that challenge or reinforce the rules in use. As forms of citizen-led activity that purposefully transcend economic and social domains, the social enterprises examined in this research have stimulated some disruptions to the institutions of local governance in our research setting.

As Lowndes (2005) observes, new institutionalism allows us to examine "different trajectories of change and continuity within the sets of rules that shape local governance" (p. 297). While our focus in this chapter is on questions of institutional disruption, we note that, consistent with Aiken (2006), our research uncovered more stories of isomorphism amongst social enterprises working with local government than it did stories of institutional transformation, or even irritation. In keeping with the potentiality of new institutionalism to illuminate "how paths widen over time as they gradually encompass smaller tracks" (Lowndes 2005, p. 299), we have nevertheless sought to present the 'stories less told' in order to understand the possibilities for institutional change produced where social enterprises – as policy actors characterised by hybridity – are engaged in local governance.

We do not wish to overstate the impacts of these disruptions. Institutional change happens slowly (Pierson 2003) and is more often accidental than purposeful. Clearly, relations of power play a significant role in the construction of so-called 'creative spaces' (Lowndes 2005) for institutional change, and our research uncovered more stories of state-led co-optation and isomorphism than it did social enterprise-led disruption. Our findings do suggest, however, that, where local governments and social enterprises are purposefully engaging with each other, the hybridity of social enterprise influences institutional practice in some instances, challenging path dependence and leading to adaptations of the rules in use by local government. This suggests that, in contrast to many existing neo-institutional analyses of social enterprises (Aiken 2006; Dart 2004; Nicholls 2010b), these organisations behave in a 'collegially disruptive' way, and are less driven by pressures toward institutional conformity. Indeed, consistent with Desa's (2012) analysis in the context of international social entrepreneurship, we found examples where the multi-resource and multi-stakeholder nature of social enterprise drives resource acquisition and local opportunity exploitation activities that (re)combine institutional resources in ways that necessarily challenge institutional norms. For organisations with relatively small resource bases, locally oriented social enterprises become active network partners and utilise their own cultural norms to shape the 'rules in use', which they deploy to assist their own opportunities in the network.

In cases where locally focused social enterprises are not working purposefully with local government, they may still influence the institutions of local governance through the transformation of civic and commercial spaces in ways that are consistent with new governance emphases on citizen participation and the co-production of social value beyond government (Ryan 2012). Recent research on social enterprise as hybrid organisations has traced the competing institutional logics that operate within them (Battilana and Dorado 2010; Mullins *et al.* 2012). The research discussed in this chapter suggests that this competition manifests externally, in ways that contest – and in rare cases reshape – the institutional norms of local governance.

Acknowledgements

The research discussed in this chapter was funded by a Victorian Public Health Research Grant. Blake Blain assisted with copy editing. Our thanks to our reviewers for their useful suggestions.

References

Aiken, M 2006, 'Towards market or state? Tensions and opportunities in the evolutionary path of three UK social enterprises', in M Nyssens (ed.), *Social enterprise: at the crossroads of market, public policies and civil society*, Routledge, London and New York.

Barraket, J (ed.) 2008, *Strategic issues for the not-for-profit sector*, UNSW Press, Sydney.

Barraket, J and Archer, V 2010, 'Social inclusion through community enterprise? Examining the available evidence', *Third Sector Review*, vol. 16, no. 1, pp. 13–28.

Battilana, J and Dorado, S 2010, 'Building sustainable hybrid organizations: the case of commercial microfinance organizations', *Academy of Management Journal*, vol. 53, no. 6, pp. 1419–1440.

Battilana, J and Lee, M 2014, 'Advancing research on hybrid organizing – insights from the study of social enterprises', *The Academy of Management Annals*, vol. 8, no. 1, pp. 397–441.

Carmel, E and Harlock, J 2008, 'Instituting the "third sector" as a governable terrain: partnership, procurement and performance in the UK', *Policy and Politics*, vol. 36, pp. 155–171.

Considine, M 2001, *Enterprising states: the public management of welfare-to-work*, Cambridge University Press, Cambridge.

Considine, M 2005, *Making public policy: institutions, actors, strategies*, Polity, Cambridge, UK.

Creswell, J 2003, *Research design: qualitative, quantitative, and mixed methods and approaches*, 2nd edn, Sage Publications, London.

Crouch, C and Farrell, H 2004, 'Breaking the path of institutional development? Alternatives to the new determinism', *Rationality and Society*, vol. 16, no. 1, pp. 5–43.

Dart, R 2004, 'The legitimacy of social enterprise', *Nonprofit Management and Leadership*, vol. 14, no. 4, pp. 411–424.

Deephouse, D L 1996, 'Does isomorphism legitimate?', *Academy of Management Journal*, vol. 39, no. 4, pp. 1024–1039.

Defourny, J and Nyssens, M 2010, 'Conceptions of social enterprise and social entrepreneurship in Europe and the United States: convergences and divergences', *Journal of Social Entrepreneurship*, vol. 1, no. 1, pp. 32–53.

Desa, G 2012, 'Resource mobilization in international social entrepreneurship: bricolage as a mechanism of institutional transformation', *Entrepreneurship Theory and Practice*, vol. 36, no. 4, pp. 727–751.

DiMaggio, P J and Powell, W W 1983, 'The iron cage revisited: institutional isomorphism and collective rationality in organizational fields', *American Sociological Review*, vol. 48, no. 2, pp. 147–160.

Eikenberry, A M 2009, 'Refusing the market: a democratic discourse for voluntary and non-profit organizations', *Nonprofit and Voluntary Sector Quarterly*, vol. 38, no. 4, pp. 582–596.

Eikenberry, A M and Kluver, J D 2004, 'The marketization of the nonprofit sector: civil society at risk?', *Public Administration Review*, vol. 64, issue 2, pp. 132–140.

Gardin, L 2006, 'A variety of resource mixes inside social enterprises', in M Nyssens (ed.), *Social enterprise: at the crossroads of market, public policies and civil society*, Routledge, London, pp. 111–136.

Greenwood, R and Hinings, C R 1996, 'Understanding radical organizational change: bringing together the old and the new institutionalism', *The Academy of Management Review*, vol. 21, no. 4, pp. 1022–1054.

Greenwood, R, Raynard, M, Kodeih, F, Micelotta, E R and Lounsbury, M 2011, 'Institutional complexity and organizational responses', *The Academy of Management Annals*, vol. 5, no. 1, pp. 317–371.

Hajer, M A and Wagenaar, H 2003, *Deliberative policy analysis: understanding governance in the network society*, Cambridge University Press, Cambridge.

Haveman, H A 1993, 'Follow the leader: mimetic isomorphism and entry into new markets', *Administrative Science Quarterly*, vol. 38, no. 4, p. 593.

Kerlin, J 2006, 'Social enterprise in the United States and Europe: understanding and learning from the differences', *Voluntas: International Journal of Voluntary and Nonprofit Organizations*, vol. 17, no. 310.1007/s11266–006–9016–2, pp. 246–262.

Kooiman, J 2003, *Governing as governance*, SAGE, Thousand Oaks, CA, viewed 30 September, 2013, http://site.ebrary.com/id/10369672.

Kraatz, M S and Zajac, E J 1996, 'Exploring the limits of the new institutionalism: the causes and consequences of illegitimate organizational change', *American Sociological Review*, vol. 61, no. 5, pp. 812–836.

Lefebvre, H 1991, *The production of space*, D Nicholson-Smith, trans. Basil Blackwell, Oxford.

Lowndes, V 2005, 'Something old, something new, something borrowed...', *Policy Studies*, vol. 26, no. 3–4, pp. 291–309.

Lowndes, V, Pratchett, L and Stoker, G 2006, 'Local political participation: the impact of rules-in-use', *Public Administration*, vol. 84, no. 3, pp. 539–561.

Lyons, M 2001, *Third sector: the contribution of nonprofit and cooperative enterprise in Australia*, Allen & Unwin, St Leonards, NSW.

Lyons, M and Passey, A 2006, 'Need public policy ignore the third sector? Government policy in Australia and the United Kingdom', *Australian Journal of Public Administration*, vol. 65, pp. 90–102.

Mason, C 2012, 'Isomorphism, social enterprise and the pressure to maximise social benefit', *Journal of Social Entrepreneurship*, vol. 3, no. 1, pp. 74–95.

Mason, C, Kirkbride, J and Bryde, D 2007, 'From stakeholders to institutions: the changing face of social enterprise governance theory', *Management Decision*, vol. 45, no. 2, pp. 284–301.

McDonald, C and Warburton, J 2003, 'Stability and change in nonprofit organizations: the volunteer contribution', *Voluntas: International Journal of Voluntary and Nonprofit Organizations*, vol. 14, no. 4, pp. 381–399.

Meyer, J W and Rowan, B 1977, 'Institutionalized organizations: formal structure as myth and ceremony', *American Journal of Sociology*, vol. 83, no. 2, pp. 340–363.

Mullins, D, Czischke, D and van Bortel, G 2012, 'Exploring the meaning of hybridity and social enterprise in housing organisations', *Housing Studies*, vol. 27, no. 4, pp. 405–417.

Nicholls, A 2010a, 'The legitimacy of social entrepreneurship: reflexive isomorphism in a pre-paradigmatic field', *Entrepreneurship Theory and Practice*, vol. 34, no. 4, pp. 611–633.

Nicholls, A 2010b, 'Institutionalizing social entrepreneurship in regulatory space: reporting and disclosure by community interest companies', *Accounting, Organizations and Society*, vol. 35, no. 4, pp. 394–415.

Odell, J 2001, 'Case study methods in international political economy', *International Studies Perspectives*, vol. 2, no. 2, pp. 161–176.

Osborne, S P 2006, 'The new public governance? 1', *Public Management Review*, vol. 8, no. 3, pp. 377–387.

Ostrom, E 1999, 'Institutional rational choice: an assessment of the institutional analysis and development framework', in *Theories of the Policy Process*, Westview, Boulder, CO.

Pierson, C 2003, 'Learning from Labor? Welfare policy transfer between Australia and Britain', *Commonwealth and Comparative Politics*, vol. 41, no. 1, pp. 77–100.

Reddel, T 2004, 'Third way social governance: where is the state?', *Australian Journal of Social Issues*, vol. 39, no. 2, pp. 129–142.

Reid, K and Griffith, J 2006, 'Social enterprise mythology: critiquing some assumptions', *Social Enterprise Journal*, vol. 2, no. 1, pp. 1–10.

Rhodes, R A W 1997, *Understanding governance : policy networks, governance, reflexivity and accountability*, Open University Press, Buckingham.

Rhodes, R A W 2007, 'Understanding governance: ten years on', *Organization Studies*, vol. 28, no. 8, pp. 1243–1264.

Røiseland, A 2011, 'Understanding local governance: institutional forms of collaboration', *Public Administration*, vol. 89, no. 3, pp. 879–893.

Ryan, B 2012, 'Co-production: option or obligation?', *Australian Journal of Public Administration*, vol. 71, no. 3, pp. 314–324.

Salamon, L M, Sokolowski, S W, Haddock, M A and Tice, H S 2013, *The state of global civil society and volunteering: latest findings from the implementation of the UN Nonprofit Handbook (2013)*, (No. 49), Center for Civil Society Studies, viewed 19 May 2015, http://ccss.jhu.edu/wp-content/uploads/downloads/2013/04/JHU_Global-Civil-Society-Volunteering_FINAL_3.2013.pdf.

Spear, R, Cornforth, C and Aiken, M 2009, 'The governance challenges of social enterprises: evidence from a UK empirical study', *Annals of Public and Cooperative Economics*, vol. 80, no. 2, pp. 247–273.

Teasdale, S 2010, 'How can social enterprise address disadvantage? Evidence from an inner city community', *Journal of Nonprofit and Public Sector Marketing*, vol. 22, no. 2, p. 89.

Thompson, J 2011, 'Reflections on social enterprise and the big society', *Social Enterprise Journal*, vol. 7, no. 3, pp. 219–223.

Tolbert, P S and Zucker, L G 1983, 'Institutional sources of change in the formal structure of organizations: the diffusion of civil service reform, 1880–1935', *Administrative Science Quarterly*, vol. 28, no. 1, pp. 22–39.

Tracey, P, Phillips, N and Jarvis, O 2011, 'Bridging institutional entrepreneurship and the creation of new organizational forms: a multilevel model', *Organization Science*, vol. 22, no. 1, pp. 60–80.

Zucker, L G 1977, 'The role of institutionalization in cultural persistence', *American Sociological Review*, vol. 42, no. 5, pp. 726–743.

11 How better methods for coping with uncertainty and ambiguity can strengthen government–civil society collaboration

Mark Matthews

Introduction

This chapter considers the implications for collaboration with government that stem from broader efforts to improve how governments cope with uncertainty, ambiguity and risk.[1] The issue of how well governments handle uncertainty, ambiguity and risk is important because it impacts upon the cost efficiency and the effectiveness with which public services are delivered. When public administration principles and systems are focused on coping with uncertainty, ambiguity and risk there is a reduced likelihood that tax-payers' funds will be wasted. This is because attempts to govern as if uncertainty, ambiguity and risk can, both in principle and in practice, be avoided tends to result in a range of inter-connected problems associated with attempts to achieve a level of precision and 'the right solutions' that are, in many cases, impossible to achieve simply because the world does not work in the sort of way that current public management principles would like it to. In contrast, if policy and its delivery are approached as processes of learning-by-doing in an ambiguous and uncertain world then effective policy will inevitably require adjustment and effective responses to unanticipated events. This approach is referred to here as *intelligence-based policymaking*. If those adjustments and responses are made more difficult by prevailing norms, procedures and guidelines that neglect the importance of intelligence-based policymaking, then public expenditure can be wasted.

These issues are discussed in detail in Matthews (2016) and include a discussion of how governing effectively and efficiently can require governments espousing 'evidence-based policymaking' to open up the black box of the technical issues faced in determining what evidence is, how it should be assessed, analysed – *and used* in practice. The book pays particular attention to the potential usefulness of Bayesian inference as a technique for implementing intelligence-based policymaking by helping governments cope with uncertainty, ambiguity and risk – particularly when standardised Bayesian approaches are used that, by design, align with the different stages in familiar policy formulation, delivery, and monitoring and evaluation cycles.

A Bayesian implementation of the policy learning cycle is advocated because it:

- Directly reflects the ways in which governments must make difficult decisions under conditions of substantive uncertainty, ambiguity and risk – decisions in which prior assumptions based on experience to date are central to grappling with what the future *may* have in store.[2]
- Provides a technically tractable means of monitoring and evaluating governments' performance when designing, testing and learning from new approaches to public policy (i.e. supports the implementation of experimentalist governance as advocated by Sabel and Zeitlin (2012)). In that approach, which resonates with a Bayesian perspective but does not explicitly adopt Bayesian methods, intended outcomes are broad, provisional and can be modified in the light of experience.[3] Governance shifts from a command and control architecture to a distributed learning architecture – a mode better suited to handling complex situations with ambiguous cause and effect relationships. In such situations, effective public policy should not be a matter of 'getting things right' ex ante, but rather, establishing the conditions for learning-by-doing in an uncertain world in which objectives are rarely 'right' in the light of hindsight and unfolding, frequently unexpected, events and experiences. However, it is worth bearing in mind that more traditional command and control stances can be satisfactory when simple problems with well-understood cause and effect relationships are faced.
- Opens up avenues for leveraging a substantial and highly relevant body of analytical work that lies at the interfaces between information theory, statistical methods, physics, astronomy and cryptography, all of which share an emphasis on information uncertainty and the concept of (Shannon) entropy and have drawn upon Bayesian inference to advance these analytical methods.
- Requires only that decision-makers use the data and insights at their disposal (however limited) and not, as sampling theory-based concepts of statistical significance require, a larger set of assumed statistical distributions against which the likelihood that the specific dataset has been observed is assessed.

Examining these matters requires a discipline, and subject area, spanning approach, due to the wide scope of Bayesian analytical work coupled with the challenge of identifying useful insights for improving how we manage the policy learning process.

The picture that emerges from analysing this broad body of (often highly mathematical) work is that the key lessons for public policy are profound but do not necessarily require sophisticated mathematical treatments to get the main messages across. In the main, these key messages stem from the ways in which research in science, engineering and medicine (and some parts of economics) all highlight the following basic principles:

- Substantive uncertainty (i.e. ignorance) should not be assumed away as an analytical inconvenience. Rather, its reduction should be treated as the primary objective of investing in improved understanding (i.e. research and learning-by-doing in implementing policy). This focus requires that measures of the impact of substantive uncertainty on current understanding be used in order to calibrate decision making.
- Risk stems from the existence of substantive uncertainty and therefore cannot be decreased without reducing substantive uncertainty itself – a process with decreasing marginal returns to investment. Consequently, risk is a fact of life in public policy that governments must learn to live with rather than treat risk management as a compliance exercise.
- Given substantive uncertainty and risk as unavoidable realities, efficient and effective governance should not attempt to attain spurious precision in 'getting a policy right' at the outset and then doggedly delivering it. Policy should be an adaptive learning process. This requires suitable metrics – metrics which we do not have readily at hand within government at present, largely because the emphasis is upon hitting well-defined performance targets rather than demonstrating whether substantive uncertainty and risk have been reduced (or not) – and estimating the social and private benefits of those impacts.
- Claude Shannon's (1948) concept of entropy in an information-related system, defined on the basis of the differential predictability of future information content, may provide a useful practical basis for measuring policy learning at a general level: the less likely an event is assumed to be, the greater the information gain *if* it is observed.[4]

This perspective creates a link between our assumptions about the likelihood of a range of events actually happening (and being observed) in the future and the value of the information we obtain by research and learning-by-doing. Research and learning-by-doing can result in information gains when unlikely events are observed because they require us to change our theories, models and hypotheses. While this is a familiar concept in financial economics (and considered to some extent in public policy from that specific angle), it would be useful to use this approach at a general level in public policy. In particular, it provides the basis for measuring the extent of learning-by-doing in policy implementation (or enhanced levels of preparedness) as an outcome from government spending. Any change in, or addition to, the set of assumed event likelihoods that may be faced in the future creates the basis for assessing changes in Shannon entropy.

We need to have postulated that an event is a 'theoretical' possibility, or have updated our likelihood estimate for its occurrence, in order to be able to assess the information gain *if* the event does happen. A Bayesian approach to public policy consequently creates the potential to think differently, and more constructively, about how we go about public management in general, and risk management in particular.

The purpose of this chapter is to focus on one specific issue within this analytical framework: *can a standardised Bayesian approach to 'evidence' open up useful new avenues for civil society to engage with, and contribute to, public policy?* This engagement issue is important because, in an uncertain, ambiguous and risky world, governments are prudent to seek to maximise both the range of information at their disposal and their capability to analyse and react to this information. If relevant information is ignored, then the likelihood that a policy intervention will fail to meet expectations, or have negative unintended consequences, increases. Consequently, it makes considerable sense for governments to find more effective ways of collaborating with both academia and civil society than are evident at present – methods that jointly exploit the tacit knowledge accumulated in civil society on strengths and shortcomings in service delivery combined with the technical/analytical expertise in academia (especially evidence in social and health policy).

The first part of the chapter establishes the basic point that, as uncertainty and risk managers of 'last resort', governments have to learn-by-doing through using the evidence-base that they currently have, i.e. to conjecture about what the future may have in store for us – and to prepare for those possible circumstances. This learning process of conjectures and tests against what actually happens is central to what governments do. For example, a poverty reduction intervention may or may not prove to be as effective as intended (or may be more effective than anticipated). Implementing the intervention is therefore a test of a hypothesis about useful solutions, and an opportunity to learn-by-doing. The aim is to increase the likelihood of getting close to what actually happens – but recognise the impossibility of being fully 'correct' in forecasts and predictions (and avoiding being pressured to be accountable for not being 'correct'). The second part explains the relevance of Bayesian inference to governments' role as uncertainty and risk manager of last resort. The third part of the chapter highlights the ways in which a standardised Bayesian framework can be developed as a tool for handling and using evidence in the policy cycle. The fourth part of the chapter explores how a Bayesian approach to public management has the potential to bring civil society entities (especially those involved in 'front line' service delivery) into the policy cycle as key actors. Finally, the fifth part of the chapter concludes by considering ways of taking this collaborative approach forward.

The key point running through these arguments is that all policy interventions are effectively hypotheses being tested via experimentation. Consequently, the formulation of these hypotheses (i.e. piloted policy interventions), as well as the processes that assess and evaluate their effectiveness, should be domains in which collaboration takes place – mainly because this maximises access to useful information and ideas.

How reading Machiavelli helps to calibrate the concept of evidence-based policy[5]

In *The Discourses*, Niccolò Machiavelli refers to Xenophon and stresses the importance of learning how to quickly recognise patterns in landscapes (Machiavelli 2003). As he remarks, "For all countries and all their parts have about them a certain uniformity, so that from the knowledge of one it is easy to pass to the knowledge of another."[6] It is useful to treat this as a metaphor for the roles of evidence and conjecture about the unknown in public policy – about handling the known *and* the unknown. If we take the time to consider the terrain that can be seen (the known) and to try to identify general patterns in the landscape, then that can help us to visualise what (for example) the unseen valley to one side might look like (the unknown). If one makes a habit of visualising the unseen valley on the basis of the known valley and then bothers to take a look into the next valley in order to see how accurate the conjecture was, one learns how to get better over time at this process of inferring the unknown from the known. As Machiavelli suggests, learning how to identify patterns in landscapes that allow us to improve conjectures about what unseen terrain might look like can be critically important in a skirmish or battle. In those frantic situations it may be necessary to visualise what the terrain in an adjacent unknown valley may look like in order to give orders to troops during a battle – with no time to scout out that valley (i.e. gather more evidence). The decision must be made on the basis of conjecture, not robust evidence.

Machiavelli's advice on constantly searching for general patterns in terrain is an important one for public policy in general. Governments must constantly learn-by-doing in improving their ability to conjecture about the unknown on the basis of the known. The unseen valley is a metaphor for what we now call 'horizon scanning' – but we only see the ridge defined by current evidence, not what lies beyond it. In Shannon's terms, the unseen valley beyond the observed ridge is entropy (i.e. the information we do not yet have – and valued in inverse proportion to the assumed likelihood of receiving different signals in the future).

This aspect can be challenging for academics and civil society entities collaborating with government because they are required to move outside of the comfort zone of the evidence base (the valley they are in) and speculate about the terrain in the valley for which they have no immediate evidence. Some are able to do this – others are not. Those that can do this are especially useful to governments because they can assist in one of the most challenging issues for governments – helping to be better prepared for dealing with the, as yet unknown, factors that may eventuate at some point in the future. Civil society organisations operating at the front line of service delivery are especially well positioned to pick up weak signals (indications of possible larger-scale changes) and to identify patterns in the present that can generate conjectures about possible future circumstances.

The existence of Shannon entropy in public policy means that the notion of 'evidence-based policymaking' it is not a panacea – it restricts us to the valley we know, not the unknown valley that we might have to make decisions about with little or no robust evidence. Taking this point further, politics and policy do not have an easy 'technocratic' relationship with each other that is 'solved' by evidence. Indeed the tensions between politics and policy are inherent to creativity, innovation and the democratic process. Politics is well suited to decision making under substantive uncertainty. Political decisions, like Machiavelli's advice on understanding terrain, must frequently be made without adequate evidence – there is no option to defer a decision until more evidence becomes available. That is a luxury for academics that policymakers do not have.

The policy process requires treatments of evidence that extend beyond detective work in the analysis of evidence from the past (what happened and why) into risk management and preparedness (what *may happen* in the future given uncertainties and risks and what could be done to reduce the likelihood of unwanted outcomes). This means that 'preparedness' is, and should always be, a key outcome from what governments do (Matthews 2009b).[7] It also means that the ability to learn-by-doing in an uncertain and changing world enhances preparedness.

Indeed, theory, in a range of guises, plays an important and valuable role in both politically driven policy and 'policy-driven' policy. Effective and practically applicable theories help us to make sense of complexity and make decisions when little evidence is available. Theory also drives policy experiments and innovation (for example privatisation in the 1980s). Theory allows us to speculate about the (as yet) unknown on the basis of what we believe we know. In contrast, evidence is currently treated as engendering 'proof' of cause and effect for things that have happened in the past – proof arrived at in the main only after lengthy and costly research activities. This would be fine *if* public policy was (say) a criminal court hearing (which it is not – unless of course things go badly wrong). In general terms, the greater the combined impact of the rate of change in pertinent conditions together with the degree of uncertainty and risk, the less useful, and indeed even dangerous, a reliance on evidence-based policymaking alone. Evidence-based approaches (as currently formulated) also suffer from long time lags and relevance deficits that reduce their utility to policymakers.

Figure 11.1 illustrates the principle that uncertainty over understanding both the future *and* past experiences should, ideally, be treated as a 'U' shaped curve that reaches its lowest point in the immediate past (lags in receiving and assessing information mean that there is always more uncertainty over the present than the immediate past). Although there is far greater uncertainty in regard to what the future may involve, we can never be certain about our understanding of the lessons from experience to date. All other things being equal, we are more uncertain the further we go into the past.

This approach to articulating the relationship between evidence-based policymaking and intelligence-based policymaking is based upon the notion

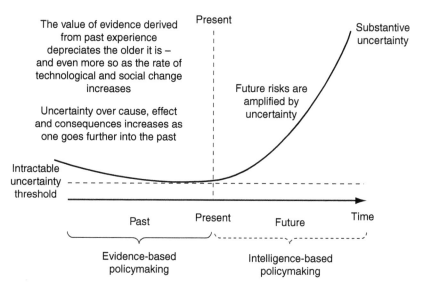

Figure 11.1 Asymmetries in uncertainty between the future and the past.

of discount rate symmetry with regard to the future *and* the past. Just as we apply a discount rate to assumptions and estimates relating to the future, we should also apply a discount rate to the past. The value of findings obtained from the analysis of the *past* (i.e. the evidence base) does not eliminate uncertainty and risk over what actually happened and what actually caused this. Consequently, from a decision-making perspective, uncertainty, ambiguity and risk do not just relate to the future – they also relate to our understanding of history and the lessons for decisions that need to be made today about what to do in the future. These points reinforce the usefulness of Bayesian methods in a public policy context because they have an explicit emphasis on valuing information gain over time against changes in entropy (the less likely the assumed incidence of an event the more information provided if it is observed).

If we have a low tolerance for uncertainty and ambiguity in the manner in which we govern, then we lock ourselves into a cost-escalation spiral driven by attempts to reduce ambiguity – especially if big data and associated ICT costs are involved. In a manner similar to the arms race dynamic, we have to spend more and more taxpayers' funds to try to re-assure ourselves that we know what our stakeholders are doing. This stance reduces empowerment and fosters a passive, compliance-oriented culture, as has occurred under many new public management reforms. In addition to fostering dependency on the state rather than encouraging self-reliance (thus increasing the burden on public expenditure), a public policy dimension of the double hermeneutic also comes into play: if I let you know the theories I have about you, you may change your behaviour in response and cause that theory to become untrue (Giddens 1984). This can drive up the cost of governance by increasing the risk that public expenditure will fail to deliver intended outcomes. This contrasts with the alternative of fostering a tolerance for uncertainty and ambiguity with the aim of breaking this cost-escalation cycle and, in so doing, encouraging self-reliance, innovation etc. The two contrasting dynamics are illustrated in Figures 11.2 and 11.3.

It is important to set clear transgression boundaries when being more tolerant of ambiguity and uncertainty (i.e. identifying the circumstances and behaviours which suggest I should stop trusting you). The ability to test the

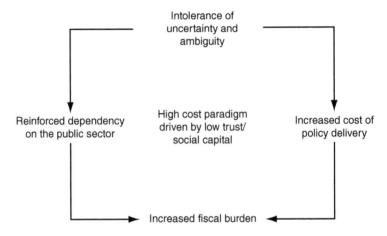

Figure 11.2 How an intolerance for uncertainty and ambiguity increases governance costs.

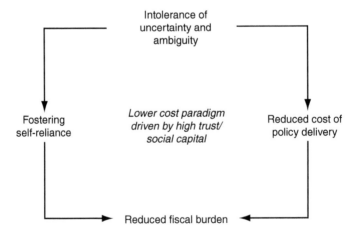

Figure 11.3 How a tolerance for uncertainty and ambiguity decreases governance costs.

relative plausibility of competing hypotheses, given current evidence, that is integral to Bayesian inference provides the basis for setting these transgression boundaries in the management of ambiguity.[8]

As outlined at the start of this chapter, a Bayesian approach to public policy may have the potential to assist governments to cope better with ambiguity (especially as regards the costs of handling ambiguity) because, in effect, the generation of public value is treated as progress in managing Shannon entropy: we need to have postulated that an event is a 'theoretical' possibility, or have updated our likelihood estimate for its occurrence, in order to be able to assess the information gain *if* the event does happen. This stance is able to cope with ambiguity, because competing hypotheses/ explanations are tested in an updateable manner when new information is obtained. There is no 'right' answer – only more or less plausible answers with better or worse support by the evidence. Interestingly, this sort of per-spective is 'core business' for the security intelligence community, who make use of competing hypotheses, and indeed Bayesian inference, to try to explain (and predict) highly uncertain and ambiguous evidence – but less common in other areas of government, see Schweitzer (1978) and also Wheaton *et al.* (2009).

Bayesian inference as a policy-learning framework

The preceding discussion used the metaphor of two valleys (one observed, one as yet unseen) to start to:

- unpick the notion that sound public policy must be evidence-based policy;
- highlight the importance of governments being able to cope effectively with uncertainty, ambiguity and risk; and
- raise the question as to whether Bayesian inference might usefully play a stronger role in helping to deliver public sector reform.

The aim in this section of the chapter is to demonstrate that Bayesian infer-ence can, indeed, play a very useful role in informing public management frameworks that are better able to cope with the uncertainties, ambiguities and risks that the two valley problem expresses – but only if simplified and standardised implementations of the methods can be developed.

Bayesian probability, and associated statistical methods, differ in marked ways from the alternative (and more established) *sampling theory* approach (sometimes referred to as frequentalist, classical or orthodox probability). In the *sampling theory* definition, probability is treated as the long-run relative frequency of the *observed* occurrence of an event. The sample set can be either a sequence of events through time or a set of identically prepared systems (Loredo 1990). In contrast, Bayesians treat probability (in effect) as the rel-ative *plausibility* of propositions when knowledge is incomplete.

The term plausibility is used here because Bayesian statisticians and classical sampling statisticians use the term probability in different ways – generating semantic confusion. To a Bayesian, the concept of probability refers to the state of knowledge, expressed in terms of the degree to which different competing hypotheses may be correct given the available evidence. To a classical statistician, probability refers to the observed frequency of different events. In other words, one definition of probability refers to hypotheses given available data, and the other data independent of hypotheses. Given this semantic confusion it is preferable to avoid use of the term probability in this context.

Figure 11.4 explains the basic (and very simple) principle behind Bayesian analysis, namely that we are able to update the assumed odds of something happening when new information is obtained. The new information may either confirm that the initially assumed odds should be retained, or may lead us to revise these odds. For the purposes of relating Bayesian inference to the policy cycle, the simple equation expressing new odds and a product of the old odds plus the analysis of new information is re-framed as a circular learning process. Estimated odds, via experience, generate new information which, when analysed, allows estimated odds to be updated. This learning loop combines a real world implementation phase (experiments in effect) with an analytical phase. Everything that government does is, in effect, in the implementation phase and consequently an experiment (either explicitly or implicitly). However, implementation/experimentation activities may not necessarily involve the new information being identified, collated and analysed. If this does not happen then the odds cannot be updated and, in effect, there has been a missed opportunity to learn (and manage risk in particular).

Linear expression of Bayesian inference

New odds = old odds + analysis of new information

Circular/learning loop-based expression of Bayesian inference

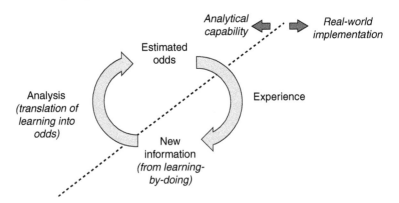

Figure 11.4 Diagrammatic explanation of Bayesian learning.

From this perspective, governments' monitoring, evaluation and learning (MEL) activities will have the greatest utility when the information obtained as a result of experience in implementing a policy intervention is related back to an initial (uncertainty and risk-based) assumption of the odds of success assumed for the intervention.[9] If MEL measures are not based on an explicit recognition of uncertainty and risk (i.e. the odds of success are not made explicit), then it is unlikely that useful learning will be captured *and used* even if useful learning takes place. This is because uncertainty and risk are marginalised rather than centralised in the analysis.

One major problem is that current approaches to MEL in the public sector favour firm targets that cannot be fudged ('Key Performance Indicators' or KPIs). These are often treated as counts of things happening – measures that can be verified as true or false. For example, people who have managed overseas development projects report that government donors tend to prefer projects that meet their KPIs even though they generate little benefits over projects that do appear to generate benefits but do not meet their contractually specified KPIs – which characteristically become outdated as a result of accumulating experience. In contrast, a Bayesian implementation of the policy-learning cycle would provide an alternative basis for MEL methods by more clearly specifying the uncertainties and risks involved in delivering a policy intervention and (where relevant) targeted by that policy intervention. As a result, outcomes from an intervention can be tracked as updated calculations of the odds that competing hypotheses are correct (calculated odds that incorporate uncertainties as reduced odds).

Figure 11.5 provides an annotated version of the logical construction of Bayesian inference. 'H' represents a hypothesis, 'P' the calculated probability that the hypothesis is correct and 'E' the evidence available to make that calculation. In essence, the calculations test hypotheses against new data on the basis of the previous estimated likelihood that a hypothesis is correct (given previously available data) combined with the theory-based likelihood that the new evidence would still be observed if that hypothesis were correct.[10]

That part of the calculation is then adjusted by the likelihood that the evidence being used was actually generated by the assumed model of the process to which the hypothesis/es relate (and includes a specific calculation relating to the impact of false positive results – an aspect that gives Bayesian methods a particular relevance to medicine). This latter element (the denominator in the equation) reflects a balance of likelihoods (including the likelihood of a false positive result) that in practice is usually complex to calculate. This limited the application of Bayesian inference to simple problems until high speed computing made it possible to calculate complex combination of circumstances in the denominator (see Lilford and Braunholtz 1996). The complexity associated with calculating the denominator tends to be associated with extremely large technical variations in how Bayesian methods are implemented. As Scott Ferson comments, Bayesian approaches are rather like snowflakes, in the sense that each one is unique (Ferson 2005). This

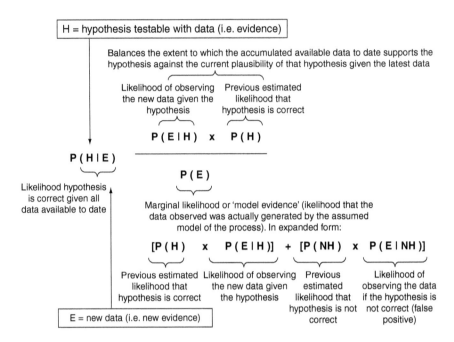

Figure 11.5 The logical construction of Bayesian inference.

heterogeneity makes it hard for non-specialists to adopt these methods in a public policy context – and reinforces the importance of developing more standardised and simplified approaches for use in public policy. Fortunately, as Gigerenzer (2002) has stressed, Bayesian inference can be simplified if conditional probabilities are avoided and the raw 'natural frequencies' of data are used instead – an approach that is particularly useful for bringing clarity to the incidence of false positives and false negatives in diagnosis.[11] Rather than the complex formula commonly required when conditional probabilities are used, the natural frequencies version of the Bayesian equation for calculating the likelihood that a particular positive test result actually means the condition is present can be collapsed to a simpler ratio which expresses the observed True Positive Rate as a proportion of the sum of the True Positive Rate and the False Positive rate.[12]

Perhaps the most famous demonstration of the power of Bayesian inference is found early on in the mathematical development of the techniques – in the seminal work of Laplace in the eighteenth century. Laplace sought to estimate the most plausible estimate of the mass of the planet Saturn, based on the (limited) astronomical data available at the time (the observed perturbations of the orbits of Jupiter and Saturn) combined with other common sense assumptions that imposed limits on what the mass could be (large enough not to lose its rings but not large enough to de-stabilise the solar system as a whole). Bayes theorem estimated that the most plausible mass of Saturn would be 1/3512 of the solar mass and specified a probability of 0.99991 that the actual mass would be within a margin of error of 1 per cent of that estimated value. The addition of another 150 years of astronomical data (and considerable additional expense and effort) improved this margin of error estimate from 1 per cent to 0.63 per cent (Loredo 1990). This is a powerful illustration of the power (and very high cost-effectiveness) of the use of conditional probabilities to interpret available but incomplete information in order to produce the most plausible estimate possible at that point in time.

Decision making in public policy shares the key characteristics exhibited by this aspect of Laplace's work: it is necessary to work with incomplete data, combined with a range of assumptions, in order to assess a situation in a manner that can inform timely decision making. The Bayesian emphasis on estimating the relative plausibility of different hypotheses is well suited to this environment. Arguably, orthodox sample theory-based definitions of probability and tests of statistical significance are better suited to an academic research context because they encourage continued investigation and debate over technical subtleties (especially as regards the wide choices to make over methods to test hypotheses) without the 'pinch point' associated with the need to make a decision *now* on the basis of everything that we believe we know and understand. The Bayesian approach also recognises that a simpler model should be preferred to a more complex model (this Occam's Razor aspect is built into the calculations via the denominator).

The distinction between sampling theory and Bayesian approaches has resulted in a long debate between the two camps characterised by misunderstood concepts and under-pinning philosophical assumptions (see Jaynes 1957 and Jaynes 1984). The orthodox stance tests hypotheses in a discrete manner (not relative to each other) and on the basis of the likelihood that a particular null hypothesis can be safely rejected as being very unlikely to have been produced randomly. The standard threshold for stating statistical significance in the social sciences is that there is a less than 5 per cent probability that random events could have produced the phenomena captured in the data.[13] Forward-looking forecasts and predictions may then (if required) be derived from model(s) that pass these significance thresholds.[14]

In contrast, Bayesian analysis works with the data that we actually have without requiring it to be treated as a random sample of a larger unobserved yet theoretically possible dataset in order to determine the degree of support for a hypothesis. The use of Bayesian methods in fields such as astrophysics (where there may be a very limited number of observations of some very hard to detect sub-atomic particles such as neutrinos) has helped to counter-balance the view that Bayesian approaches are reliant on subjective assumptions (Loredo 1990). Significantly, in 2006, the US Food and Drug Administration (FDA) published guidelines (published in draft form in 2010) on the use of Bayesian inference in testing medical devices. The FDA guidance stressed the importance of basing Bayesian prior distributions (i.e. initially assumed odds in the learning cycle) based only upon previous Randomised Control Trial (RCT) studies (FDA 2010). This approach removes the subjectivity objection of the anti-Bayesian camp, who have (understandable) reservations about the robustness of results that are based in part upon prior assumptions.

The final key point about Bayesian inference is that it provides a direct measure of the relative plausibility of different competing hypotheses – simply by comparing the different values of the Bayesian calculation with the latest information available. A similar measure of the *Weight of Evidence* (known as a Ban and its log derivative the Deciban) was used to particular effect by Alan Turing and colleagues in efforts to break the German Enigma code in WW2 (see Good 1979). However, Turing did not explicitly base his code breaking work on Bayesian inference – when asked by a colleague whether he was using Bayesian inference, he reportedly responded "I suppose so" (Gillies 1990), although, as Gillies argues, technical details of the approach adopted by Turing (which was a classified government secret for many years) suggest that it is closer to Popper's concept of the *Severity of a Test* (Popper 1934). The concept of the *Severity of a Test* asserts that the preferred test of hypotheses should be the severity of the tests applied, and not simply the number of corroborating instances that have been counted.

Turing's metric proved itself to be very useful as a numerical guide to which decryption solution(s) had the greatest promise, given available (ambiguous and uncertain) data. Such a metric is especially useful as a research resource allocation tool, because it provides a clear indicator of the relative plausibility of different explanations that can be updated as new data becomes available (in Turing's case on a daily basis). As such, this kind of summary metric provides a particularly useful metric for use in the policy learning process.

Building a Bayesian policy cycle

Figure 11.6 illustrates one way of linking Bayesian inference to the policy cycle, treated here using Deming's familiar plan-do-check-adjust loop.[15]

Figure 11.7 builds upon the previous one by adding a measure of the Weight of Evidence specific to competing hypotheses – treated as radial distance (the stronger the weight of evidence, the further from the centre the trajectory). This illustrates the way in which learning by doing (and its analysis) can lead to updated odds of different hypotheses being correct. In this illustration, Hypothesis/intervention 1 (H1) exhibits an increasing Weight of Evidence over the policy cycle, while Hypothesis/intervention 2 (H2) does not – and is abandoned early as a result.

One advantage of expressing the weight of evidence measure in this visual (and cyclical) manner is that it facilitates scrutiny of relative rates of change over time in the weight of evidence in favour of competing hypotheses.[16] This is particularly useful as a means of communicating Bayesian inference as decision-support information to non-specialists.[17] In this approach, 'evidence'

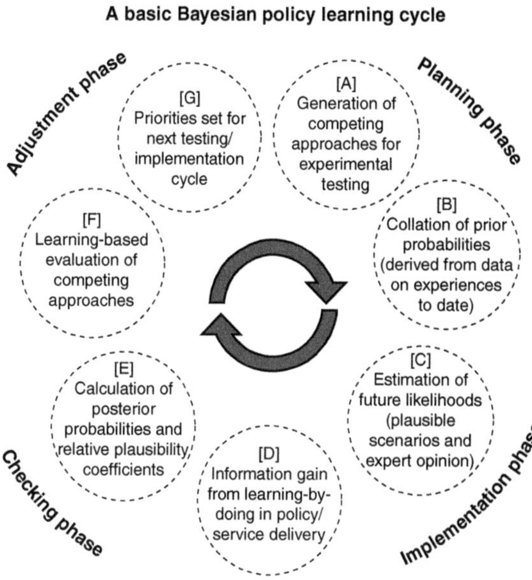

A basic Bayesian policy learning cycle
Planning phase
[A] Generation of competing approaches for experimental testing
[B] Collation of prior probabilities (derived from data on experiences to date)
Implementation phase
[C] Estimation of future likelihoods (plausible scenarios and expert opinion)
[D] Information gain from learning-by-doing in policy/ service delivery
Checking phase
[E] Calculation of posterior probabilities and relative plausibility coefficients
[F] Learning-based evaluation of competing approaches
Adjustment phase
[G] Priorities set for next testing/ implementation cycle

Figure 11.6 A basic Bayesian policy learning cycle.

Competing hypotheses in a basic Bayesian learning cycle
Weight of Evidence in favour of each hypothesis family
1.0
0.0
H1
H2
H1 exhibits increasing Weight of Exidence with accumulating experience and analysis
H2 exhibits decreasing Weight of Evidence with accumulating experience and analysis. Curtailed early as a result.
Generation of hypotheses
Collation of prior probabilities
Estimation of future likelihoods
Information gain from experience
Calculation of updated probabilites
Evaluation of learning
Specification of updated priorities
Hypothetico-deductive reasoning

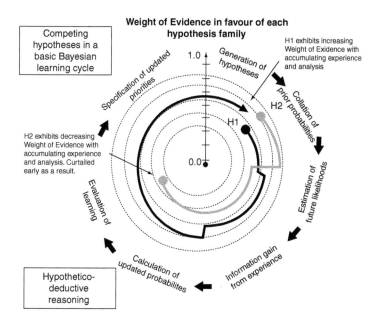

Figure 11.7 Introducing weight of evidence measures into a Bayesian policy learning cycle.

(a term used so frequently now but with so little epistemological precision) is treated as the Bayesian pathways followed by competing hypotheses in the policy learning cycle.

This section has introduced a simplified and standardised implementation of Bayesian inference of potential utility in a public policy context. The following section considers how this approach can be used to foster more effective collaboration between government, academia and civil society.

Using a Bayesian policy cycle to drive collaboration between government, academia and civil society

Figure 11.8 illustrates the concept of a Bayesian-influenced policy cycle in which collaboration between government, civil society (and academia) is treated as integral to the policy process. In each stage in the cycle, both government (at the centre of the cycle) and those preparing for or handling implementation (at the periphery and including civil society entities) are able to contribute to the process of suggesting hypothesis/interventions to test, together with the subsequent phases and activities in this Bayesian learning cycle. This capability is especially useful given the different insights and

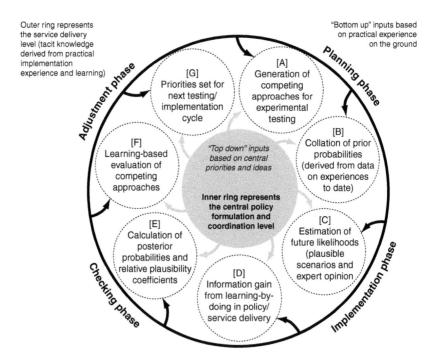

Figure 11.8 Using a Bayesian policy learning cycle to foster collaboration between government and civil society.

experiences of those delivering public service 'on the ground' (whether as government employees, contractors of civil society actors). This place-based understanding can be an especially rich source of new ideas – concepts that this framework allows to be thrown into the mix of options for potential pilots and experiments. For example, positive unintended consequences can be spotted quickly, investigated, and used to generate new pilot concepts when civil society actors are engaged fully in this sort of policy experimentation cycle.[18]

Given the current interest within many OECD governments in using RCTs to test and select between different potentially innovative approaches, coupled with a lack of emphasis on examining the methodological issues raised by the need to analyse and act on the results from RCTs (should Bayesian or classical sampling methods be used to assess the results), the current swathe of RCT projects may provide the leverage for academia and civil society to start to explore explicitly Bayesian approaches to policy innovation. In such circumstances, an attractive and feasible tactic for civil society would be to participate in RCT projects in order to use Bayesian methods to design the trials and to analyse – and learn from – the results obtained.[19] This would demonstrate, in concrete terms, how Bayesian methods can be applied to the policy learning cycle by leveraging the existing emphasis on RCTs. Adopting a standardised Bayesian approach has the additional advantage of providing a formal structured method for identifying and analysing useful knowledge obtained from 'frontline' policy implementation, in situations where timelines and budget limitations do not allow RCTs to be used. The proposed approach therefore encompasses both RCT and non-RTC methodologies.[20]

Conclusions

Governments' ability to deliver cost-effective public policy is being held back by a reluctance to think about some of the fundamental conceptual and methodological issues over what the concept of 'evidence' means and an over-enthusiastic focus on facts (detective work on the past) that has been de-coupled from the conceptual thinking and the testable hypotheses that are better positioned to help us grapple with what the future may have in store for us.

If we avoid using Bayesian inference, we risk basing policy decisions on false positives or false negatives because these tend to be counter-intuitive results from 'common sense' analyses. The Bayesian concept of the 'weight of evidence', expressed as the odds in favour of competing hypotheses, provides a suitable and easily grasped means of measuring the extent to which the experience gained from policy delivery is changing the odds in favour of the hypotheses that these policy interventions are testing. Using a simplified and standardised Bayesian approach to assessing how policy delivery impacts upon the weight of evidence supporting different hypotheses may provide the basis for an open and collaborative approach to public policy that is likely to be more effective than the current stance. In the approach advocated here, evidence is treated as the Bayesian pathways that are followed by competing hypotheses in the policy learning cycle.

Using Shannon's concept of entropy (information is what we know, entropy is what we do not know, and the size/'significance' of new information is greater the less likely the *assumed* likelihood of observing that information) then governments can play their distinctive role effectively if:

- they seek to maximise the set of assumed likelihoods (especially low likelihood – large consequences events); *and*
- maximise the information they are able to access about evolving experiences; *and*
- adopt analytically tractable (that is to say simplified and standardised) Bayesian methods.

Collaboration with academia and with civil society provides the key to achieving all three of these capability objectives. Civil society organisations are especially well placed to accumulate and use tacit knowledge on strengths and weaknesses in service delivery (generating new intervention concepts and assessing delivery effectiveness) and universities are well placed to deploy analytical methods to design, develop and demonstrate the advantages of a standardised Bayesian approach to the policy innovation cycle.[21] Consequently, a trilateral partnership between government, civil society and academia has the potential to catalyse this sort of transformation in ways that are less likely than with government acting alone.

One useful aspect of future work in this area will be to develop 'value for money' estimates based on the cost of achieving advances in understanding as reflected in updated odds of competing hypotheses being correct. This will have the advantage of reflecting decreases in uncertainty as improved odds of certain hypotheses being true – in so doing allowing a return-on-investment calculation ('truth comes at a price': public investment is a means of buying more favourable odds in the future). This sort of approach would be particularly useful in providing a basis for expressing the return on investment in academic research rather than relying on research commercialisation concepts.

Acknowledgements

This work was initiated when I was working at the HC Coombs Policy Forum in Australia and was supported by the 'Enhancing Public Policy Initiative' of the Commonwealth–ANU Strategic Relationship. The discussion of the use of Bayesian inference in the policy cycle draws upon research being supported by the Australian Centre for Biosecurity and Environmental Economics (ACBEE). I would like to give particular thanks to Geoff White, Gemma Carey and one anonymous referee – both of whom have provided very useful comments during the drafting of this chapter. In addition, useful comments and advice as these ideas were being developed was provided by Michael Cooney, Edward DeSeve, Jenny Gordon, Paul Harris, Tom Kompas, Ian Marsh, Tarik Meziani, Ben Reilly, John Young, and Grant Woollett.

Notes

1 The term uncertainty is used here in the sense of Knightian or epistemic uncertainty: situations in which there is immeasurable risk (it is not possible to calculate likelihoods). This differs from quantifiable uncertainty, often expressed as even odds-situations, in which likelihoods are quantifiable but there is insufficient information to determine whether one (or more) situations are more likely to occur than others. See Bammer and Smithson (2008) for a broad spectrum of views on the nature and consequences of uncertainty.

2 Fenton and Neil (2013) provide a useful and accessible introduction to Bayesian inference from a risk management perspective.

3 The importance of adaptive learning based on keeping options open in an uncertain and changing world is a well-established general managerial principle, see Klein and Meckling (1958) for an influential contribution. After nearly 60 years, the fact that there are still pleas for governance to transition to a more adaptive learning based and 'experimentalist' mode is a telling consequence of the rigidities associated with managerialism in the public sector.

4 In technical terms, Shannon entropy (derived from Bayesian inference) is calculated on the basis of the predictability of the relative frequencies of a set of symbols. It yields a metric, known as Metric Entropy (ME) that tells us the potential for surprise in a set of symbols (a ME of 1.0 tells us that the sequence is an equally distributed random (i.e. a maximum potential, for surprise) and a value of zero that there is no potential for surprise because the sequence is fixed. In a public policy context, Shannon entropy can be applied to the 'lexicon' of hypothesis tests (either explicit or implied by practice) that characterise government interventions (Matthews 2016). This creates a framework for applying the concepts of grammar and syntax to understanding how policy is articulated and evolves via learning-by-doing.

5 This section of the chapter is based upon a keynote address by the author at a workshop on government–academic collaboration in Canberra, organised by the Australian Government's *Department of Prime Minister and Cabinet* on 13 June, 2014.

6 The passage is taken from 'That a General ought to be equated with the lie of the land' in *The Discourses*.

7 See Berkowitz (2003) for a brief discussion of the key differences between detective work (and the concept of 'proof') and intelligence work (aimed at enhancing preparedness).

8 This is most easily achieved by setting up two competing hypotheses: (a) behaviour suggests that an agent can be trusted; (b) behaviour suggests that an agent cannot be trusted – each hypothesis assessed on the basis of the relative Weight of Evidence given available evidence. Indeed, many national tax authorities and credit card issuers already use pattern recognition systems that use learning-based Bayesian inference to make such assessments.

9 See Matthews and White (2013) for a discussion of an experimental project that used structured hypothesis testing as an MEL methodology.

10 This method is derived from the principles of conditional probability in mathematics.

11 Natural frequencies are simply the counts of the occurrences of possible permutations expressed in raw terms (and ideally using a graphical mapping of the structure of these permutations. This is both simpler and (for many people) a more intuitive way of dealing risks and uncertainties (see Gigerenzer (2002) for an explanation using a range of examples).

12 Details of how this natural frequency-based approach can be used to test hypotheses in a public policy setting using worked examples and systematic reviews of evaluations of public sector programs and projects (and including further elaboration on a Bayesian expression of the policy cycle) can be found online at: http://marklmatthews.com/false-positives-false-negatives-project/.

13 In some branches of physics where large amounts of data are available a deviation of three standard deviations from the mean is used as the criteria for attributing the status of 'evidence' and five standard deviations from the mean for attributing a 'discovery'.

14 See Ziliak and McCloskey (2014) for a discussion of the shortcomings in classical statistical significance testing.

15 There are other more specific models of the policy process, see for example Althaus *et al.* 2007; however the Deming model is used here to avoid complicating the picture. Most if not all specific versions of the policy cycle align with Deming's broad stages – but with differing flourishes and levels of detail. Feinberg (2011) discusses Bayesian inference in a governance context.

16 Implementing this cyclical approach requires that the Weight of Evidence is calculated continuously.

17 Schweitzer (1978) discusses how linear plots of Bayesian likelihoods (posterior estimates) were used by the Central Intelligence Agency (CIA) to inform decision makers over the nature and extent of consensus between different analysts in relation to specific threat assessments. This was especially useful in giving a clear sense of the diversity of conclusions and changes over time in intelligence assessments (as new information is received and analysed).

18 Issues raised when attempting to deliver innovative approaches in a federal governance context are discussed in Matthews (2009a).

19 Contemporary statistical analyses in medicine demonstrate how a range of analytical methods, including Bayesian inference, can be used in assessing RCT-type results (see for example Ma *et al.* 2009).

20 The applicability of RCTs to complex situations can, in any case, be limited – in those situations, Bayesian inference can have major advantages.

21 It may be useful to aim to produce a draft technical standard for the use of simplified and standardised Bayesian inference in the policy learning cycle.

References

Althaus, C, Bridgman, P and Davis, G 2007, *The Australian policy handbook*, 4th edn, Allen & Unwin, Sydney.

Bammer, G and Smithson, M (eds) 2008, *Uncertainty and risk: multidisciplinary perspectives*, Routledge, London.

Berkowitz, B 2003, 'The big difference between intelligence and evidence', Commentary in the *Washington Post*, Re-published by the RAND Corporation.

FDA 2010, *Guidance for the use of Bayesian in medical device clinical trials*, US Food and Drug Administration, Draft issued in 2006.

Feinberg, S E 2011, 'Bayesian models and methods in public policy and government settings', *Statistical Science*, vol. 26, no. 2, pp. 212–226.

Fenton, N and Neil, M 2013, *Risk assessment and decision analysis with Bayesian networks*, CRC Press, Boca Raton, FL.

Ferson, S 2005, *Bayesian methods in risk assessment*, Paper prepared for Bureau de Recherches Géologiques et Minières (BRGM), France.

Giddens, A 1984, *The constitution of society*, Polity, Cambridge, UK.

Gigerenzer, G 2002, *Reckoning with risk: learning to live with uncertainty*, Penguin. London.

Gillies, D 1990, 'The Turing–Good weight of evidence function and Popper's measure of the severity of a test', *British Journal of the Philosophy of Science*, vol. 41, pp. 143–146.

Good, I J 1979, 'Studies in the history of probability and statistics. XXXVII A. M. Turing's statistical work in World War II', *Biometrika*, vol. 66, no. 2, pp. 393–396.

Jaynes, E T 1957, 'Information theory and statistical mechanics', *Physical Review*, Series II, vol. 106, no. 4, pp. 620–630.

Jaynes, E T 1984, *Bayesian methods: general background: an introductory tutorial*, Paper presented at the Fourth Annual workshop on Bayesian/Maximum Entropy Methods, August 1984, Calgary.

Klein, B and Meckling, W 1958, 'Application of operations research to development decisions', *Operations Research*, vol. 6, no. 3, pp. 352–363.

Lilford, R J and Braunholtz, D 1996, 'The statistical basis of public policy: a paradigm shift is overdue', *British Medical Journal*, vol. 313, pp. 603–607.

Loredo, T J 1990, 'From Laplace to supernova SN 1987A: Bayesian inference in astrophysics', in P F Fougere (ed.), *Maximum entropy and Bayesian methods*, Kluwer Academic Publishers, The Netherlands.

Ma, J, Thabane, L, Kaczorowski, J, Chambers, L, Dolovich, L, Karwalajtys, T and Levitt, C 2009, 'Comparison of Bayesian and classical methods in the analysis of cluster randomized controlled trials with a binary outcome: the community hypertension assessment trial (CHAT)', *BMC Medical Research Methodology*, vol. 9, no. 1, p. 37.

Machiavelli, N 2003, *The discourses*, Penguin Classics, London.

Matthews, M 2009a, 'Fostering creativity and innovation in cooperative federalism – the uncertainty and risk dimensions', in, J Wanna (ed.), *Critical reflections on Australian public policy*, Australia New Zealand School of Government (ANZSOG), Monograph.

Matthews, M 2009b, *Giving preparedness a central role in science and innovation policy*, Discussion Paper commissioned by the Federation of Australian Scientific and Technological Societies (FASTS).

Matthews, M 2014, *Innovation in governance: the productivity benefits of fostering a greater tolerance for uncertainty and ambiguity*, Paper given at the ANZSOG workshop on 'Twenty-first Century public management: the experimentalist alternative', 11–12 February, Crawford School of Public Policy.

Matthews, M 2016, *Transformational public policy*, Routledge, (Forthcoming).

Matthews, M and White, G 2013, *Faster and smarter: using a hypothesis-testing methodology to reduce the time and cost of evaluations*, Discussion paper prepared for consideration by the OECD Expert Panel on the Evaluation of Industrial Policy, available on request.

Popper, K R 1934, *The logic of scientific discovery*, 6th Impression, Hutchinson 1972 (quoted in Gillies 1990).

Sabel, C and Zeitlin, J 2012, 'Experimentalist governance', in D Levi-Faur (ed.), *The Oxford handbook of governance*, Oxford University Press.

Schweitzer, N 1978, *Bayesian analysis for intelligence: some focus on the Middle East*, Note on analytical techniques (declassified without redaction), Central Intelligence Agency, Virginia.

Shannon, C E 1948, 'A mathematical theory of communication', *The Bell System Technical Journal*, vol. XXVII, July, pp. 379–423.

Wheaton, K J, Lee, J and Deshmukh, H 2009, 'Teaching Bayesian statistics to intelligence analysts: lessons learned', *Journal of Strategic Security*, vol. 2, no. 1 pp. 38–58.

Ziliak, S T and McCloskey, D N 2014, *The cult of statistical significance: how the standard error costs is jobs, justice and lives*, The University of Michigan Press, Ann Arbor, MI.

12 Performance budgeting

The power to persuade, control or deceive?

David Hayward

Introduction

In his now classic text, *Respect: the formation of character in an age of inequality*, Richard Sennett (2004) identifies ways to reshape the welfare state so that its clients feel respected in an age of inequality. A core part of his argument is the importance of autonomy, the legitimacy of dependence, and the significance of allowing recipients of welfare to have a say "in the condition of their existence".

In elaborating his argument, Sennett takes aim at modern managerial approaches to welfare, which have 'hollowed out' (see Rhodes 1994) the state and undermined social policy good intentions. Interestingly, and Sennett's powerful critique notwithstanding, these modern approaches to welfare share with Sennett a common desire to transform the state in ways that will improve clients' experiences. They try to do this by focusing on new technologies of management that will force providers of welfare to consider the effects of their interventions instead of concentrating on the inputs at their disposal. Initially begun under the rubric of Program Budgeting, this literature has morphed into a body of work called The New Public Management (NPM), a name it still enjoys even though it is more than a quarter of a century old.

NPM is concerned with how we might use measures of output and outcome to increase accountability in order to improve performance. While the adoption of NPM across the OECD has been patchy, Australia stands out as one of its leading proponents, along with the UK (where it began), the US and New Zealand. While NPM is not necessarily linked to an annual budgeting process, this has increasingly been the case and once again Australia stands out as a world leader in attempts to do this (Schick 2014; de Jong *et al.* 2012; Bach and Bordogna 2011). Using this approach, funds might be allocated and redistributed based on how well agencies deliver the outputs and outcomes they say they are trying to deliver. While there are different iterations and versions of the NPM, this chapter focuses on that which has become influential in the framing of social policy budgets, particularly at the state level in Australia (the tier most responsible for service delivery in education, health, housing and disability services).

This chapter explores the NPM and its significance as a technology of persuasion. It also explores various critiques of the NPM. Of particular interest are those that reject it on the basis that much of social policy cannot be readily measured and that the very process of doing so damages and distorts the system of public administration in ways that impede the achievement of genuinely effective results. The chapter concludes by exploring whether or not it is possible to overcome some of the flaws in the NPM by accommodating Sennett's plea to allow those who use welfare to have a say in the conditions of their existence. It is argued that a potential solution lay with splitting budgeting and performance management into two separate activities, on the grounds that they are fundamentally different. It is also argued that we need to shift performance management away from definitions and measures agreed to by policy and bureaucratic 'experts', and require instead clients of services to be given a central role in defining what outcomes, including measures, are important to them.

Performance budgeting in the Australian federation: where it all began

Up until the 1980s, Australian State governments and the Commonwealth framed annual budgets by departments on a line item basis. Focusing only on cash, their budgets were neither transparent nor uniform.[1] (Evatt Research Centre 1989; OECD 2012). In the early 1980s, the newly elected Cain government in Victoria began a public sector revolution, which among other things modernised the State's public accounts and budget system to make it more strategic and managerial (Considine and Costar 1992; Evatt Research Centre 1989). A core reform was the introduction of program budgeting.

Program budgeting was first introduced into public finances by the United States Defence Department under Secretary Robert McNamara in the 1960s. Its central feature was to align spending decisions with programs, which in turn were required to be focused on objectives instead of pre-existing organizational arrangements. "Its essence", as West puts it, "is to think about activities and spending in terms of their contributions to organizational goals" (West 2011, p. 9). For example, instead of a long list of line item cash payments, program budgets were developed in which items of expenditure were grouped according to function and aligned with agreed objectives. Theoretically, this would enable the Department (or Secretary McNamara) to work out annually how budgets should be deployed to secure the best set of defence programs within a given budget constraint. It would be possible to have more tanks and fewer missiles, more submarines and fewer planes, and so on, with each dollar of additional expenditure being allocated to generate the best return relative to the program's objectives (for an excellent account see West 2011, Chapter 3).[2]

The introduction of program budgeting in Victoria was linked more generally to a purpose built budget system that included a cabinet level expenditure review committee, with spending proposals, their program objectives and intended effects being considered systematically prior to being approved (Considine 1992; Evatt Research Centre 1989).

In Victoria, in the first half of the 1980s the Government wrapped program budgeting around a broader Keynesian Economic Strategy, and then in the latter half of the 1980s a Social Justice Strategy, enabling the Government to better assess spending decisions in light of longer-term policy considerations (Davidson 1992; Wiseman 1992; Evatt Research Centre 2009).

It did not take long before Victoria's lead was picked up by other states. By the late 1980s and for the first time, a bureaucratic capability was being developed across the country (albeit patchily) to be clear about program objectives and the funds required to secure these on an annual basis. Before they were more broadly embraced, however, the policy innovations being driven from Victoria were effectively undermined by the global recession of the early 1990s (Considine and Costar 1992; Davidson 1992). The State Labor government found itself facing a severe recession prompted by the failure of the State Bank of Victoria and the private Pyramid Building Society. Labor was swept from office, as was the system of public administration which it had painstakingly built up over the previous decade (Considine and Costar 1992; Hayward 1999).

The newly elected conservative Kennett government immediately rejected the Economic and Social Justice Strategies and shifted the budget framework dramatically rightward, following the recommendations of an Audit Commission established shortly after winning government (Hayward 1999). Interestingly, amidst the policy wreckage, program budgeting was picked up and dusted off and transformed into a new budgeting framework based on what has come to be known as the New Public Management.

Program budgeting in a new set of clothes: the rise of New Public Management

Implemented within a framework of austerity, the New Public Management approach formally distinguished between inputs (staff, consumables, assets) and outputs (e.g. number of patients treated or number of homeless people assisted) associated with government programs (Alford and O'Neil 1994). When added to the pre-existing model that focused on objectives, the result was a formidable budget model, at least in theory. Budgets began to be prepared on the assumption that the amount of funding and the delivery mechanism was less important than the outputs being delivered to achieve agreed objectives. Greater efficiency could deliver more for less. Implemented as part of a broader framework of privatisation (including asset sales and outsourcing), the underlying idea was to use the power of the private market to make the public sector as efficient as possible (Alford and O'Neil 1994; Costar and Economou 1999; Hayward 1999).

Victoria once again stood out in the 1990s as the leading reformer in the country, developing and implementing this new approach with great speed.

The budget papers were re-crafted to reflect this new emphasis on outputs. A budget paper was prepared that showed by department and program the objectives being pursued, the outputs being 'purchased', with annual targets being specified along with actual performance from the year before. The new system was fully put into effect in the 1998–9 budget, when Victoria became the first administration in the country to move to accrual accounting. This budget coincidentally turned out to be the Kennett government's last.[3]

The other states followed Victoria's lead in the subsequent decades, partly as a result of their own Commissions of Audit, following changes of government from Labor to Coalition. This model was also adopted by the Commonwealth Government in the late 1990s and early 2000s, following the recommendations of its own Commission of Audit (which was chaired by the same person who chaired the Victorian Commission of Audit earlier in the decade) (OECD 2012).

Under this new model, narratives shifted from the amount of money going into a particular social policy area to the level of outputs being delivered. Governments were simultaneously able to argue that what mattered was not whether the service was being delivered publicly or privately but results, thereby heeding the advice of Osborne and Gaebler's (1993) influential text on *Reinventing Government*, which recommended governments should focus on 'steering' not 'rowing'. The OECD recently explained the Commonwealth government's approach this way:

> Between the 1999–2000 to 2008–2009 budgets, Australia's budget process was based on an outcomes and outputs framework. This reform was meant to focus the budget process on ends rather than means, by more directly linking expenditure to outputs produced and outcomes achieved. Under the outcomes and outputs framework, every agency was required to identify comprehensive and explicit outcomes which form the legal basis for appropriations approved by the Parliament.
>
> (OECD 2012, p. 130ff.)

NPM: the critique

It did not take long for the NPM budget model to be subjected to sustained critique from a variety of quarters. One strand of argument is founded on traditional ideas of pluralist democracy and public administration and is critical of NPM because it tries to impose a market model onto a public sector that should serve non-commercial ends. Early advocates included Rhodes (1994), who saw a 'hollowing out of the state', courtesy of privatisations, the increased use of government businesses and private contractors to deliver public services in ways that were decreasingly subject to democratic scrutiny and control (for a useful summary see Davis 1997). Others took issue with the idea inherent in NPM that it was either possible or desirable to introduce private sector management techniques into the public sector. Adcroft and

Willis (2005) go a step further arguing that the main purpose of NPM is to commercialise and de-professionalise the public service rather than genuinely improve its effects.

A different argument is developed by West (2011). He argues that pluralist democracies do not lend themselves to the type of managerialism evident in NPM-inspired performance budgeting. In the case of the US, he argues that institutional structures and incentives within the broader political system have frustrated performance-planning management, and these frustrations have been amplified by bicameral legislative structures, federal systems and party political differences that necessarily accompany pluralist democratic systems. Put slightly differently, democracy and efficiency are not necessarily happy bedfellows, but stem from fundamentally different values. He writes:

> The most basic point is that the institutional preconditions for comprehensive planning and co-ordination may not be desirable … the assumption that a rational administrative system can be reconciled with our current political system ignores all that this implies…. (T)here is not a management system that can solve the complex issues that bureaucracy must confront. Public management is instead more art than science.
>
> (West 2011, pp. 131, 134)

There is much in this critique that has merit. It is important to be wary of simplistic technical solutions drawn from private sector practice as a way of solving public sector problems. However, while pluralist democracy, social democratic values and public sector bureaucracies are not necessarily compatible with the efficiency principles embedded in NPM, it is another matter altogether to conclude that they are enemies of managerial accountability. Similarly, while it is reasonable to question whether contestable markets are an effective vehicle for the delivery of public services, it is surely reasonable to expect public sector managers to be able to explain what it is their departments are seeking to do and how they know if the job is being done effectively. The core issue is then not so much about attempts to measure and hold providers of services to account. Perhaps it is more about the way the measures are developed, implemented and managed.

This leads to a second set of criticisms that are potentially more significant than the first in that they question the very idea of being able to measure most of what the public sector does, particularly in the area of social policy and welfare involving highly skilled professionals and complex issues (Pidd 2007). In practice it can be very difficult, if not impossible, to specify objectives or to distinguish easily between inputs and outputs. Even in cases where this is the case, what is important is not inputs and outputs but outcomes, which are notoriously difficult to measure (Hatry 2002; Perrin 2003; Sheil 1997, 1998). Even more important is the issue of effect, which begs questions of history, biography and social structure and is simply not able to be measured in any meaningful way.

In the most difficult social policy areas, Department officers agonise over what it is they are trying to do and how to measure this. They often end up choosing measures that are meaningless or which are so ambiguous they can be interpreted in a variety of ways. It is difficult trying to measure what it is that a central agency such as a Premier's Department, or the Department of Treasury and Finance do, much less measure it. Measures end up being chosen which are effectively meaningless, such as the numbers of letters sent, the number of speeches written or the number of ministerial briefings.

Even seemingly straightforward measures can prove to be tricky. To take policing as an example, it is not at all clear whether a fall in the number of reported crimes is evidence of success, in that crime might have fallen, or failure, in that people have lost confidence in police and are therefore no longer reporting crimes like they used to. Nor is it clear whether the Department of Justice (against whom this is reported in most jurisdictions) is in any way responsible for the change in the measure. Measures of child protection and support are also ambiguous and open to interpretation. Are increasing rates of substantiated abuse a sign of success or failure, and who is ultimately responsible in any case (see for example Queensland Government 2014)?

Forced to find measures for which they will be held to account, Departmental officers often end up defaulting to what is easiest to measure, and this is typically measures of output, input and throughput, not outcome or effect. For example, in the area of homelessness, the measures frequently and still chosen are either the number of people provided with homelessness assistance, or the amount of time clients spend in homeless shelters (see for example Victorian Government 2014; Queensland Government 2014). Both are flawed measures of throughput that ignore outcomes. What matters most is not the number of people provided with assistance or the amount of time they are provided with shelter, but whether the assistance is effective in providing clients with long-term secure housing into the future, something that is hard to measure given the time frames involved. The problem as Schick points out is that, "The cost of acquiring relevant performance data partly explains why so many performance budgeting systems that aim for outcome measures end up with output data" (Schick 2014, p. 12). Or as Lowe has put it rather pointedly:

> Our desire for outcome information outstrips our ability to provide it. Information about outcomes can either be simple, comparable and efficient to collect, or it can be a meaningful picture of how outcomes are experienced by people. It cannot be both.
>
> (Lowe 2013, p. 214)

In many cases, the adoption of NPM within an output and outcome budget context has resulted in less meaningful information being published and the level of accountability therefore declining. This is because the measures are vague, while no or limited data have been published on inputs. It is no longer possible to tell how much cash is being allocated to programs year-on-year, or over a longer time frame. Yet for most policy analysts this is the most critical issue of them all. As the then Commonwealth Minister for Finance argued shortly after winning office in 2008:

> Some outcomes are so broad and general as to be virtually meaningless for budget accounting purposes leading taxpayers to only guess what billions of their dollars are being spent on.... The Outcomes and Outputs Framework is intended to shift the focus of financial reporting from inputs ... to outputs and outcomes.... While this is worthy in theory, it has not worked. Basic information on inputs was lost in the changeover, and reporting of outcomes is seriously inadequate.
>
> (Tanner 2008, quoted in McKay 2011, p. 23)

A related criticism is that, in many areas of social policy, inputs are inextricably entwined with the outcome, in that the process used to deliver services is crucial to the success of the program. The delivery of disability services, health, homelessness assistance, public housing and education to name but a few social policy areas depends fundamentally on a vibrant and well-trained service of professionals able to make judgments about the best way to deliver a service (Pidd 2007). In these areas, the desire to reduce costs can damage the professionalisation of the services needed to deliver effective outcomes. These complex areas, typically involving the delivery of care, are a very different enterprise to factories making cars or widgets. It is in the interaction between clients and service delivery professionals that a successful intervention is determined. Relatedly, inputs and outputs are inextricably interwoven across portfolios and it is how they interweave that determines whether or not the intervention is a success. For example, the number of homeless people is at least partially a reflection of the overall state of the economy and unemployment as well as previous investments in education.

This in turn leads to the criticism that as soon as the focus shifts from the professional nature of the intervention (see Radin 2006, Chapter 4) to something that is measured with accountability targets attached, the measure itself becomes the object of concern rather than the service. We confuse the 'is' and the 'ought', and encourage actors to confuse and obfuscate along the way. This is nicely summarized as Goodhart's Law, which was neatly restated by Marilyn Strathern as: "When a measure becomes a target, it ceases to be a good measure". The measure is effectively given a life of its own and Departments end up spending their time gaming it rather than trying to genuinely achieve their social policy objectives. Episodes of care are increased by churning the same people through the same service, without improving well-being. An alternative is to keep changing measures (targets) that are not met, making it impossible to assess changes over time and therefore to work out whether policies are working (for a summary see Pidd (2007); see also Lowe (2013, p. 216). So routinely are the measures changed that Departments now report this (see for example Queensland Government, 2014). Harris *et al.* (2014) summarise the problem of 'gaming' this way:

> when outcomes are positioned as targets and key measures of perform-ance they have perverted practice. This perversion of practice comes in the form of 'parking' service users that may struggle to achieve the pre-determined outcome, creaming or cherry picking service users that will easily achieve the pre-determined outcome, fraudulently claiming out-comes for clients that don't exist and manufacturing outcomes by means that deliver a statistic but have no value to the service user themselves. We have seen this happen in the employment services sector within Aus-tralia and our own train system in Victoria. Not stopping at stations so that you can meet punctuality outcomes may deliver for the company but it does very little for the passengers standing on the platform.

By focusing on outcome measures and targets in areas where there can be no effective measures, the NPM has encouraged the formation of a whole new layer of bureaucracy that was not there before. This sees agencies like the Productivity Commission spending vast sums gathering data and refining flawed data on a quest that can never succeed (Sheil 1997, 1998). It sees armies of public servants employed generating and auditing data sets and endless arguments about their meaning instead of delivering the front line ser-vices that might actually make a difference, while those delivering these ser-vices end up focusing on defining and meeting targets that have little meaning or point.

This waste of resources stands in marked contrast to the promise of the NPM to deliver more efficient public services. In a recent assessment, the OECD applauded Australia for its overall level of public sector efficiency, but drew attention to what it saw as a flawed approach to outcome and output budgeting:

> the extent to which outcomes and outputs were actually used for the purpose of budgeting was very low.... (I)t has been noted that outcome definitions are brief and broad, hence vague, widely different between agencies in terms of their nature and specificity, subject to permanent reformulation, hence not comparable over time. Furthermore, it has been noted that the information provided by agencies concerning the connec-tion between outputs and outcomes as well as the output and outcome information itself is often of low quality.... The combination of output steering and budgeting in an annual exercise conducted as part of the budget cycle, is increasingly seen as ineffective, bureaucratic and distor-tive (leading to perverse incentives).
>
> (OECD 2012, p. 131; see also Hood and Peters 2004)

More recent developments

There is, then, much that is wrong with NPM. Nevertheless, it does not necessarily follow that we should abandon efforts to identify and in some way measure the purpose and effect of public policy interventions. It is one thing to accept that much of public policy is grey and ambiguous so that it does not lend itself to easy measurement, but it is quite another to suggest that public policy operates in an accountability free zone (Noordegraaf and Tineke 2003). Similarly, it is one thing to point out that there are complex interdependencies between policy areas, service delivery agencies, individual biographies and history, but it is quite another to suggest that there is then no way of knowing what the point or effect of intervention might be. Finally, it may well be the case that there is too strong a tension between the twin tools of budgeting and performance measurement to allow the two to be brought together in any meaningful way. Budgeting is focused on the allocation of resources based on last year's allocation, while performance systems are intended to focus on change and improvement. It may well be better to sever the two, while keeping both (Schick 2014) and resisting the futile approach of trying to bind the two together in reams of meaningless budget papers. It may be better to keep them apart but to allow the result of performance assessments to inform budget considerations.

Seen pragmatically, it is difficult to argue against a focus on outcomes from social policy intervention. The flaw in the NPM position is not about this focus so much as the way it has ended up being done, that is via systems enabling powerful central agencies to determine allocations of resources based on performance measures designed by groups of experts who determine the outcomes and assemble the measures they consider to be best. This is a 'top down' system, that effectively treats service users with little respect, and which sits rather uncomfortably with the explicit goal of the NPM to encourage the public sector to be client focused (Harris et al. 2014; West 2011).

This disregards the views of those whom the interventions are seeking to assist. Service delivery clients are denied, in Sennett's (2004) language, the right to participate in the conditions of their own existence. Recently an alternative approach has been suggested, which shifts the terms of the engagement into a very different terrain. This alternative approach argues that the clients of services are the ones who should determine the outcome measures that work best for them. This is done at the level of a specific program intervention, but there is no reason in principle that these outcomes as they apply to individual clients cannot be aggregated to give a picture of service delivery effects as a whole.

This approach should not just be seen as another way of refining the NPM approach to social policy: far from it. By engaging with clients in this way, this new outcome based approach is designed to focus service delivery agencies on the needs and understandings of those they serve; it is structured in a way that gives the clients of services a degree of autonomy they would otherwise be denied, a degree of autonomy crucial in order to provide for a respectful relationship. As Sennett puts it,

> in education or medicine we grant autonomy to teachers or doctors when we accept that they know what they are doing, even if we don't understand it; the same autonomy ought to be granted the pupil or the patient, because they know things about learning or being sick which the person teaching or treating them might not fathom ... I conceive in this way, autonomy is a powerful recipe for equality. Rather than an equality of understanding, a transparent equality, autonomy means accepting in the other what you do not understand, an opaque equality. In so doing, you are treating the fact of the autonomy as equal to your own.
>
> (Sennett 2004, p. 1,602 of Kindle Edition)

Shifting the power to determine what is measured and how this is to be done to a conversation with the client has the potential to become a powerful driver of public sector performance. This approach has the added and important advantage of requiring welfare clients to think carefully about what it is they are trying to achieve by being a recipient of support and to help them find a way to voice their views as clearly and constructively as possible. As Harris and Andrews explain: "This situates the client as an expert in their own life and holds the service accountable to respond to their voice" (Harris *et al.* 2014).

It would be possible to see how this approach could be used in a variety of social policy and welfare delivery settings. While it is intended to operate in the context of a conversation between an individual client and a case manager (or equivalent), it would be possible for the outcomes to be reported back in an aggregated way across a program or program area. This would enable accountability to operate both at the micro and macro levels.

Conclusion

This chapter has examined the New Public Management approach to performance budgeting in the Australian public sector. It has shown how over the last three decades Australian governments have progressively moved from a line item cash-based system of budgeting to one increasingly interested in output and outcomes, most clearly reflected in a purposefully designed separate volume to annual budget papers.

The chapter provided a detailed summary of criticisms of the NPM by focusing in particular on social policy and welfare. The chapter highlighted those who argue that the NPM's private sector genesis renders it unsuitable for the public sector, as well as those who claim that pluralist democracy does not lend itself to performance measurement. Efficiency and democracy are fundamentally different values and we should not judge the latter by the standards of the former.

The chapter argued that, however much criticisms like this might be valid, they do not provide a persuasive argument as to why the public sector should not be held accountable for its performance. A stronger set of criticisms were summarised showing that the main problem with this particular approach to performance budgeting and measurement is that it is best understood as a system of central control that enables powerful central government agencies to have great say over what it is that the agencies of the public sector do and how much they will fund them to do it. The public sector does not lend itself to this type of measurement, particularly in social policy and welfare. The effect in Australia has been the allocation of vast sums of money on a system of performance budgeting that involves the creation of and reporting on meaningless measures.

An alternative model was proposed in which performance and budgeting are separated, and in which the former is put under the microscope using measures and targets determined by clients, who are encouraged to develop the skills and abilities to communicate their objectives and better understand their current position. It would be possible for service agencies to report back to funders annually on how well they delivered on the outcomes agreed with clients, thereby enabling performance to be a consideration in the next budget round. An approach to performance management that empowers those served to specify the outcomes and have a say in whether they are met is consistent with Richard Sennett's call for a respectful form of welfare by allowing the clients of government services to have a say in the conditions of their own existence.

They are given the power to persuade.

Notes

1 The Tasmanian Parliament did not have a Hansard until 1979.
2 Program budgeting was initially seen to be highly successful, and President Johnson ordered it to be implemented across the federal public services. Despite this, a variety of implementation problems meant it never ended up being adopted anywhere seriously, except within Defence. This failure was partly to do with the peculiar nature of Defence, which lent itself to hierarchical objective setting and measurement, partly because of the politics of existing organisational arrangements, and partly because of the complexity of the public sector, which did not readily lend itself to easy measurement and therefore lacked the crucial data necessary for it to be implemented (West 2011, pp. 19ff.).
3 It is important to distinguish between program budgeting in which funds are allocated for the achievement of specific outputs and outcomes, and program budgeting that acts as a guide for what it is that is to be delivered. Australian systems have been of the latter rather than former variety (see Schick 2014).

References

Adcroft, A and Willis, R 2005, 'The unintended outcomes of public sector performance measurement', *International Journal of Public Sector Management*, vol. 18, no. 5, pp. 386–400.

Alford, J and O'Neil, D (eds) 1994, *The contract state*, Deakin University Press, Waurn Ponds, Vic.

Bach, S and Bordogna, L 2011, 'Varieties of new public management or alternative models? The reform of public service employment models in industrialized democracies', *The International Journal of Human Resource Management*, vol. 22, no. 11, pp. 2281–2294.

Considine, M 1992, 'Labor's approach to policy-making', in M Considine and B Costar (eds), *Trials in power. Cain, Kirner and Victoria, 1982–1992*, Melbourne University Press, Carlton, Vic.

Considine, M and Costar, B 1992, 'Introduction', in M Considine and B Costar (eds), *Trials in power. Cain, Kirner and Victoria, 1982–1992*, Melbourne University Press, Carlton, Vic.

Costar, B and Economou, N 1999, 'Introduction', in B Costar and N Economou, (eds), *The Kennett Revolution*, UNSW Press, Sydney.

Davidson, K 1992, 'The Victorian economy and the policy of the Cain/Kirner government', in M Considine and B Costar (eds), *Trials in power. Cain, Kirner and Victoria, 1982–1992*, Melbourne University Press, Carlton, Vic.

Davis, G 1997, 'Toward a hollow state? managerialism and its critics', in M Considine and M Painter (eds), *Managerialism: the great debate*, Melbourne University Press, Carlton, Vic.

de Jong, M, van Beek, I, and Posthumus, R 2012, 'Introducing accountable budgeting: lessons from a decade of performance budgeting in the Netherlands', *OECD Journal on Budgeting*, vol. 2, viewed 4 October, 2014, www.keepeek.com/Digital-Asset-Management/oecd/governance/introducing-accountable-budgeting_budget-12-5k455r12vs37#page1.

Evatt Research Centre 1989, *State of Siege: Renewal or Privatisation for Australian State Public Services?* Pluto Press, Sydney.

Evatt Research Centre 2009, State of Siege. Renewal or privatisation for Australian state public services? Pluto Press, Leichardt, NSW.

Hatry, H 2002, 'Performance measurement: fashions and fallacies', *Public Performance and Management Review*, vol. 25, no. 4 pp. 352–358.

Harris, L, Andrews, S and Plant, J 2014, 'The potential and limitations of an outcomes measurement framework for the homelessness sector', *Parity*, February edition.

Hayward, D 1999, 'A budget revolution?', in B Costar and N Economou, (eds), *The Kennett Revolution*, UNSW Press, Sydney.

Hood, C and Peters, G 2004, 'The middle aging of new public management: into the age of paradox', *Journal of Public Administration Research and Theory*, vol. 14, no. 3, pp. 267–282.

Lowe, T 2013, 'New development: the paradox of outcomes – the more we measure, the less we understand', *Public Money and Management*, vol. 33, no. 3, pp. 213–216.

McKay, K 2011, 'The performance framework of the Australian government, 1987–2011', *OECD Journal on Budgeting*, vol. 3, viewed 4 October 2014, www.keepeek.com/Digital-Asset-Management/oecd/governance/the-performance-framework-of-the-australian-government-1987-to-2011_budget-11-5kg3nhlcqdg5#page1.

Noordegraaf, M and Tineke, A 2003, 'Management by measurement? Public management practices amidst ambiguity', *Public Administration*, vol. 81, no. 4, pp. 853–871.

OECD 2012, *Value for money in government: Australia*, OECD Publishing, Paris.

Osborne, T and Gaebler, D 1993, *Reinventing government. How the entrepreneurial spirit is changing government*, Plume, New York.

Perrin, B 2003, 'Effective use and misuse of performance measurement', *American Journal of Evaluation*, vol. 19, no. 3, p. 367.

Pidd, M 2007, 'Perversity in public service performance measurement', in A Nealy (ed.), *Business performance management. Unifying theories and integrating practice*, 2nd edn, Cambridge University Press, Cambridge.

Queensland Government 2014, *State budget 2014/15, service delivery*, Budget Paper No 5. Queensland Treasury, Brisbane.

Radin, B 2006, *Challenging the performance movement*, Georgetown University Press, Washington DC, Kindle Edition.

Rhodes, R 1994, 'The hollowing out of the state: the changing nature of the public service in Britain', *The Political Quarterly*, vol. 65, no. 2, pp. 138–151.

Schick, A 2014, 'The metamorphoses of program budgeting', *OECD Journal on Budgeting*, vol. 2, viewed 4 October 2014, www.keepeek.com/Digital-Asset-Management/oecd/governance/the-metamorphoses-of-performance-budgeting_budget-13-5jz2jw9szgs8#page1.

Sennett, R 2004, *Respect: the formation of character in an age of inequality*, Penguin Books, Kindle Edition.

Sheil, C 1997, 'Heart of darkness: new managerialism and its contradictions', in C Sheil (ed.), *Turning point: the state of Australia*, Allen & Unwin, Sydney, pp. 292–307.

Sheil, C 1998, 'New managerialism revisited', in C Sheil (ed.), *The state of the states, 1998*, Evatt Foundation and Public Sector Research Centre, Sydney.

Victorian Government 2014, *Victorian budget 2014/15. service delivery*, Budget Paper No. 3, Victorian Treasury, Melbourne.

West, W 2011, *Program budgeting and the performance movement. The elusive quest for efficiency in government*, Georgetown University Press, Washington DC.

Wiseman, J 1992, 'The social justice strategy', in M Considine and B Costar (eds), *Trials in power. Cain, Kirner and Victoria, 1982–1992*, Melbourne University Press, Carlton, Vic.

13 Creating joined-up government

Challenging intuitive logic

Gemma Carey and Brad Crammond

Introduction

The aspiration to link different parts of government is not a new goal; it is, in fact, one of the oldest preoccupations in public administration (6 1997; Pollitt 2003). However, the packaging of these ideas as 'joined-up government' by the Blair Government in 1997 brought such approaches to the fore amongst commonwealth countries such as Australia, New Zealand and Canada (6 1997; Christensen and Laegreid 2007; O'Flynn 2009).

Joined-up government continues to have both political appeal and policy relevance, as governments continue to search for ways to address wicked policy problems. Broadly, joined-up government seeks to improve the efficacy of policies by removing tensions and contradictions, to create more efficient use of resources, improve cooperation, and provide citizens with more integrated services (Pollitt 2003). Joined-up government (JUG) is an umbrella term; how 'joining-up' is done depends on both the nature of the problem and the government (Davies 2009; Richards 2001). At present, much of the work on joined-up government is theoretical rather than empirical, meaning that little is known about the real world effectiveness of joined-up government initiatives. Increasingly, public administration scholars are turning their attention to how whole of government approaches are created and whether they are appropriate or effective in combating the problems they set out to address (Christensen and Laegreid 2007; Pollitt 2003; Ross *et al.* 2011).

Along side the rise of joined-up government, we have seen discourses of evidence-based policy take hold. The evidence-based approach is thought to provide a means by which to improve policy outcomes by strengthening decision-making processes and accountability mechanisms, drawing politicians away from seemingly arbitrary ideologically driven decision making (Bacchi 2009; Donald 2001). However, proponents of evidence-based policy have been primarily concerned with evidence of problems and solutions, and far less concerned with evidence of effective processes. As Colebatch notes, our attention naturally goes to the object of policy – 'what's the problem and how is the government trying to address it?' (Colebatch 2006, p. 1). Far less attention is given to the policy process, in part because it is seen as overly complex and difficult (Colebatch 2006).

In this chapter, we provide a synthesis of the empirical public policy research on joined-up government, identifying characteristics associated with success. We then use this synthesis as the basis for reflection upon a recent joined-up initiative in the Australian context at the federal level (the Social Inclusion Agenda). Drawing on these two pieces of work, we put forward a number of recommendations for how to strengthen and improve joined-up initiatives.

What does the research tell us?

Bacchi has argued for the importance of research synthesis for policy: for policy, 'meta-analysis' provides a forum by which disparate empirical studies can be reduced to a common metric (Bacchi 2009). At present, there are no agreed upon methods of qualitative research synthesis, and debate in this area has continued for some time (Dixon-Woods *et al.* 2005; McDermott *et al.* 2004). Thematic approaches to meta-analysis seek to uncover concepts and their meanings from the data (rather than pre-determining them), using inter-pretive approaches to ground the analysis of that data (i.e. existing studies).

In order to identify relevant empirical research on JUG, searches were conducted in Expanded Academic, Academic Complete, JSTOR, Web of Science and Science Direct between 1990 and 2014. Prominent journals in the field, including the *International Journal of Public Administration* and *International Public Management Journal*, were also searched independently. Search terms included joined-up government, joined up governance and whole-of-government.

In total, 823 papers were identified once duplicates were removed. Abstracts of these studies were screened for studies that were empirical evaluations of a past or existing national-level JUG initiative. To be classed as an empirical evaluation, studies had to have collected qualitative or quantitative data on the success of an initiative according to any indicator. Twenty-seven such studies were identified, and Eleven of these were then excluded either for not collecting empirical data or for addressing international governance. The remaining 16 studies were subject to further analysis of their quality, using a framework adapted from McDermott *et al.* (2004), upon which one study was excluded due to poor quality.

Fifteen empirical studies are included in the review. In total, these studies comprise evaluations of 26 joined-up initiative case studies. From these 26 case studies, characteristics associated with success or failure of joined-up initiatives were identified through thematic analysis. Here, like data (in this case, findings, observations and analysis) are grouped together, forming cat-egories and subcategories (Strauss 1987). Guided by the work of Keast (2011), these characteristics are organised into six categories, reproduced in Table 13.1.

Table 13.1 Characteristics associated with successful joined-up government initiatives

	Factors found to aid joined up approaches	Supporting studies
Operational Level	Target multiple levels: • Strategic Government • Managerial • Practitioner • Community	(Burnett and Appleton 2004; Cowell and Martin 2003; Darlow et al. 2007; Karré et al. 2013; Keast 2011; Larner and Craig 2005; Moran et al. 2011; Naidoo 2013; O'Flynn et al. 2011; Ross et al. 2011; Scott and Thurston 2004)
Top-down/ Bottom-up	Top-down and bottom-up	(Askim et al. 2009; Burnett and Appleton 2004; Cowell and Martin 2003; Keast 2011; Larner and Craig 2005; Naidoo 2013; O'Flynn et al. 2011; Signoretta and Craglia 2002)
Nature of control	Decentralised	(Askim et al. 2009; Burnett and Appleton 2004; Cowell and Martin 2003; Keast 2011; Lips et al. 2011; O'Flynn et al. 2011; Ross et al. 2011; Scott and Thurston 2004)
Membership	Reflects the multiple levels targeted for change (i.e. strategic government, managerial, practitioner, community)	(Askim et al. 2009; Burnett and Appleton 2004; Cowell and Martin 2003; Davies 2009; Karré et al. 2013; Keast 2011; Larner and Craig 2005; Moran et al. 2011; Naidoo 2013; O'Flynn et al., 2011; Ross et al. 2011)
Focus	Designed based on both the purpose and the context	(Burnett and Appleton 2004; Davies 2009; Keast 2011; Moran et al. 2011; O'Flynn et al. 2011)
Instruments and their functions	Fulfil a range of functions depending on objectives. For example: • Governance and structure (e.g. committees/taskforces, creation of shared leadership)	(Burnett and Appleton 2004; Cowell and Martin 2003; Darlow et al. 2007; Karré et al. 2013; Keast 2011; Lips et al. 2011; Moran et al. 2011; Naidoo 2013; Scott and Thurston 2004)
	• Managerial changes (e.g. to improve relationships)	(Askim et al. 2009; Larner and Craig 2005; Lips et al. 2011; Moran et al. 2011; Sang et al. 2005; Signoretta and Craglia 2002)
	• Adjusted systems, processes and finances	(Askim et al. 2009; Burnett and Appleton 2004; Darlow et al. 2007; Karré et al. 2013; Keast 2011; O'Flynn et al. 2011)
	• Cultural and institutional change	(Askim et al. 2009; Burnett and Appleton 2004; Davies 2009; Keast 2011; Lips et al. 2011; Naidoo 2013; O'Flynn et al. 2011; Scott and Thurston 2004; Signoretta and Craglia 2002)

While, as Keast (2011) notes, joined-up initiatives can create some progress with only a few key elements and need to be 'fit-for-purpose', a number of clear commonalities emerged from the review. For effective integration, research has found that 'joining' must happen at multiple levels and be supported by a range of cultural and structural interventions (Klijn 1997; O'Flynn *et al.* 2011; Ross *et al.* 2011).

First, joined-up initiatives appear to be most effective when they targeted a range of actors, or levels, of government and the policy process, from strategic decision making in government through to practitioner relationships at the service delivery level. Consistent with this, research also indicates that initiatives need to be both 'top-down' and 'bottom-up'. Efforts to create joined-up government can target either vertical (e.g. linking national and local actors) or horizontal (e.g. forming partnerships between actors at the same level) integration (Ling 2002; Matheson 2000; Stewart 2002). Depending on which approach they favour, these initiatives are often described as following 'top-down' (vertical integration) or 'bottom-up' models (horizontal integration at the practitioner level) (Keast 2011; Matheson 2000). As Keast has argued, "Successful joined-up approaches draw from top-down and bottom-up models to shape hybrid arrangements which draw on the strengths of both, thus forming new models" (Keast 2011, p. 227). Mechanisms for creating integration at the local level include: establishing shared problems, seeking agreed solutions, intersectoral planning, and inter-agency models (Keast 2011). Alongside these 'bottom-up' methods, integration can be encouraged from the 'top' through funding and incentives and the creation of a culture that values joined-up working.

Enabling top-down and bottom-up strategies to function simultaneously requires decentralised control. This is because governments are reliant on individuals, groups and organisations that exist within the policy environment, but are external to government. Research into joined-up approaches within the public policy literature indicates that initiatives need to engage this broad, and dynamic, set of actors. Centralised approaches have also been found to have limited effectiveness in promoting change within government itself, being unable to break down programmatic and departmental silos (Davies 2009; Keast 2011; O'Flynn *et al.* 2011).

In their landmark work, de Bruijn and de Heuvelhof (1997) articulate three approaches to JUG:

- institutional – focused on establishing the rules of engagement as well as organisational frameworks that can set the stage for ongoing interactions and strategy development;
- instrumental – focused on how governments seek to exercise legitimate authority by altering dependency relationships;
- interpersonal – where the aim is to shape the interactions between a range of actors to generate innovative responses (Carey *et al.* 2014a; O'Toole and Hanf 1997).

Interestingly, our analysis of the empirical evidence suggests that initiatives are more likely to be successful if they utilise instruments that operate across these different levels, shaping structures, processes, cultures and relationships.

The Australian Social Inclusion Agenda

In 2007, the Australian Federal Government launched a 'joined-up' approach to addressing social inequality. Through the Social Inclusion Agenda (SIA), the Labor Government sought to strengthen the Australian welfare state, reducing inequality and disadvantage while building social, economic and civic participation (Carey *et al.* 2012; Commonwealth Government of Australia 2009; Commonwealth of Australia 2011, 2009; Gillard and Wong 2007). Running until 2013, the targets of reform included education, employment, health, and infrastructure such as law, 'financials' and economic services (Commonwealth Government of Australia 2009).

Under the SIA, 'joining-up' was pursued on two levels: first, between government departments and, second, between government and non-government organisations (Commonwealth of Australia 2009). This was pursued by the use of a policy narrative of 'social inclusion', aimed at creating cultural and institutional change (Christensen and Laegreid 2007; de Bruijn and Heuvelhof 1997; Kickert *et al.* 1997), along with changes to structure. These included the creation of an advisory board (the Social Inclusion Board) to provide direction on issues relating to social inclusion from experts outside of government, and a Social Inclusion Unit – an interdepartmental working committee located in the Department of Prime Minister and Cabinet (Carey *et al.* 2012).

Creating integration under the SIA

Embedded in the SIA was a centralised and top-down approach to creating joined-up government. As described in the previous section, initiatives that are directed from an 'authoritative core' at strategic levels of government are limited in their ability to create integration (Kickert *et al.* 1997; Klijn 1997). Joined-up government is as much about lower-level politics and relationships as it is about political leadership and change within government (Christensen and Laegreid 2007). Beyond this relatively straightforward observation, the SIA reveals the complex ways in which instruments for joined-up government can interact and derail integration and cohesion.

Policy narratives are instruments aimed at creating important cultural and institutional change – reshaping values, norms and how problems are perceived and understood by policy actors (Christensen and Laegreid 2007; Kickert *et al.* 1997). This is based on the rationale that actors will be more open to process-level changes where there has been a prior shift in their values. They are not, in themselves, aimed at bringing about process-level changes in a direct way. Despite this, under the SIA policymakers attempted to operationalise the concept of 'social inclusion' in the design and conceptualisation of policies and programs (Carey *et al.* 2015, 2014b). Perhaps not surprisingly, this lead to debate, as policymakers grappled with what social inclusion meant and whom it applied to (Carey *et al.* 2015, 2014b).

To resolve this conflict, policymakers subsumed the concept of social inclusion back into existing practice. While aimed at broad scale social policy change and a push towards universal policy delivery (Labonte 2004), in the Australian context social inclusion was used to support greater means testing in policy through a focus on 'the most excluded' (Carey *et al.* 2015). The 'practice norm' for policymakers is to generate policy solutions that are sufficiently targeted towards 'problem populations' separated off from the rest of society (Jamrozik 1998). As O'Flynn *et al.* (2011) suggests, embedded ways of knowing and doing can restrain innovation when it comes to implementing new policy approaches. Hence, during implementation those within government began to gravitate towards targeted approaches. The statements below indicate that policymakers were more comfortable with targeted approaches and the intuitive logic of focusing on those most in need.

> I think there was some confusion initially in government about how hard they were focusing on it, what the breadth of the definition was.... There was a lot of discussion about [the balance] in the bureaucracy.... How do we implement this Agenda? Do we do a big broad picture and try and attack everything or do we target? And in the end my understanding is that they decided to target.
>
> (Carey *et al.* 2015)

> So the social inclusion vision is that all-encompassing thing, but the social inclusion ... mission is about making a system more accessible for the most vulnerable people.
>
> (Carey *et al.* 2015)

The disjuncture between the broad vision encapsulated by the concept of social inclusion and the continuation of normal practice had an undermining effect on joined-up efforts; policymakers across government interpreted this inconsistency as a sign that joining-up had been abandoned (Carey *et al.* 2015). Hence, while political commitment and mandates for change are important (as suggested by the literature), they are insufficient on their own to guide implementation.

The second point of intervention for the implementation of the SIA was the creation of new administrative structures, aimed at creating integration and coordination between different departments in order to more effective policy solutions. The Social Inclusion Unit was principally responsible for driving and coordinating action on social inclusion across government and creating alignment between policies developed in different areas of government. While the Unit was placed in the Department of Prime Minister and

Cabinet (PMC) to give it greater authority, policymakers felt that this created an odd structure, where the Unit was detached from the Minister for Social Inclusion (the Ministry for Social Inclusion was associated with the Department of Education, Employment and Workplace Relations). This arrangement was described as limiting the ability of the Social Inclusion Unit to work across government, and with ministers, to drive the implementation of the SIA:

> There was an odd political structure where you've got it sitting in the Department of Prime Minister and Cabinet and it *sort of* makes sense but ... if the minister is somewhere else while they're still sitting in the Prime Minister's Department. So they've got two or three masters so they're not quite sure how to work with them...
>
> (Carey *et al.* 2015)

The Social Inclusion Unit had no formal authority over other departments, limiting its ability to influence activities across government departments. This is consistent with previous work, which has found that interdepartmental groups of this nature can create 'serious dysfunction', due to the separation in responsibilities between policy design and implementation (Davies 2009; James 2004; Keast 2011; Kickert *et al.* 1997; O'Flynn *et al.* 2011). They can in fact end up creating new administrative siloes (O'Flynn *et al.* 2011). The case of the SIA also revealed similar issues with cross-sectoral advisory boards which are linked to a central department (see Carey *et al.* 2014b). Interestingly, participants conceptualised strong mechanisms as being based *within* the existing siloed departmental structure, undermining the SIA at its most basic level.

When it came to creating better integration between government and non-government organisations, and between non-government organisations, the SIA did not fare much better. The high profile reform agenda – promoted through the policy narrative and placement of related committees within a high profile ministry – raised the expectations of non-government actors with regard to the speed and nature of change (see Carey *et al.* 2014b). When these expectations were not met, the resulting frustration and disappointment impedes trust between government and non-government sectors – creating 'reform fatigue' and impacting the likely uptake of future reform efforts (Carey *et al.* 2014b). This problem is captured in the following quote, taken from a working paper produced by Australian Catholic Social Services, a major peak body representing over 180 welfare organisations:

> While dramatic narratives of reform can help build support, the downside is that they set the stage for disappointment. When success fails to come easily or quickly, the direction of the story can shift abruptly.... 'Social inclusion' may lose its shine and fall from use.
>
> (Carey *et al.* 2015)

Paradoxically, this statement suggests that the more ambitious the reform vision and the higher the profile it is given, the greater likelihood it will be assumed to be ineffective, and the more chance it will be ignored by non-government organisations (thereby contributing to its ineffectiveness).

The experiences of the SIA demonstrate the need for greater attention to be given to process-based evidence. Experiences documented in the literature indicate that the type of top-down approach taken by the SIA, and lack of accountability mechanisms, was unlikely to produce good results. Specifically, the case of the SIA raises questions about how to improve the functionality of these units without reverting to traditional siloed structures, and how governments can deliver the message about a cultural shift towards joined-up government, without creating a backlash among non-government organisations. These are questions we tackle in the final section of this chapter.

What can be done differently?

Increasingly, the evidence suggests that joined-up government requires a robust 'supportive architecture', in order to support horizontal and vertical integration (O'Flynn *et al.* 2011). In this final section, we outline what this supportive architecture might look like, based on the research presented in the first two sections of this chapter. Table 13.2 outlines the different components of a strong horizontal and vertical integration matrix to support joined-up government.

Skill development and training has emerged as an important area of intervention for joined-up government (Ling 2002; Pollitt 2003). In a review of joined-up government initiatives and recommendations, Ling (2002) found that relational skills such as new leadership skills, networking, shared agenda and goal settings, and understanding wider operational contexts are important, alongside unlearning certain skills developed from horizontal working. Joining-up creates professional and bureaucratic tensions. Negotiating these tensions requires: problem-solving skills, coordination skills (getting people to the table), brokering skills (seeing what needs to happen), flexibility, deep knowledge of the system and, for front line workers, both knowledge of how to work with their community and how to obtain information about their community (demographics, needs and so on), and a willingness to undertake the emotional labour associated with relational working. These skills are particularly important for leaders.

Many joined-up initiatives focus on changing structures through, for example, new administrative units. While structural change is important, the mistake is to think that structure alone can drive cultural change (Pollitt 2003). For successful integration, the emphasis must be on knowing what types of structures are appropriate for both the context and the desired outcome (Keast 2011). For example, Keast (2011) argues that, if the outcome is to share information and improve cooperation, the linkages between

Table 13.2 Horizontal and vertical integration matrix

	Horizontal	Vertical
Politics	Skill development	Strategic focus on collaboration; Cultural change; Incentive and accountability mechanisms (including between government departments); Mandate for change; Dedicated resources and financing; Local control and leadership
Central government Government agencies	Shared objectives and targets training and skill development Changes to structures Changes to processes	
Between government and non-government sectors	Networking events Cross-sectoral forums Secondments Board appointments	
Non-government sector	Training and skill development Shared control of resources Inter-organisational forums Shared goal and agenda setting Memoranda of understanding	
Service delivery	Information sharing Joint case management Co-locations	

members can be quite loose, such as efforts to increase networking and collaborative agenda setting. If, however, the desired outcome is to achieve systems change (or collaboration), the linkages must be much tighter and more complex. These arrangements will need to include, for example, clear lines of accountability along with effective incentive mechanisms (these are discussed in more detail below). Legislative changes to ensure information sharing and shared budgets are also critical, which may include shared revenue streams, pooled budgets and other ways to ensure shared resources (Darlow *et al.* 2007; Keast 2011; Mulgan 2005; Pollitt 2003).

As noted throughout this chapter, a key ingredient for creating joined-up government is cultural and institutional change. This change must permeate all levels through strong vertical mechanisms, such as a strategic focus on collaboration at all levels. Capturing the interests of politicians is one component of this and helps to ensure policymakers have a mandate for change (Blackman *et al.* 2010; Karré *et al.* 2013); as Pollitt (2003) notes, politicians cannot create joined-up government on their own, but they can undermine it. A strategic focus on joining up can ensure clear vision and secure shifts in values and culture (Ross *et al.* 2011). Yet, this focus must penetrate to the street level, as creating a collaborative culture on the ground is as important – if not more – in the long run (Lipsky 1980).

Joined-up government often relies on interdepartmental groups. When interdepartmental groups are not integrated into existing horizontal structures, departments continue to carry the burden of accountability and implementation, while interdepartmental groups generate ideas but lack the capacity to get things done (thereby creating tensions between new and existing structures (Davies 2009; James 2004; Kickert *et al.* 1997; O'Flynn *et al.* 2011). Strong accountability and incentive mechanisms can support integration and create formal relationships and structures between interdepartmental committees, advisory bodies and departments. These include formal mechanisms, such as performance-based accountabilities built around output and outcome measurements, through to more informal accountability arrangements, such as dialogue (Roberts 2002; Romzek and Dubnick 1987). These need to be accompanied by dedicated resources, such as funds earmarked for cross-cutting policies (Ling 2002).

One of the strongest lessons emerging from the empirical literature on joined-up government is the need for multiple interventions and flexibility, so that mechanisms can be added, removed or refined as 'joining up' progresses. Joining up is a dynamic process and the instruments and mechanisms used to create and support such efforts need to be equally dynamic and flexible. Achieving success requires a balancing of horizontal and vertical mechanisms and a willingness to abandon unsuccessful tools and approaches 'mid-stream'. Critically, when it comes to creating joined-up government, the stakes are high. As noted in the authors' previous work (Carey *et al.* 2014b), when joined-up initiatives are poorly implemented the resulting distrust and frustration can derail future reform efforts.

Conclusion

Joined-up government is a complex, expensive and elusive goal, which has captured public administrators' attention and imagination since the 1950s. It offers great promise for tackling the complex, or 'wicked', policy problems that concern the governments of industrialised countries. However, the challenges are perhaps as great as the promise. As Richards (2001) has noted, there is a 'glibness' in the way joined-up government is used, which disguises the major structural and systemic changes required within government and between government and other sectors. To overcome the barriers, we must move away from popular instruments that have intuitive appeal (but little empirical weight), in order to develop new strategies and approaches for creating integration. In this chapter, we have argued that joined-up government needs a 'matrix' style supportive architecture, where multiple horizontal efforts and supported by strong vertical mechanisms.

References

6, P 1997, *Holistic government*, Demos, London.

Askim, J, Christensen, T, Fimreite, A L and Lægreid, P, 2009, 'How to carry out joined-up government reforms: lessons from the 2001–2006 Norwegian welfare reform', *International Journal of Public Administration*, vol. 32, pp. 1006–1025, doi:10.1080/01900690903223888.

Bacchi, C 2009, *Analysing policy: what's the problem represented to be?* Pearson, NSW.

Blackman, D, Buick, F, Halligan, J and Marsh, I 2010, *Australian experiences with whole of government: constraints and paradoxes in practice*, viewed 22 May 2015, http://ssrn.com/abstract=1927603 or http://dx.doi.org/10.2139/ssrn.1927603.

Burnett, R and Appleton, C 2004, 'Joined-up services to tackle youth crime', *British Journal of Criminology*, vol. 44, pp. 34–54.

Carey, G, Crammond, B and Keast, R 2014a, 'Creating change in government to address the social determinants of health: how can efforts be improved?', *BMC Public Health*, 14:1087, doi:doi:10.1186/1471–2458–14–1087.

Carey, G, Crammond, B and Riley, T 2014b, 'Top-down approaches to joined-up government: examining the unintended consequences of weak implementation', *International Journal of Public Administration*, 1–12, doi:10.1080/01900692.2014.903276.

Carey, G, McLoughlin, P and Crammond, B 2015, 'Implementing joined-up government: lessons from the Australian social inclusion agenda: implementing joined-up government', *Australian Journal of Public Administration Online First*, doi:10.1111/1467–8500.12096. Also now published as (2015) vol. 74, no. 2, pp. 176–186.

Carey, G, Riley, T and Crammond, B 2012, 'The Australian government's "social inclusion agenda": the intersection between public health and social policy', *Critical Public Health*, vol. 22, pp. 47–59, doi:10.1080/09581596.2011.559535.

Christensen, T and Laegreid, P 2007, 'The whole-of-government approach to public sector reform', *Public Administration Review*, vol. 67, pp. 1059–1066.

Colebatch, H 2006, *Beyond the policy cycle: the policy process in Australia*, Allen & Unwin, New South Wales.

Commonwealth Government of Australia 2009, *Principles for social inclusion – everyone's job*, Commonwealth Government of Australia, Canberra.

Commonwealth of Australia 2011, *Foundations for a stronger fairer Australia*, Commonwealth Government of Australia, Canberra.

Commonwealth of Australia 2009, *The Australian Public service social inclusion policy design and delivery toolkit*, Commonwealth Government of Australia, Canberra.

Cowell, R and Martin, S 2003, 'The joy of joining up: modes of integrating the local government modernisation agenda', *Environment and Planning C: Government and Policy*, vol. 21, pp. 159–179, doi:10.1068/c0135.

Darlow, A, Percy-Smith, J and Wells, P 2007, 'Community strategies: are they delivering joined up governance?', *Local Government Studies*, vol. 33, pp. 117–129. doi:10.1080/03003930601081457.

Davies, J S 2009, 'The limits of joined-up government: towards a political analysis', *Public Administration*, vol. 87, pp. 80–96. doi:10.1111/j.1467–9299.2008.01740.x.

De Bruijn, J and Heuvelhof, E 1997, 'Instrument for network management', in W Kickert, E-H Klijn and J Koppenjan (eds), *Managing complex networks: strategies for the public sector*, Sage, London, pp. 166–191.

Dixon-Woods, M, Agarwal, S, Jones, D, Young, B and Sutton, A 2005, 'Synthesising qualitative and quantitative evidence: a review of possible methods', *Journal of Health Services Research and Policy*, vol. 10, pp. 45–53.

Donald, A 2001, 'Commentary: research must be taken seriously', *British Medical Journal*, 278–279.

Gillard, J and Wong, P 2007, *An Australian social inclusion agenda*, Australian Labor Party, Canberra.

James, O 2004, 'The UK core executive's use of public service agreements as a tool of governance', *Public Administration*, vol. 82, pp. 397–419.

Jamrozik, A 1998, *The sociology of social problems: theoretical perspectives and methods of intervention*, Cambridge University Press, New York.

Karré, P M, Van der Steen, M and Van Twist, M 2013, 'Joined-up government in the Netherlands: experiences with program ministries', *International Journal of Public Administration*, vol. 36, pp. 63–73. doi:10.1080/01900692.2012.713295.

Keast, R 2011, 'Joined-up governance in Australia: how the past can inform the future', *International Journal of Public Administration*, vol. 34, pp. 221–231, doi:10.108 0/01900692.2010.549799.

Kickert, W, Klijn, E-H and Koppenjan, J (eds) 1997, *Managing complex networks: strategies for the public sector*, Sage, London.

Klijn, E-H 1997, 'An overview', in W Kickert, E-H Klijn and J Koppenjan (eds), *Managing complex networks: strategies for the public sector*, Sage, London, pp. 166–191.

Labonte, R 2004, 'Social inclusion/exclusion: dancing the dialectic', *Health Promotion International*, vol. 19, pp. 115–121, doi:10.1093/heapro/dah112.

Larner, W and Craig, D 2005, 'After neoliberalism? Community activism and local partnerships in Aotearoa New Zealand', *Antipode*, vol. 37, pp. 402–424.

Ling, T 2002, 'Delivering joined–up government in the UK: dimensions, issues and problems', *Public Administration*, vol. 80, pp. 615–642.

Lips, A M B, O'Neill, R R and Eppel, E A, 2011, 'Cross-agency collaboration in New Zealand: an empirical study of information sharing practices, enablers and barriers in managing for shared social outcomes', *International Journal of Public Administration*, vol. 34, pp. 255–266, doi:10.1080/01900692.2010.533571.

Lipsky, M 1980, *Street-level bureaucracy*, Sage, New York.

Matheson, C 2000, 'Policy formulation in Australian government: vertical and horizontal axes', *Australian Journal of Public Administration*, vol. 59, pp. 44–55.

McDermott, E, Graham, H, Hamilton, V and Glasgow, L 2004, *Experiences of being a teenage mother in the UK: a report of a systematic review of qualitative studies*, Centre for Evidence-based Public Health Policy, University of Glasgow, Glasgow.

McDermott, Elizabeth, Hilary Graham, Val Hamilton, and Lancaster Glasgow 2004 Experiences of Being a Teenage Mother in the UK: A Report of a Systematic Review of Qualitative Studies. Lancaster: Institute for Health Research.

Moran, N, Glendinning, C, Stevens, M, Manthorpe, J, Jacobs, S, Wilberforce, M, Knapp, M, Challis, D, Fernandez, J-L, Jones, K and Netten, A 2011, 'Joining up government by integrating funding streams? The experiences of the individual budget pilot projects for older and disabled people in England', *International Journal of Public Administration*, vol. 34, pp. 232–243.

Mulgan, G 2005, 'Joined-up government: past, present, and future', in V Bogdanor (ed.), *Joined-up government*, Oxford University Press, New York, pp. 175–187.

Naidoo, V 2013, 'The challenges of policy coordination at a programme level: why joining up is hard to do', *Development Southern Africa*, vol. 30, pp. 386–400, doi:10. 1080/0376835X.2013.817309.

O'Flynn, J 2009, 'The cult of collaboration in public policy', *Australian Journal of Public Administration*, vol. 68, pp. 112–116, doi:10.1111/j.1467–8500.2009.00616.x.

O'Flynn, J, Buick, F, Blackman, D and Halligan, J 2011, 'You win some, you lose some: experiments with joined-up government', *International Journal of Public Administration*, vol. 34, pp. 244–254. doi:10.1080/01900692.2010.540703.

O'Toole, L and Hanf, K 1997, 'Managing implementation processes in networks', in W Kickert, E-H, Klijn and J Koppenjan (eds), *Managing complex networks: strategies for the public sector*, Sage, London, pp. 137–151.

Pollitt, C 2003, 'Joined-up government: a survey', *Political Studies Review*, vol. 1, pp. 34–49.

Richards, S 2001, *Four types of joined-up government and the problem of accountability*, Annex to National Audit Office *Joining Up to Improve Public Services* (HC 383 2001–2002), TSO, London.

Roberts, N 2002, 'Keeping public officials accountable through dialogue: resolving the accountability paradox', *Public Administration Review*, vol. 62, pp. 658–669.

Romzek, B S and Dubnick, M J 1987, 'Accountability in the public sector: lessons from the Challenger tragedy', *Public Administration Review*, vol. 47, p. 227, doi:10.2307/975901.

Ross, S, Frere, M, Healey, L and Humphreys, C 2011, 'A whole of government strategy for family violence reform', *The Australian Journal of Public Administration*, vol. 70, no. 2, pp. 131–142, doi:10.1111/j.1467–8500.2011.00717.x.

Sang, N, Birnie, R V, Geddes, A, Bayfield, N G, Midgley, J L, Shucksmith, D M and Elston, D 2005, 'Improving the rural data infrastructure: the problem of addressable spatial units in a rural context', *Land Use Policy*, vol. 22, pp. 175–186, doi:10.1016/j.landusepol.2003.08.008.

Scott, C M and Thurston, W E 2004, 'The influence of social context on partnerships in Canadian health systems', *Gender, Work and Organization*, vol. 11, pp. 481–505.

Signoretta, P and Craglia, M 2002, 'Joined-up government in practice: a case study of children's needs in Sheffield', *Local Government Studies*, vol. 28, pp. 59–76, doi:10.1080/714004127.

Stewart, J., 2002, 'Horizontal coordination – how far have we gone and how far can we go? The Australian view', *The Public Interest*, July 2002, pp. 21–26.

Strauss, A 1987, *Qualitative analysis for social scientists*, Cambridge University Press, Cambridge.

14 Collaboration as cultural performance

Agency and efficacy

Helen Dickinson and Helen Sullivan

Introduction

Despite the fact that collaboration is a core concept within the scholarship and practice of public administration, it has received remarkably little critical analysis. Much of what has been written about collaboration is inherently rationalist and treats it as an instrumental tool intended to bring about particular ends such as reduced inequalities or improved service user outcomes. Yet, the evidence to support a clear link between collaboration and improved outcomes is weak at best. We have previously argued (e.g. Dickinson and Sullivan 2013; Dickinson 2014) that this lack of evidence may be because collaboration is treated instrumentally so missing the work it does as cultural performance expressed through social efficacy. In this chapter, we seek to demonstrate the ways in which collaboration can be seen as an expression of cultural performance. We do this by re-reading evidence from case studies of collaborative working from England and Wales, where we have been involved in assessing collaborative performance. In doing so, we illustrate the persistent appeal of the concept of collaboration to policy makers and practitioners.

The chapter is structured as follows. In the first section we provide an account of collaboration, its use in public policy and key criticisms. We then provide an overview of cultural performance and its application to the concept of collaboration. We then use this approach to re-read the evidence from three case studies of collaboration. We conclude that examining collaboration in terms of social efficacy reveals a great deal about why policy makers and practitioners persist with this idea and practice in the face of a lack of evidence of effectiveness and significant struggles to make collaboration work on the ground.

Collaboration and its critics

Mainstream discussions of governance suggest that in recent years we have moved away from hierarchies and markets as governing modes towards networks. The case for networks is often made as a reaction to the tensions that arise from hierarchies and market modes of governance. While hierarchies are often portrayed as slow and inflexible, public sector market-based relationships may be mistrusted, as competitive relationships are seen as anathema to the delivery of public goods. In addition the terms associated with hierarchy and markets can be perceived negatively when viewed against those of networks, which are often seen as 'relational', based on 'reciprocity' and effectively playing to 'complementary strengths', as opposed to being based on 'formal rules' or 'contracts'. It is proposed that within networks, actors are working towards the same aims and objectives and therefore generate trust between them. This trust reduces transaction costs and avoids the formal structures associated with hierarchies (although actors will likely be bound by shared understandings or informal rules). Trust allows partners to work together more effectively as they perceive less uncertainty between stakeholders and are better able to predict the actions of their partners (Putnam 2003; Rowlinson 1997).

Networks reflect the aspiration of policymakers to promote collaboration, though in practice this aspiration may be represented in a range of different structural forms. In the UK the emphasis on collaboration was most overtly expressed by the New Labour governments (1997–2010), who used this in an attempt to achieve a number of different, though linked, policy goals including: diversifying public services through public–private partnerships; reducing fragmentation in policy and services by 'joining-up' through collaborative action in key sites and spaces; and, maximising the engagement of all interested stakeholders by promoting collaborative governance. The policy rhetoric reflected the apparently benign features of networks, emphasising the way in which the private sector could 'add value' to public services through partnership arrangements, how professionals could work better together if particular organisational or professional barriers were removed, and how diverse and disparate communities could be brought together to work with the state in a spirit of consensus and co-operation (Sullivan and Skelcher 2002). It quickly became apparent though that the New Labour agenda contained a number of tensions and contradictions, not least that appeals to collaboration and co-operation were accompanied by instruments of performance management and control that were centrally driven and incentivised sole rather than joint activity (Barnes *et al.* 2005).

While collaboration proliferated under New Labour in the UK and developed apace in Europe, North America and Australia, claims that network had replaced hierarchy as the dominant mode of governance proved unfounded. Davies (2007) is one among a number of critics who have consistently questioned the demise of hierarchy. Others have noted how attempts at forms of collaborative governance often replicated modernist practices (Newman 2001; Marinetto 2003; Larner & Craig 2005). Rather than producing new ways of working which fundamentally changed the nature of interactions between individuals, populations and public institutions collaborative efforts often served to 'managerialise' complex debates. Instead of engaging in discussions about how structural inequalities might be addressed, debates have instead focused on technical issues of how to achieve collaboration (be this through structural means, different types of roles and responsibilities or sharing budgets). This critique offers an important challenge to the normative discourse of collaboration as a 'good thing', but it is also limited. Specifically the role of agency is neglected or treated crudely with actors described either as Machiavellian agents seeking to serve their own interests, or as passive recipients of others' actions, which ultimately perpetuates the dominance of those with resource, positional or authority power. In this chapter we adopt a cultural performance approach in an attempt to provide a more complete account of the agency of individuals in engaging in collaborative efforts.

Performing collaboration

In exploring collaboration as cultural performance we draw heavily on the work of Jon McKenzie (2001) and his analysis of the different facets of performance within contemporary society. McKenzie identifies three inter-linked performance paradigms – organisational, technological, and cultural. In Table 14.1 we provide an overview of these approaches and set out further detail in relation to these concepts below.

Organisational performance prioritises *efficiency*, achieving more for less by employing tools of performance improvement such as setting targets, identifying relevant performance indicators and measures, and initiating regular reviews and assessments. These tools are employed within a culture of worker 'empowerment', decentralising decision making to teams and individuals in order to foster creativity and innovation. This paradigm dominates public management systems in the global north and is immediately familiar to those who work in and/or study them. Assessments of collaborative performance mimic these tools, for example devising targets for and indicators of collaborative performance. They also assume a rational basis for collaborative action – collaboration will lead to improved outcomes that are tangible and measurable (see Sullivan *et al.* 2013 for a discussion). Importantly for our argument and analysis, the workings of the organisational performance paradigm can be understood as simultaneously liberating, freeing individuals to be creative in pursuit of efficiency, and constraining, regulating how that freedom is exercised through the institutionalisation of performance regimes.

Technological performance is concerned with *effectiveness* and the ways in which technological advancements can enhance the performance of everyday objects as well as highlighting the creation of a niche group of 'high performance' objects constituted by 'cutting-edge' technologies working together. The technological paradigm becomes relevant in the context of our argument because of the contribution of machines and innovations, particularly computers and telecommunications to improving the overall performance of other systems, including public policy and/or service delivery systems. Ironically perhaps, public policy and public service collaboration often experience technology as a barrier to enhanced collaborative activity with examples of incompatible IT systems preventing rather than promoting improved performance (Sullivan and Williams 2009).

Table 14.1 Features of different forms of performance

	Efficiency	Effectiveness	Efficacy
Paradigm	Performance Management	Techno–Performance. No specific paradigm although closely aligned with computer science.	Performance Studies
Contributing disciplines/areas of study	Human relations, systems theory, economics, organisational development, information processing and decision making	Computer science, engineering, rocket science, product design.	Theatre studies, anthropology, ethnography, sociology, psychology, linguistics.
Challenge	Working better and costing less. Maximising outputs and minimising inputs.	Executability – the technical 'carrying out' of prescribed tasks, successful or not.	Embodiment of symbolic structures in living behaviour and the transformation of those structures through discourses and practices of transgression, resistance and mutation.
Tools and techniques	Setting targets, performance indicators and measures, pay for performance, restructuring.	Computers, statistical modelling, computer aided design.	Dramaturgy, reflexive practices, storytelling, ethnography.
Performance is…	Rational, it can be controlled for, predicted, managed and ultimately delivered	Satisficing, different facets of performance are weighed up against one another. It is the result of a long and open series of negotiations and compromises.	Always interactional in nature, it can both reaffirm existing traditions and beliefs or resist and adapt these.

Cultural performance privileges *social efficacy*, the constitution of meaning and affirmation of values that is achieved via an engagement with social norms. Drawing on Performance Studies literatures, McKenzie identified cultural performance as an expression of staged or ritualised representations or enactments of particular social and cultural traditions. Performances may be transformative or transgressive, encouraging and securing conformance to a set of traditions and values or promoting subversion of those same traditions and values in pursuit of others. Cultural performance can offer both a means of reaffirmation and resistance. This paradigm offers an opportunity to view collaboration differently, to explore it as a "performance act, interactional in nature and involving symbolic forms and live bodies [that] provides a way to constitute meaning and affirm individual and cultural values" (Stern and Henderson 1993, p. 3).

Adopting a cultural performance perspective means that we cannot simply look at the actions and interactions of individuals and organisations as primarily motivated by rational motives: their meaning goes beyond this. Decisions to collaborate are similarly complex and are driven by motivations that are not rational but reflective of particular values or meanings that are attached to collaboration. Exploring these motivations can provide helpful insights into why actors choose to collaborate and persist in the face of limited evidence of its capacity to improve outcomes.

Dickinson (2014) argues that in order to develop a complete view of collaborative performance we need to take all three perspectives into account. She applies the different dimensions of performance to the context of collaboration to generate examples of the sorts of questions that are considered within the different paradigms (see Table 14.2). In the sections that follow we

Table 14.2 Questions to interrogate different aspects of performance

Organisational efficiency	*Technological effectiveness*	*Cultural efficacy*
• What different forms of partnerships exist and how do their features differ from one another? • Do partnerships lead to improved services? What measures demonstrate this? • Do partnerships lead to improved outcomes for service users? What measures demonstrate this? • Are partnerships cost-effective compared to other forms of arrangements?	• What types of technology are being used? • To what degree do technologies manage to execute their prescribed tasks? • What negotiations and compromises are made between possible technology performances?	• What discourses of partnership are present and what performative work do discourses do? • How do actors perform a collaborative self? • What are the affective dimensions of discourses and performances? • What kinds of metaphors and symbols are present?

apply these ideas and questions to a re-reading of case studies of collaboration to try to develop a more rounded understanding of collaboration and actors' engagement with it.

Re-reading collaboration cases studies

In this section we set out three case studies that illustrate the cultural performance of collaboration in different ways. The case studies were not undertaken for this purpose; rather we are re-reading cases undertaken for other research and evaluation projects which were exploring collaborative performance in the context of efficiency or more often effectiveness. Re-examining the cases through the lens of cultural performance and efficacy allows us to consider the ways in which individuals gain meaning and fulfilment from engaging with collaboration beyond the achievement of pre-determined goals or outcomes. The cases share a health and social care focus, though they are situated in countries with distinct policy agendas – England and Wales.

Chronic care condition management programme

Williams and Sullivan (NLIAH 2009) undertook a case study of the 'Pathways to Work – Condition Management programme' in Neath Port Talbot and Swansea as part of an all Wales review of learning about and from collaborations in health and social care. The Condition Management Programme (CMP) was one element of a wider welfare reform programme aiming to provide a single gateway to financial, employment and health support for people claiming incapacity benefits. Provided through the local NHS, the CMP aimed to enable people to understand and manage their health condition so that they could get back to work. A partnership between the Department of Health and Department of Work and Pensions financed and managed the CMP, while Jobcentre Plus offices delivered the programme. Although the CMP worked to a particular model of delivery, local actors had flexibility to reflect local circumstances and needs in its local application.

The CMP comprised a project manager and administrative staff employed directly by the Local Health Board and a team of clinical staff employed or seconded by Abertawe Bro Morgannwg University NHS Trust. A Steering Group with representatives from Neath Port Talbot County Borough Council, the NHS Trust, Swansea and Neath Port Talbot Local Health Boards, Job Centre Plus, Neath Port Talbot Communities First and Neath Port Talbot Council for Voluntary Service oversaw the work of the Programme – a 12-week Condition Management Course delivered from 27 community venues scattered throughout the Neath Port Talbot and Swansea areas. The course was a cognitive educational programme directed at people with cardio-vascular, mental health and muscular-skeletal problems; it was a complement to traditional medical interventions delivered through conventional routes.

CMP participants offered a number of stories about the benefits of participating in the Programme including improvements to self-belief and self-confidence and in some cases a return to part and full-time working. 'The powerful boost of patient stories' reinforced the commitment of the Steering Group and CMP team to the Programme – "all those tears and tantrums and difficult discussions have been worth it – the stories are so emotional about people's life changes". However it was acknowledged that the contribution of the CMP to increasing levels of employment amongst people receiving Incapacity Benefit was small and that establishing causal links between CMP and return to work was difficult. Reviewing the case study material through a lens of cultural performance provides an opportunity to explore the reasons why workers retained such enthusiasm for the CMP and for collaboration.

An obvious feature of the interviews and case notes associated with the CMP study was the way in which collaboration had been normalised as a way of working in the locality. Interviewees referred frequently to the existence and importance of a culture of partnership working particularly in the Neath Port Talbot area. As well as formal meetings between Chief Executives of the Abertawe Bro Morgannwg University NHS Trust, Neath Port Talbot Local Health Board, Neath Port Talbot County Borough Council and Neath Port Talbot Council for Voluntary Service, respondents claimed that a mature framework of partnership structures including the Local Service Board, Health, Social Care and Well Being Partnership and Children and Young People's Partnership institutionalised collaboration as a legitimate aspect of local governance.

However, alongside claims of normalcy were other representations of collaboration as somehow outside the mainstream, the territory of a select few who drew on high levels of social capital to function across organisational and professional boundaries. Key individuals associated with CMP considered themselves to be part of what one respondent referred to as "the local partnership mafia".

Importantly, collaboration was not seen as a 'cover' for unpalatable activity; rather participants were at pains to point out that the partnership was based on a common understanding that the purpose of the CMP Programme was to improve individual wellbeing and that considerable work had been done "to allay any fears that it was about forcing people back to work".

Considerable emphasis was placed on the contribution of personal relationships to the CMP as "they can be the making or breaking of collaborative arrangements". Interviewees expressed their confidence in their colleagues, referring to trusting relationships amongst themselves and an ability to work well together: "it's a very effective and well functioning group; the people are supportive, fully engaged and see the benefits of the service; nobody seems to be professionally precious and everyone has something to contribute" and "discussions have been open and frank since the start". Interviewees readily acknowledged conflicts and disagreements in the partnership, "most of them have been about approach because people come with different perspectives grounded in different models – medical, social and voluntary sector – but we've all rubbed each other's edges off". This emphasis on individual professionals' being willing and able to acknowledge that they worked with different 'models' of health and social care, and being prepared to try to reconcile such diverse perspectives for the purposes of the CMP highlighted a key performance challenge for the collaboration. In the words of one respondent,

> there was a degree of learning at the start – why are we here, what do we each want – but the coming together was a nice process – it could have easily been derailed if each partner stuck to a medical or social model rather than seeing it in its broader context – it's not about pills and exercises.

Interviewees repeatedly asserted that the process of collaboration was challenging but enjoyable. In part this was linked to the challenge of working with different models of care but it was also linked to individuals' reported desire to take risks, to do things differently and find fulfilment in their work. Collaboration offered workers an opportunity to do this and the fact that the CMP was a 'special project' meant that individuals volunteered to get involved: they were not forced into a 'partnership' arrangement. This voluntarism seemed to offer a freedom to be different but in a safe space as workers retained their substantive posts in the NHS or other organisation. The clinical lead for the CMP described this as building a team from a set of practitioners "who have stepped outside their traditional models of working – who want to do things differently outside their traditional constraints – are attracted by a new project and are prepared to take risks". Likewise the practitioners involved in the project reported that "they find it very exciting to employ their skills in an environment of partnership, a situation that is community-based, and an arena where they feel they can make a difference by getting people back into employment".

The chair of the CMP steering group was identified as a key player in the collaboration, someone able to exercise the right kind of leadership for the group. The interview with the chair revealed the performative dimension to her leadership role, albeit in two very different ways. The chair was keen to emphasise her leadership as an expression of collaborative performance:

> I promote a collaborative approach to a shared agenda; it is not a directive role – it involves a balance between setting an agenda and sharing it; setting it together instils a greater sense of ownership and commitment; it is important to promote mutual respect amongst partnership members and an open process to allow full stakeholder involvement throughout the different stages of the partnership process.

However she was equally keen to distance herself from what she saw as the ritualised partnership performances that operated in place of genuine collaboration:

I find it very frustrating when I see other agencies being nice to each other around tables, especially when you know there are real issues – people play this game around partnership tables then have different discussions outside the room – we don't do that in CMP.

Forensic mental health 'partnership'

Dickinson and Glasby (2010) set out an account of a partnership between a specialist forensic mental health trust (Springfield Mental Health Trust) and a more generalist mental health trust (Shelbyville Mental Health Trust) in England. Springfield is nationally renowned, financially robust and seen as a leading provider of care, while Shelbyville is smaller, based out of town, provides more community-based services and has previously received negative reports from health care inspectors about some aspects of the quality of care it provides. These two trusts formed the 'Forensic Mental Health Partnership (FMHP) which involved Shelbyville staff working in forensics transferring their employment to Springfield who were the lead partner managing the overall forensic services provided at both sites. The arrangement was presented from the start to staff, service users and other stakeholders deliberately as a 'partnership' where there would be mutual learning and sharing between the two organisations. Shelbyville would benefit from the expertise, reputation and resources of Springfield, who would in turn learn about community-based services.

However, the research that Dickinson and Glasby undertook a year after FMHP had been established suggested that it was perceived not as a 'partnership' but as a 'takeover'. Many of the frontline staff at Shelbyville were unhappy with this, feeling that this should be a partnership of equals. Yet, in terms of how FMHP had been established, it did seem that Springfield was performing a takeover: they were the dominant group of staff on the board; all meetings took place at the Springfield site; and those at Shelbyville felt disowned by their own organisation now their management had been delegated to Springfield. The procedures, approach and culture of FMHP were all perceived to be Springfield-dominated with little of Shelbyville visible.

Further, FMHP staff found it difficult to be clear about the types of outcomes that they were aiming to achieve through the partnership. While they agreed it was about better services and being more innovative, on closer interrogation many of the aspirations were about the more efficient use of scarce resources (e.g. single point of access, preventing duplication, simplifying procedures) or were altogether vastly aspirational and well beyond the stated remit of the partnership (e.g. bring in more interpreters, 'sort out' another hospital in the local area not involved in the partnership, improve the health of children in the city as a whole, create better relationships with the local authority, who again were not a partner). Although the brochures and the publicity material talked very much about FMHP being driven by service-user outcomes, the overriding impression from staff was that FMHP was designed to benefit partner organisations. This was further confirmed when in interviews senior managers suggested that part of the initial motivation had come from both organisations attempting to respond to local and national political issues. As Dickinson and Glasby outline:

> At the time the Partnership was first discussed, Shelbyville had recently experienced a high profile mental health homicide and a very critical serious case review was expected shortly. Also at this time, the region was reviewing the current configuration of mental health services, and Shelbyville was one of the organizations rumoured to be at risk of closure or merger. Meanwhile, Springfield was fighting hard to throw off a reputation of being aloof and autocratic, arguing that it should be at the centre of a regional mental health system. Against this background, FMHP was a timely development, as it gave important messages to national policy makers that Shelbyville was dedicated to improving its services and that Springfield was working hard to be a more collaborative member of its local and regional health community.
>
> (Dickinson and Glasby 2010, p. 818)

Staff at Shelbyville had essentially bought into FMHP as they fundamentally believed that a 'true' partnership would mean that there would be sharing across the organisations and therefore that staff and service users alike would benefit. Further, staff believed that this would not simply offer a way of sharing across organisations but would also fulfil a range of fantastical outcomes which went well beyond the remit of the managerial relationship between the hospitals. Staff never questioned the notion that a partnership might not mean mutual sharing and could involve a takeover. Publicly, the organisational drivers identified above were not articulated but they were certainly dominant in the rationale for the establishment of the partnership. Calling the arrangement a 'partnership' helped win staff over and establish the FMHP, which involved significant change to processes of accountability, finance and human resources; changes that could not be easily reversed when staff realised they were unhappy with the outcome.

Newfield health, homelessness and substance misuse teams

Dickinson (2010) reports on a local government with teams engaged in promoting health and social care objectives from within other service areas, specifically housing and environmental health. One team provided mental health and homelessness services, while the other comprised a substance misuse bond scheme. Both teams were relatively small in scale: mental health and homelessness had four full-time staff; the substance misuse bond scheme had five full-time staff; and there were two full-time heads of service who were also involved in these arrangements. These teams were part of a directorate recognised nationally as an area of good practice, receiving a 3 star adult social services rating in December 2006, winning National *Community Care* magazine and *Foundations* awards for the Home Improvement Agency, receiving positive inspections of their services and receiving recognition from CLG and Trading Standards in relation to several of their services. Senior members of the directorate were interested in further legitimising their reputation by participating in an independent research project.

The teams themselves were described as having developed 'organically'; a need had arisen in relation to these specialised areas and although teams existed to service these particular needs there were no structural or management arrangements in place to 'formalise' these teams in a traditional sense. Despite the senior level 'buy-in' to the research, attempts to engage the teams proved difficult. Research workshops were sparsely attended with the reason given that they were small teams and so needed to cover for each other and provide a presence for the service. Repeated invitations to staff to complete the research survey were met with no response – only one of the relevant heads of service actually completed this. Given staff's apparent unwillingness to engage with the research programme, a series of telephone calls were made in order to establish why this was. These calls proceeded on the premise that there might be a problem with the research process and tools – that they may be experienced as inaccessible or inapplicable to the work of the teams.

During these conversations members of the two partnerships repeatedly used terms such as 'organic' and 'bottom-up' to describe relationships that were built on the basis of 'trust' and 'longstanding' interactions between a series of specific individuals. These respondents repeatedly stressed their desire for their partnerships to remain small, informal arrangements which operated to some degree 'under the radar'. By engaging in the research they feared that they would no longer be able to do this. It was feared that the more recognition that they were exposed to locally, the greater the danger that they would be required to 'formalise' in a structural sense or would be more open to 'top-down' direction. This was a process that the team had witnessed in other local teams and believed had compromised the services that those teams had previously offered. The team members were not negative about the research, but were worried that this might in some way serve to undermine the long-term activities that had gone into making these partnerships a reality. It was not possible for the research to proceed on this basis and the case study ceased at that point.

Collaboration as cultural performance – discursive performatives and embodied performances

In this section we consider the case studies together and illustrate the ways in which these examples demonstrate that collaboration has an important meaning for actors across the case studies, including but going beyond its purported contribution to service-user outcomes. Writing about culture and collaboration is not in itself new. A number of authors have written about culture and collaboration (e.g. Peck and Crawford 2004), often citing differing cultures as part of a post hoc rationalisation for why a collaborative endeavour has not succeeded (Peck and Dickinson 2009). In these cases different groups perform different types of professional or organisational cultures and in so doing demonstrate different values and beliefs about public service and care. In this chapter, we argue for a more nuanced and dynamic consideration of culture and performance in respect to collaboration.

The performative work of discourse is evident, albeit in very different ways, across the case studies. In CMP the discourse of 'joined-up' delivery and improved co-ordination drove the initiatives with the promise of better outcomes for service users. In FHMP two discourses were in operation at the same time: the one offered by frontline staff described how bringing the two services together would improve outcomes (effectiveness); the other expressed by senior managers highlighted how bringing the two services together would enable better use of resources and improved compliance with central policy directives on finance and quality standards (efficiency). The tensions at play between these two discourses were masked over by the appeal to 'partnership' that accompanied both – an appeal which "has an inherently positive moral feel about it [to the extent that] it has become almost heretical to question its integrity" (McLaughlin 2004, p. 103). In Newfield the effectiveness discourse in operation locally was accompanied by an evidence-based policy discourse – which promised to authorise and legitimise the teams' work by codifying it as 'good practice'. In each case collaboration was identified as the appropriate response to the circumstances in which different actors found themselves. However, in two cases the performative work of the discourses generated difficulties in practice. In FHMP the tensions between the efficiency and effectiveness discourses manifested themselves in discontent and disappointment among front line staff once the 'partnership' was established. In Newfield, front-line staff anxious about the potential of the evidence-based policy discourse to disrupt their local practices resisted engaging with the research initiative that would draw attention to their work.

Despite the shared appeal to collaboration, collaborative performance in each of the cases was designed and structured very differently. The CMP emphasised a form of stakeholder democracy with each member of the partnership having a say in how things were done and sharing responsibility for the outcomes, regardless of their professional position or organisational resource. In addition, to 'perform' in CMP meant to take risks, to be prepared to experiment and to do things differently – performance was as much about process, decision making and ways of working as it was about outcomes for service users. In some ways this confirms findings of more traditional studies of partnerships which, it is argued, focus predominantly on *process* (how partners work together), rather than *outcomes* (what the partnership actually achieves) (Dickinson 2008). However, where our study differs from these more traditional accounts is that rather than simply describing the experience of partners and noting an absence of a focus on outcomes, we are able to theorise *why* there might be such an absence. In the case of CMP it appears that the performance, or enactment, of a 'collaborative' way of working was seen to be so important that this became the focus of activities, rather than the end product. In FHMP, collaborative performance centred on the effective integration of previously separate structures and systems, though in practice one group of actors experienced these new systems as a 'take-over' by another 'preferred' group. In Newfield, the intention was for collaborative performance to be expressed by regularisation of the local teams' work as a result of its participation in a research programme, but local actors opted out of the process before it could begin.

This diversity continued in the ways in which actors performed a collaborative self (Sullivan 2015), composing and representing their identities through their engagement with the collaboration. In CMP actors described their collaborative selves as an extension of their professional selves, indeed a sign of their authenticity as professionals in a world dominated by 'managerialism' and ideas about techno-bureaucratic performance. The collaborative self was both creative and conflictual – actors identified these as key ingredients for turning collaborative action into service improvement. Performing a collaborative self in CMP also emphasised the distinctiveness of those involved in the collaboration from 'others' – those actors not in the 'partnership mafia'. In FMHP performing a collaborative self came to mean taking on the characteristics of the 'preferred partner' and becoming 'efficient professionals', rather than developing a new collaborative self comprised of the best elements of both partners. This is where we see the affective realm of performance displayed strongly. Given the tensions evident in the discourses of performance at FMHP, actors projected phantasmic outcomes (Fotaki 2010) onto the partnership and ones which could never be realistically associated with the activities of the partnership. Although these might never have been achieved in practice, given the activities of FMHP these were held as unfulfilled promises once the take-over became apparent. In Newfield, performing a collaborative self meant continuing to do what had developed organically but doing it informally and without drawing the attention of those who might wish to regularise and formalise it and so risk limiting its impact.

Cultural performance and efficacy highlight the affective dimension of collaborative discourses and performances. In CMP affect featured in the attention given to the power of user stories, and the expressions of joy, anger and satisfaction at the experience of interacting with each other and with users. In FMHP by contrast, actors expressed frustration, disappointment and anger at the consequences of the 'partnership'. Here too was bewilderment – how could a commitment to collaboration lead to a take-over? And resentment – how could we have been duped in this way? And self-criticism – why didn't we resist, what was it about the promise of partnership that swayed us? In Newfield, the affective dimension remained off limits to those not directly engaged in the teams' work, though the sense of self-protection illustrated in the teams' resistance to the researchers hints at an emotional as well as professional attachment to their collaborative practice and a fear of diluting the impact of what they do by being exposed to a wider audience and cited as good practice.

Conclusion

In this chapter, we have explored the persistent appeal of collaboration among policymakers and practitioners in the face of repeated failure to achieve expectations. We have suggested that collaboration's appeal is vested in it as an expression of cultural performance associated with efficacy rather than efficiency or effectiveness. We have sought to argue this case by re-reading three case studies through the lens of cultural performance: to identify the discourses and cultural values inhabiting each which promote collaboration as an appropriate response to any given circumstance; and to examine the role of agents, the meanings they attached to collaboration and how these continued to motivate their pursuit of collaboration in the face of well-recorded difficulties.

The concept of collaboration has a high degree of penetration in a UK public policy context. In addition to being vague and definitionally slippery, collaboration is widely used precisely because it has a high degree of efficacy (cultural salience). In this sense, collaboration is a keyword in UK public policy. Raymond Williams famously defined 'community' as:

> the warmly persuasive word to describe an existing set of relationships, or the warmly persuasive word to describe an alternative set of relationships. What is most important, perhaps, is that unlike all other terms of social organization ... it never seems to be used unfavourably, and never to be given any positive opposing or distinguishing term.
>
> (Williams 1975, p. 76)

Williams suggests that keywords usually have two main characteristics. First, they are capable of incorporating multiple meanings (which might even be contradictory), but certainly these meanings often bear little relationship to each other. Second, the connotations of keywords are usually positive and difficult to argue against. Being against collaboration within contemporary public policy is akin to being against choice or against empowerment. Calling something 'collaboration' sets the expectation that this is a 'good thing', without necessarily being specific about how or why that may be so.[1] Collaboration has become a mobilising force in driving processes of change and modernisation.

As we illustrate in the case studies, under the guise of improving service user outcomes collaboration has been used to drive significant organisational changes which otherwise may have been resisted. The political discourses of collaboration have been used in governance terms not simply as a movement from hierarchical or market-based relationships to network forms but, instead, as an active tool in influencing actors to engage in processes of change through altering perceptions of what and how health and social care services should be delivered. The implication of this type of argument is that in assessing the relative success of collaborative efforts, rather than assuming that this is a means–ends mechanism to bring about particular outcomes, we need to ask quite different questions of individuals and organisations.

As our case studies reveal, however, we do not see actors as passive dupes in these processes of change. Rather they are active agents engaged with the discourses and practices of collaborative performance for a variety of reasons. For actors the 'rightness' and 'goodness' of collaboration may be a matter of faith, rather than evidence – it is the 'right' way to work. Collaboration may be perceived as a means of finding work fulfilment in a system that prioritises technocratic responses and performance management regimes that dominate public, and more latterly third sector, organisations. The very challenges associated with collaboration such as negotiating diversity and interdependence, the possibilities for creativity and the inevitability of conflict stretch individuals and require them to make use of skills such as judgement that cannot be read off a performance chart but instead need to be honed through experience.

We believe that examining collaboration through the lens of cultural performance provides the opportunity to fill an important gap in our understanding of how collaborations perform and why actors continue to be motivated to engage in collaborative activity. It enables researchers to ask different questions of collaboration and the actors involved focusing on what and how collaborations mean. It also offers researchers a way into understanding agency in collaboration that goes beyond a commitment to improving outcomes, important thought that is, and offers the opportunity to examine collaboration as an instrument of control and liberation, opportunity and constraint, creativity and conflict.

Note

1 This is not to say that 'collaboration' is always understood in this way. To historians of World War II, for example, 'collaboration' may be understood as a 'bad' rather than a 'good thing', reflecting the cultural specificity of the use of the term.

References

Barnes, M, Bauld, L, Benezeval, M, Judge, K, Mackenzie, M and Sullivan, H 2005, *Health action zones: partnerships for health equity*, Routledge, London.

Davies, J S 2007, 'The limits of partnership: an exit-action strategy for local democratic inclusion', *Political Studies*, vol. 55, pp. 779–800.

Dickinson, H 2008, *Evaluating outcomes in health and social care*, Policy Press, Bristol.

Dickinson, H 2010, *The importance of being efficacious: English health and social care partnerships and service user outcomes*, PhD thesis, the University of Birmingham.

Dickinson, H 2014, *Performing governance: partnerships, culture and New Labour*, Palgrave Macmillan, Basingstoke.

Dickinson, H and Glasby, J 2010, 'Why partnership working doesn't work', *Public Management Review*, vol. 12, no. 6, pp. 811–828.

Dickinson, H and Sullivan, H 2013, 'Towards a general theory of collaborative performance: the role of efficacy and agency', *Public Administration*, vol. 92, no. 2, pp. 161–177.

Fotaki, M 2010, 'Why do public policies fail so often? Exploring health policy making as an imaginary and symbolic construction', *Organization*, vol. 17, no. 6, pp. 703–720.

Larner, W and Craig, D 2005, 'After neoliberalism? Community activism and local partnerships in Aotearoa New Zealand', *Antipode*, vol. 37, no. 3, pp. 402–424.

Marinetto, M 2003, 'Governing beyond the centre: a critique of the Anglo-governance school', *Political Studies*, vol. 51, no. 3, pp. 592–608.

Mckenzie, J 2001, *Perform or else: from discipline to performance*, Routledge, London.

Mclaughlin, H 2004, 'Partnerships: panacea or pretence?', *Journal of Interprofessional Care*, vol. 18, no. 2, pp. 103–113.

Newman, J 2001, *Modernising governance: New Labour, policy and society*, Sage, London.

NLIAH 2009, *Getting collaboration to work in Wales, Lessons from the NHS and partners*, NLIAH, Cardiff.

Peck, E and Crawford, A 2004, *'Culture' in partnerships – what do we mean by it and what can we do about it?*, Integrated Care Network, Leeds.

Peck, E and Dickinson, H 2009, 'Partnership working and organisational culture', in J Glasby and H Dickinson (eds), *International perspectives on health and social care: partnership working in action*, Wiley-Blackwell, Oxford.

Putnam, R 2003, 'The prosperous community: social capital and public life', in E Ostrom and T K Ahn (eds), *Foundations of social capital*, Edward Elgar Publishing Limited, Cheltenham.

Rowlinson, M 1997, *Organisations and institutions*, Macmillan Press Ltd, Basingstoke.

Stern, C S and Henderson, B 1993, *Performance: texts and contexts*, Longman, London.

Sullivan, H 2015, 'Performing a collaborative self', in D Alexander and J Lewis (eds), *Making policy decisions: expertise, skills and experience*, Routledge, London, pp. 88–210.

Sullivan, H and Skelcher, C 2002, *Working across boundaries: collaboration in public services*, Palgrave Macmillan, Basingstoke.

Sullivan, H and Williams, P 2009, 'The limits of co-ordination: community strategies as multi-purpose vehicles in Wales', *Local Government Studies*, vol. 35, no. 2, pp. 161–180.

Sullivan, H, Williams, P, Marchington, M and Knight, L 2013, 'Collaborative futures: discursive realignments in austere times', *Public Money and Management*, vol. 33, no. 2, pp. 123–130.

Williams, R 1975, *Keywords: a vocabulary of culture and society*, Fontana, Glasgow.

Conclusion

Emerging themes and important lessons
for progressing cross-sectoral policy design
and implementation: a discussion

Kathy Landvogt, Jo Barraket and Gemma Carey

In the introduction, we described this volume as a 'toolbox' of ideas, perspectives and strategies related to policy approaches and their translation for action. The volume is also purposefully designed to function as a conversation between those from 'inside' and 'outside' the policymaking tent, and between people from policy, practice and academia (who have varying relationships to policy development and implementation). In keeping with the latter, we present our reflections and conclusions on the collection as a dialogue between the editors, who span practice and academic domains. Kathy Landvogt, a long-term policy actor from within the community sector, leads this discussion, and Jo Barraket and Gemma Carey respond from their academic perspectives. Through this dialogue, we identify where problems are located, identify what questions are critical and draw out the potential solutions as highlighted by different chapters in this book.

KATHY: My first reflection on the collection relates to the overall stance and perspectives presented, particularly that *some policy actors are more equal than others.* Across the continents and policy domains represented, there are mutually recognisable problems and solutions. The differences in perspective that emerge do not reflect local (Australian, UK, US, Canadian) interests, or subject (health, environment, poverty, etc.) interests. They are differences in whom the authors are speaking to, where they are positioned in relation to the problems they address and the specific goals of their chapters. In some ways, this highlights the sheer diversity of people, perspectives and angles associated with 'doing public policy'. As a whole, the arguments put by the contributors thus invite reflection on our own particular position on policy processes, and debate over the underlying nature of the problem(s) we are trying to solve in our efforts to find new ways of achieving good policy outcomes. I wonder whether, fundamentally, our struggle to achieve these outcomes is a problem of power rather than of technical skill? If so, perhaps the book's stance is somewhat liberatory, in that it exposes, openly acknowledges, and proposes strategies to counter these unequal power dynamics (for example, the contributions of Wiseman, Doggett and Chesterman).

The book is generally addressed to policy actors who are not at the epicentre of policy production, but are within what Wiseman calls the 'shadow networks'. By drawing on contributions from across these networks, it directly acknowledges that (though not central in terms of power) civil society is a key actor in public policy making that cannot and should not be ignored. Moreover, it is addressed to a particular quarter within the growing and competitive sphere of decentralised, sometimes marginal, policy actors; those who work for public policy that promotes a healthier, fairer, more sustainable society. The ultimate, sometimes implicit, vision of the book is 'better' policy. Here, 'better' means 'policy for the common good'. This speaks to the (usually explicit) goal of the community services (or third) sector. I do wonder how the book speaks to academic actors. Over to you, Jo and Gemma...

JO AND GEMMA: While the book is primarily aimed at revealing a range of perspectives on policy to practitioners, a number of the chapters grapple with (and progress) issues central to scholarly debates in policy making. For example, Bryant and Raphael propose a progression of theories of policy processes through synthesis of different models. Dickenson and Sullivan openly challenge conventional thinking on collaboration within the public sector, progressing it beyond technocratic discussions. They urge researchers to consider collaboration as a cultural practice that needs to be studied as such (i.e. to adopt a more fine-grained analysis of the nature and object of the problem and assumed solutions).

The diversity of perspectives also reminds us in academia of just how non-linear policy development and changes are, and that our models and theories are always partial. Critically, policy actors (and indeed all those who contribute to this volume) occupy multiple subject positions – i.e. observer, influencer, researcher and so on. While not always as explicitly declared (particularly in comparison to the community sector), we feel that the volume reminds us academics that, when it comes to policy, we all have normative agendas.

Academics are trained to attend to the analytic goals of 'what is happening', but more often than not this question becomes entwined with normative questions of 'what should happen' (both in terms of process and policy outcomes). As Newman (2013) has recently argued, in doing so they also shape the context of public management: "the 'knowledge work' of academics and policy researchers does not simply describe the world but has a generative power of its own" (Newman 2013, p. 35). Each author in this text – whether drawing on academic or practitioner backgrounds (or both) – writes from a position of wanting to see policy develop in a particular way – arguably, a 'better' way. We can see this in the academic contributions, from Clark and Haby's chapter on evidence-based policy (i.e. better evidence of the problems, for better solutions, and therefore better policy) through to Dickinson and Sullivan's piece on collaboration (i.e. we need to better understand collaboration for cross-boundary policy to function more effectively, thereby making the most of diverse world views). Similarly, our own chapters on unsettling the 'status quo of policymaking' (as well as Matthew's contribution) begin from the position that things can be done 'better'. What 'better' means may not be as clearly articulated as in the contributions from those who occupy practitioner (or community sector) spaces, but it does allude to the fact that we have more in common across the academic–practitioner divide than many may realise (or openly acknowledge).

KATHY: Yes, the book does show those commonalities between policy academics and practitioners, sometimes tackling the question directly within a chapter (such as in Chesterman's and Wiseman's chapters), but more often by the implicit dialogue created between chapters.

The second question that this volume raised for me (related to the above) is that *The policy process is problematic.* While an underlying theme of the book is that the policy process is inherently political and this should be understood as normative and worked with, the different accounts present a range of overlapping diagnoses of the policy problems we are confronting at this point in time, including:

- that the policy process is frequently overly influenced by the political machinations of government and this is something to be resisted because it undermines the assumption that policy should serve society through the transparent and rational processes of government;
- that we hold ourselves too aloof from this political process and, as members of civil society and policy actors, we should more proactively and more frequently roll up our sleeves and get into that political process ourselves as behind-the-scenes lobbyists and/or as public activists;
- more sinisterly, that the policy process is corrupted by the non-democratic power of vested interests and this is something to be fought by developing better understanding of the policy mechanisms making this possible, in order to build different forms of collaboration, find new sources of power, and create more effective tools to reverse it.

The policy process should therefore be seen as contested. Indeed the book enters this contest itself, suggesting a set of ideas and practical tools to effect change.

JO AND GEMMA: We're not sure that the volume is speaking to contestability of 'the policy process' but rather, the contestable domain simultaneously inhabited by a diversity of processes, interventions and designs underpinned by differing policy logics and governance models. Chapters in this volume variously depict policy processes as unidirectional and 'neat' (i.e. Clark and Haby's chapter on evidence-based policy, and Wyatt's contribution on policy cycle models) through to inherently messy interventions operating in complex environments on the edge of chaos, such as Matthew's which suggests that governing has become little more than a matter of managing risk in an uncertain (and complex) world. So, the volume does indeed enter into the contest, but we are not sure that it is seeking a single prize.

KATHY: This dialogue itself shows some of the challenges as well as benefits of academic–practitioner projects: the term 'policy process' evokes a maximum of perhaps two or three alternative conceptual frameworks and interpretations for me, but many times more than that for an academic!

The authors may not be seeking a single prize then, but a number of the chapters written from practice perspectives suggest that *(Civil society) policy actors need a critical but practical framework for action.* We need useable theories that allow for reality's contradictory and shifting ground while providing reliable tools to assess and act on that reality. The book helps us to question the taken-for-granted in our lived experience, as practitioners.

Many of the contributions to the book question some traditional assumptions about the policy process. They frequently identify gaps between rhetoric and reality, although I am left thinking there are very few in the policy domain who still carry assumptions of the rationality and linearity of policy-making processes. The need for this particular critique perhaps springs more from the rhetoric that those at the policy centre use to engage, co-opt, compete with, or otherwise interact with the world of policy actors sitting outside core government policy processes. The 'story' of a policy as told by its creators inevitably smooths out rough edges and omits inconsistencies to the point, often, of becoming mere rhetoric.

In the search for useable frameworks and tools, a 'hearts and minds' approach emerges. Contributors such as Liberman and Connolly Youngblood, and McMahon and Gratta draw strongly and explicitly on their respective value bases while pioneering new forms of knowledge. It is the combination of rational science and deep belief that creates the power to persuade in this context. As Doggett along with Clark and Haby also remind us, both the story and the evidence have to stack up.

Elsewhere in the book, critiques of the linear and rational assumptions implicit in much policy rhetoric and processes are explicitly offered. For example Barraket's reflections on new public governance and Matthew's talk of 'distributed learning architecture' identify useful adaptations to the networked nature of governance that characterises our current policy world.

While some contributors do question the assumed rationality in gathering evidence, however valid and novel, to present at the appropriate point in the policy cycle process, the book's message overall is one of 'critical plurality'. Many types of evidence from many types of contributors are needed, from local actors to knowledge-seekers (such as academics) to the political elite. Indeed the nature of the policy process is increasingly understood as inherently dynamic, complex, and based on multiplicity.

We can more confidently continue to put one step in front of the other in our various policy missions when we see our own role as part of the whole. Offering diverse points of analysis on the way we all 'do' policy, the book avoids taking us down the rabbit-hole of endless deconstruction until no decision-making scaffolding remains. It gives grounded examples of action, while simultaneously taking our eye to the horizon where new possibilities are always emerging.

Of course, pursuing a 'policy mission' from the sidelines of policy processes leads to questions of agency (agency being the power to act on our own behalf in ways that are significant to our lives).

JO AND GEMMA: There is a focus on agency in many chapters in the book and we like the characterisation of these as frameworks for action. We would add that some of the contributions – particularly in the last section of the book – also encourage us to think about how new *interactions* (between more or less explicit policy actors) inform policy change. Creating these new interactions – relationships and dialogues – is a key form of agency for policy actors.

KATHY: Yes, and on that note, there is a clear message in the book that *Policy-making cannot and should not be left entirely to the state*. It is really clear throughout the chapters on policy advocacy, the use of evaluative evidence, and hybrid forms of organising that the social and intellectual capital of non-state actors are resources that are needed within the policy process. I would think that even cynical policy managers could see the value of sharing the inevitable policy risks with civil society.

In fact, some of the most important work happens at the boundaries between civil society and other entities (such as this very conversation). Boundary experiences help us make sense of our world, what to do, why and how. As Crosby et al. (2010) suggest, it helps us to connect "people, ideas and other kinds of actors into a way forward" (Crosby et al. 2010, p. 205).

JO AND GEMMA: We think the 'cannot' part is more significant than the 'should not' part of this observation. Although the volume does contain individual contributions (i.e. written from individual or single perspectives), co-produced by policy insiders and civil society actors (or community sector practitioners), the overarching picture is one of interdependence between the state and civil society in the configuration of resources and responses to wicked problems. As Wiseman and

Chesterman both note, the rise of corporate power is also a significant factor in the production of policy responses. There is no question that some aspects of contemporary policy making are well and truly decentred. This is articulated in recent depictions of new public governance (Osborne 2010, 2006) and reflected in a number of chapters in this volume. For example, as Hayward argues, New Public Management approaches have been revealed to be insufficient forms of governing, and make too little use of the knowledge and skills that exist outside of government due to their technocratic approach. Like New Public Governance, in this volume policy is understood to involve coordination and collaboration across sectors, levels and spheres of governance (which go beyond just government and the community sector). Hence, contemporary policymaking requires the navigation of a number of rationalities arising from different governance logics of hierarchies, markets and networks, where approaches coexist rather than eclipse each other. This affects where and in what contexts non-traditional policy actors have a voice in the process.

KATHY: Yes, exactly. For example, there's another interesting point of difference between practitioner and academic in this paragraph. I speak readily of 'shoulds' even though I know that will invite critique about assuming a normative position, because the community organisation I work for freely espouses mission-based values. Academics do not have that liberty, or at least not to use that language.

Speaking of voice, another reflection on what the collection says to me is that *the policy process itself should reflect the democratic nature of our society*. This is a corollary of achieving policy 'for the common good'. There are a number of suggestions proposed for how this can be accomplished. For example, collaboration and networking.

Yet each of these is also subject to the play of power, with the potential to be a form of agency or of constraint. Collaboration is now normalised; it has become a new mantra in service delivery and policy making. We therefore need to analyse, as Dickinson and Sullivan do, whose interests are being served by adopting this new paradigm. Putting our own agency into the 'collaboration' process rather than taking on the version of collaboration that suits other (usually dominant) policy actors, requires an analysis of power.

If we needed reminding, a major theme of the book is that 'the policy process is about power'. The lesser power held by community actors is seen as a problem. Although the authors come from a variety of power bases, this book generally pushes that power downwards, and/or bolsters the power of those with lesser agency through promoting collaborative action. The questions of "Who has agency? And how?" often run between the lines of the book. As policy actors from civil society we need a power analysis to understand where our own agency and constraint lie. The agency held by the powerful central policy actors is usually assumed, but Barraket's focus on informal systems as, even occasionally, trumping the 'main game' directly challenges this assumption. It is empowering to reflect on non-traditional opportunities for influence especially through policy implementation where the community sector has enormous agency.

Beyond the role of community sector practitioners in policy processes, *individual citizens as users of public services need to be empowered as policy actors*. Several chapters reference this in different ways. For example, Hayward speaks of the importance of 'bottom-up knowledge', Carey and Crammond of horizontal and vertical integration, and Matthews of the value provided to policy decision makers by 'weak signals from the coalface'. Still, overall there is much more to be done on enabling the recipients of policy to become co-producers, especially along the lines of Liberman and Connolly Youngblood's work.

JO AND GEMMA: The popular interest in co-production, which is touched on by many of the chapters in Parts II and III of the volume, reflects this sentiment. As Osborne (2010) notes, co-production is inevitable insofar as citizen-consumers interact with services delivered through policy programs. Yet, there is an appetite – echoed in the chapters by Liberman and Connolly Youngblood, McMahon and Gratta, and Matthews – for more explicit commitments to co-production both to improve service quality and redress democratic deficits observed across jurisdictions over the last 30 years.

KATHY: Yes, and there is great potential for scholars, researchers and practitioners to do this work together. On the matter of policy improvements, we typically place a lot of emphasis on evidence-based approaches. Chapters in this collection suggest that *Policy uses evidence … sometimes*. The use, and usefulness, of evidence in the policy-making process is sometimes accepted and sometimes contested. The importance of evidence as a basis for policy is reinforced through advocacy for new types of evidence to be used and for better communication of the evidence.

JO AND GEMMA: 'New types of evidence' is critical here. A number of chapters illuminate the function of non-privileged systems of knowledge in policy advocacy and invite us to think differently about what constitutes evidence. For example, Liberman and Connolly Youngblood, and McMahon and Gatta argue that evidence can enter into policy processes in unexpected ways, from unlikely disciplines, to shape services which could then be scaled up by governments, while Carey and Crammond suggest that process evidence is too infrequently considered.

KATHY: In other parts of the book, a critical stance is taken on the way evidence is squeezed out of policy making by political interests. This stance assumes evidence can be and should be present. Elsewhere it is the nature of evidence itself that is seen as the problem. Scientific, generalisable evidence is not actually available to the degree commonly assumed.

Johnson *et al.*'s case study is an instructive exception – the exception that proves the rule perhaps. If this is accepted, we can go beyond the evidence, concentrate on dealing with the inherent uncertainties in the policy process and focus on what we can know, even though it is a very incomplete knowledge base.

And finally – or perhaps ultimately – the contributions to this volume remind me that *policy-making is not a rational process but thinking about it is*. The nature of rationality – of evidence, and of policy making – is itself under discussion at times. As perhaps the most fundamental conceptual tool used by policy managers and actors (as Wyatt explains), the 'policy cycle' implies a more-or-less logical progression through a number of stages, a progression that is rarely illustrated unproblematically in these pages. 'Reason' is less present than 'power' in most of the discussions. Yet, to undertake action in a complex world does require rational mental frameworks such as the policy cycle to sort and order reality. And certainly, the presentation of ideas in a book is an attempt at imposing order on complexity!

References

Crosby, B, Mclaughlin, K & Chew, C 2010, 'Leading across frontiers', in S Osborne (ed.), *The New Public Governance*, Routledge, New York, pp. 200–222.

Newman, J 2013, 'Constituting context', in C Pollitt (ed.), *Context in public policy and management: the missing link?*, Edward Elgar, Cheltenham, UK, pp. 35–44.

Osborne, S (ed.) 2010, *The new public governance*, Routledge, New York.

Osborne, S P 2006, 'The new public governance?', *Public Management Review*, vol. 8, pp. 377–387.

Index

Page numbers in *italics* denote tables, those in **bold** denote figures.
End of chapter notes are indicated by a letter n between page number and note number.